"I Would Not Step Back…"

"I Would Not Step Back..."

Squadron Leader Phil Lamason RNZAF, DFC and Bar

Hilary Pedersen and Associated Writers

An imprint of
MENTION THE WAR PUBLICATIONS

First published in the United Kingdom in 2018 by Mention the War Ltd. Merthyr Tydfil, CF47 0BH, Wales.

Copyright 2018 © The Phil Lamason Heritage Centre Trust Incorporated.

Cover design: Topics – The Creative Partnership www.topicdesign.co.uk

A CIP catalogue reference for this book is available from the British Library.

ISBN 9781911255390

The Phil Lamason Heritage Centre Trust (Inc) has been established for a Charitable Purpose. Best efforts have been made on the part of the Trust, as owner, to acknowledge the sources of information and images included in this publication. In this regard we greatly appreciate the genuine interest and support shown by the many people and organisations, locally, nationally and internationally who have taken a special interest in Phil Lamason's war story. Such support has enabled this biographical project to be undertaken. If we have inadvertently overlooked an acknowledgement, please accept our sincere apologies. Our intention in this work is to present an important New Zealand biography and military story with worthiness and accuracy, so it may be preserved for the appreciation and inspiration of future generations.

The Trust's share of any profits from the publication of this work will be donated towards furthering the goals of the Trust. These goals are listed on our website and in the acknowledgements at the end of this book.

www.phillamason.com

Contents

Foreword

by Mike Dorsey

Filmmaker, "The Lost Airmen of Buchenwald"
Grandson of former Buchenwald prisoner,
Lt.Col. E.C. "Easy" Freeman, USAF

Phil Lamason with Mike Dorsey at the Lamason Farm, Rua Roa, Dannevirke, New Zealand in 2010, during the filming for the documentary 'The Lost Airmen of Buchenwald. (Photograph courtesy of Mike Dorsey)

When the 168 Allied airmen arrived at Buchenwald Concentration Camp, they didn't know what they were dealing with yet. And in Phil Lamason, the Germans didn't know what they were dealing with yet, either.

Even in his 90s I found Phil to be an intimidating figure. I couldn't imagine disagreeing with him or doing anything else that could put us at odds. The last time I saw him, he gave me a bit of old school advice. As I walked with him to his car to say goodbye for what would be the last time, he told me that he had always done what he said he was going to do. If he said he'd be up working on the farm at 4 o'clock in the morning, then that's exactly where you would find him. We've probably all received such advice throughout our own lives, but it meant so much more coming from Phil. Context is everything.

I didn't know Phil for the first 90 years of his life. I don't know what shaped the man who came to stand on that train platform outside the Buchenwald gates in 1944, surrounded by guards and snarling German

Shepherds; possibly the only man in the middle of that chaos who immediately recognised where they were and what needed to be done.

I tell people that Phil's actions over those next two months were a lesson in leadership. His story should be required reading for everyone from the military to the corporate boardroom. And we must remember: he did this *in his 20s!* I remember the foolishness of my 20s, and what he did simply boggles my mind. I've interviewed airmen who, even in their 90s, said they would still follow him just about anywhere. To understand what he did, one must first understand the Buchenwald Concentration Camp.

It's estimated that 240,000 prisoners were held at the camp throughout its existence from 1937 to 1945. Of those poor souls, 56,545 are estimated to have perished there, either by starvation, disease or execution. We say "estimated" because the records are incomplete; the real numbers could even be higher. If you got sick, there was no treatment; why would your captors worry about restoring you to good health when there's another trainload of slave labor arriving tomorrow? The airmen imprisoned there called the camp's infirmary a "death camp." If you couldn't stand for roll call, you were beaten to death right where you fell. Simply clenching your fists in the presence of a guard was grounds for execution. Food consisted of cabbage soup with worms and a type of bread that was largely sawdust. And the prisoners were worked to the bone in the camp's factories, building armaments for the German war machine. But more on that later...

Scientists can study tree rings not only to tell the tree's age, but to note any historical cataclysms, such as floods or fires, that left permanent marks on the tree's life. The children and grandchildren and now the great grandchildren of Buchenwald's former prisoners have felt the impact of their ancestor's experiences there. We grew up hearing these stories around the dinner table, we've found ways to record those accounts in books and films and audio recordings, and we've travelled with our loved ones to commemorations in Germany and to documentary film screenings and to memorials in our nations' capitals. Buchenwald was a place of such evil terribleness that its impact reverberated through the men who suffered there and continued in subsequent generations, leaving its mark like a ring in our family trees. We exist because *they* survived.

It was understood in the Allied militaries that once captured, you were to continue to act as a member of the military, and you were to locate the most senior officer in your group and take his orders. It could be a senior officer from any military, so long as it was Allied. As I understand it, there were other officers in the group of Buchenwald airmen that were equal to Phil, but they all fell in behind *him*. Imagine that for a moment. There were 82 Americans, 48 British, 26 Canadians, 9 Australians and 1 Jamaican, but they all decided that they would take orders from one of only two New Zealanders in their group. What does that tell you about Phil's presence and leadership?

Maybe they had all seen how he'd handled the German guards out on the railway line on their five day journey to the camp from France. Here's how Phil told one story:

"A German there around the bend who was bloody mad – he had a bit of wood about three feet long, and he was just bashing at these prisoners just standing by the railway lines. And everyone was trying to run past him, *but I wasn't gonna run*. I sort of walked up to him, and an English voice said 'Shoot him.' I turned around and there was about half a dozen guards with rifles on me. He said, 'None of them are gonna get within five yards of you, and if you get within five yards they're gonna shoot ya. So you make sure they don't.'"

"But I wasn't gonna run" is a line that still comes to mind at odd moments in my day. Another similar line from Phil, and the title of this foreword: "I wouldn't step backwards."

Buchenwald was a work camp. If you were a prisoner there, you were put to work, and if you didn't work, you were no good to the Germans. But Phil and his airmen refused to work. No one said "no" to the Germans, but they did. One day, a German commander marched a unit of armed guards with a German Shepherd up to Phil and ordered him one last time to send his men to work in the factories. This is how Phil responded, after receiving an earlier tip from a fellow prisoner that he was going to be shot:

"They called me up to shoot me there. They brought an amazing number of soldiers. I said with a bit of irony, 'I didn't realize it took 20 guys to shoot me.' Bloody dog was jumping up, snapping at my throat. More or less was trying to talk me into cooperating to some extent with them. And I said, 'No, we don't work, we don't do this. We are servicemen, we want out of this place.' And he just stood, and he had about 20 as I say, soldiers around me, and he gave the order and they all trained their guns on me. He said, 'Are you gonna work or not?' I was looking straight at him, and he looked at me. He looked quite a decent sort of a guy, the officer in charge. And we looked at each other for a minute, and he gave the order to ground arms and he marched them out again. I will admit I'm a pretty scary person, I guess I got pretty scared with all this. *But I wouldn't go backwards. I stood still and I didn't walk back.* I think it probably saved my life."

I asked Phil if he was afraid of being shot, but he said that he knew there were other men behind him ready to pick up where he left off. I think about how many of his men survived Buchenwald – nearly all of them. And I think about how much of that survival rate would have suffered had he capitulated and sent them to the factories. Never mind the moral dilemma of building armaments that would be used to kill your fellow countrymen in battle; the factories were dangerous. They were even bombed by the Americans while Phil's airmen were there. I am amazed by the story of Phil's defiance – *still* amazed and I've watched it hundreds of times.

The airmen never did work in those factories. Thanks to Phil's efforts and the connections that he made with Buchenwald's underground groups, word was smuggled out to the regular German military, who were reportedly at odds with the Nazi SS. Luftwaffe officers arrived at Buchenwald, and the airmen were taken out of that hell and sent to a regular POW camp. Only two of them perished in Buchenwald, both from illness. Their names are carved into a stone plaque that now sits in the middle of the camp.

Every airman who made it through that place handled the impact in different ways. For some, it reportedly ruined their lives. Others suffered from nightmares, but otherwise lived full lives, taking from their Buchenwald experience a renewed appreciation for their freedoms. Some suffered from negative long-term health effects from their time in the camp, while others like Phil lived into their 90s.

I don't know how Buchenwald affected Phil. I suspect that some of his decisions haunted him late into his life. I suspect that, despite his toughness, some of what he witnessed there haunted him too. I don't think he was the sentimental type, but I thanked him the last time that I saw him, and I thank him here again. I exist because he and his men survived.

Squadron Leader Phil Lamason, 1942. (Photograph courtesy of Lamason Family Collection)

Preface

The story that emerges of this gritty New Zealander appears to be better known elsewhere than in the hero's own country. Why?

For those who returned from combat nursing mind-numbing experiences that are outside our comprehension, it's become a recognised fact that they were seldom mentioned. Phil Lamason was no exception. "I know very little about Dad in the war," his daughter Patricia Simmonds says more than 70 years later.

Like his comrades Phil Lamason could never erase the memories. But nor did he wish to discuss them. So other than snippets like flying exploits and life in the mess that he volunteered to mates as time went on, little was said. During Phil's later life however, he agreed to the occasional interview. Thus, in a newspaper article published on April 24, 1999, a glimpse of life in a concentration camp was related to 'Dominion Newspaper' reporter Warren Barton.

"I've always tried to put what happened behind me and to get on with my life. But I do have memories, particularly of things like Buchenwald." He then speaks of a visit to the toilet where he found "a couple of bodies, stripped, lying there." Sights like that were commonplace. On another occasion, "I saw a door I hadn't noticed before so I pulled it open. The room was full of naked bodies. It was bloody awful." Whatever you heard about Buchenwald, "it was worse." Only in the final months when facing death through cancer did he fully release the burden of memory that had been carried for so long.

In the Ulysses tradition the Oxford dictionary defines a hero as 'A man of superhuman qualities favoured by the gods; demigod; illustrious warrior; one who fought for his country.' To some, there would be times during his life when Phil Lamason was all of these. As 165 Allied airmen who survived Buchenwald would testify. But interestingly, hand in hand with these lofty attributes lurked the tendency to combine the heroic with the comic; the 'heroi-comic.' The 'larrikin.' These traits within the quintessential Phil demonstrated another more lighthearted – some would say headstrong – aspect of the Lamason approach to life.

As a young man emerging from boyhood teens into adulthood Phil was someone who knew what he wanted. And with ability and determination he achieved his aims. From stockmanship, to flying, to his thirst for the land. And when unimagined aspects of his life were tested to the limit, hard-won powers of endurance enabled him to meet the challenges.

This is a man who stood tall. Literally. A broad-shouldered, blue-eyed man of six feet who looked the world in the eye. Lamason, a man of equality looked up to few. But neither did he look down. His story is one of courage, of tenacity and self-belief, of wits, vigour and bloody-mindedness. Of someone who was prepared to push boundaries to achieve his aims. Above everything his is a story of sheer, unadulterated guts. How else to describe someone who has a Luger pressed to his temple whilst eyeballing the German guard who holds it?

In the Phil Lamason story you will find an extraordinary cast of characters and range of circumstances. Of opportunities, some taken, some missed. Find friendships, personal tragedy, royalty, betrayal, loyalty, the humble and the powerful. Find inhumanity, the stench of death, pathos and humour.

So who were the people and what were the events and influences that shaped this extraordinary New Zealander's life?

Hilary Pedersen

Squadron Leader Phil Lamason pictured in 1942 while on a visit to the Cadzow's Farm near Edinburgh, Scotland. (Photograph courtesy of Lamason Family Collection)

The Making of the Man

Phillip John Lamason was born on September 15, 1918 to William and Violet Lamason. He was the third of six children. The family history spans generations in which some common themes emerge. Ability, enterprise, determination, resilience and conviction. These were individuals who were unafraid to follow their aspirations.

The Lamasons were of French origin and are understood to be weavers from the district of La Mason near the Belgian border. The family's religious background however, was the product of a long history and a hard won tradition born of persecution. Inspired by the writings of early 16th century reformer John (Jean) Calvin, the Lamasons were French Protestants or Huguenots, victims of the Spanish Jesuits and, in 1572, of the orchestrated St Bartholomew Day massacre. When religious persecution saw adherents fleeing to other more tolerant Protestant countries the Lamasons did likewise. They escaped to England during the reign of Henry VIII, settled in Devon at Ashburton-on-Dart and for a time continued their occupation as weavers. Further down the centuries tombstones reveal that the Lamasons became brush makers. Later still there was a sweet shop – the sweets were a family specialty product.

Fast forward the generations to Phil's grandparents Thomas Ryder Lamason and his wife Martha. Thomas Ryder Lamason was born in Devonshire, UK and is described as 'a well-educated engineer and a good musician who specialised in hydraulic engineering.' He emigrated with the mining boom to the gold fields of Bendigo and Ballarat in Victoria, Australia. It was there that Thomas met and later married Martha Hayman in 1869. Martha was the daughter of Abraham and Sarah Hayman and was also born in Devonshire

The Haymans were living in the settlement of Port Phillip where Abraham had a carrying business involving large stables of draught horses and working bullocks to haul his numerous wagons. His territory was large, covering the area from Port Phillip and passing through Adelaide to the young city of Melbourne. The countryside had no formed roads at that time.

A story is told about Abraham, Sarah and Martha travelling in their horse-drawn dray – or large cart – to Melbourne when a heavy dust storm blew in from the outback. Forced to take shelter from the swirling debris, the two women sought shelter on the leeward side of the heavy four-wheeled dray. Suddenly, a particularly strong gust caught the dray, rolled it over and pinned Sarah to the ground, breaking her back. Sarah survived the ordeal but remained an invalid. Ever dutiful, Martha nursed her mother for the rest of her days. It was during this time that Tom and Martha were married.

Martha is recalled as a patriotic, good Victorian and "dressed like the Queen." A seal skin coat in her possession adds an interesting story of resilience to the Lamason family history. Her enterprising gold mining brother Aaron, having decided to trade his own gold in California, set sail on the ill-fated three-masted barque 'General Grant.' En route the ship foundered and was wrecked off Auckland Island in New Zealand's stormy sub-Antarctic waters. Along with the tragic loss of 68 lives was a single boatload of 16 survivors including Aaron. Unable to immediately reach a food depot known to be on the island, the men made do with sheath knives and slaughtered birds, seals and sea elephants to stay alive. Later they replaced their worn out clothing with sealskin. Aaron and his companions were eventually discovered on Auckland Island and returned to Australia. Meanwhile the resourceful Aaron had assembled a bale of 'choice sealskins' which he had dressed and prepared for sale. He presented a coat to his sister Martha which 'was much admired.'

When gold was discovered in Westland, in the South Island of New Zealand, Tom and Martha Lamason along with thousands of Australian gold seekers, crossed the Tasman Sea and moved to the rugged West Coast. Settling at the gold-town of Ross, Tom was soon putting his engineering skills to good use, operating a very successful sluicing claim. Here, the gold was extracted from the rocks and streams using early hydraulic technology. This continued until gold deposits became too deep and uneconomic for surface extraction.

Later, the rapidly growing family moved further north up the West Coast to the settlement of Kumara. It was in Kumara they became neighbours of Richard John Seddon, later to become 'King Dick,' Premier of New Zealand and a man still regarded as one of the country's most colourful politicians. Lancashire-born Seddon, who was ousted from school by the headmaster (his own father) had, like Tom Lamason, followed gold to Victoria and then to Westland. He then moved to Kumara after staking a claim on a newly-discovered goldfield, establishing the Queen Hotel and also operating a butcher's shop and a store. Miners' rights were dear to Seddon's heart and continued to be

Richard John Seddon, Prime Minister of New Zealand, 1893-1906. (Photograph courtesy of Alexander Turnbull Library)

throughout his political career. Never one to back down from an argument he was once described as 'a rough ex-goldfields publican.' Seddon and Lamason became partners in a group with five other miners. In keeping with the current mining laws each pegged out their own claim and by mutual agreement operated as a single entity. Seddon was the business manager. The claim was productive and envied by some other miners who bought out some of the original claimants. The newcomers then became jealous of Lamason's success to the point where his life was endangered. On one occasion a pick was dropped upon him whilst he was down in a shaft examining deposits.

Tom and Martha had a family of eight children; Sarah, Barbara Mary, Lucy Anne, Thomas Isaac, Agnes, Robert, Elizabeth and William, born July 18, 1881 in Kumara. William was to become Phil Lamason's father. Thomas Lamason continued his life in Kumara until his death there in 1904. Miners were tough men and Tom Lamason was no exception. "The Kumara rush was no place for feather-bed miners," a journalist from a South Island newspaper wrote in 1876. "Digging here means hardship and downright hard work… The gold must be wrought for and striven for, and even when it's got at, it means nothing more than wages." Accidents would have been commonplace. Tom once had a large stone fall on him, pinning him to the ground below the knee and breaking the leg in two places.

Tom Lamason's combination of toughness of character and natural intelligence would have laid a path for his children to follow. This was apparent in his youngest son. William Lamason attended Kumara School, which was a tough place. Attendances were irregular and school inspections record it as "the most slovenly in the district." Later, following the educational reform of 1887, a general improvement in the appearance of the written work of the upper classes (seniors) was noted. Children were often expected by their parents to go to work "as soon as they were able." Not so the Lamasons. William was aged 16½ when he passed his Junior Civil Service examination in 1898. Given that many children left school at just 13 years of age – Standard Four, at that time in New Zealand – William's equivalent, a 'proxy' Standard Seven was considered a high level of achievement. William would have been positively influenced by his older sister Barbara Mary who achieved the rare distinction of being recommended for a scholarship by the Westland Education Board and later became a teacher at Kumara School.

William advanced in his learning to train and work as a draughtsman and also as a surveyor's assistant. Initially his work was at Kumara, but after his mother moved to live nearer relatives at Hawera in the North Island province of Taranaki, William's work extended from Wellington to some of the remote country areas in Taranaki. This skilled professional career ensured that employment was always readily available for William.

In 1911 William Lamason married Violet Curtis, the eldest in a family of eight children. Her parents, Phil's grandparents, Charles Curtis and Barbara Lloyd were both born in Gwynedd, Wales and had subsequently migrated to New Zealand. Barbara died aged just 40 years, which for some time left Violet as a surrogate mother to her younger siblings before her marriage to William. Sometime during the early WWI years William and Violet moved across to Napier on the North Island's East Coast. Here, he joined the New Zealand Public Works Department as a draughtsman. Later he was an appointed to the position of Building Overseer, to be followed in 1935 by a promotion to Inspector of Works.

Phil's early life

William and Violet had six children; Nelly, William (Bill), Phillip (Phil), Dorothy, Noeline and David. Their mother is described as a "beautiful Welsh woman," who was "very hard working and hospitable and always having people for dinner," and their father as "tall, handsome and uncompromising." As parents they would have been a united couple in a family life strongly influenced by their religion.

19

William and Violet Lamason, parents of Phil Lamason. (Photograph courtesy of Lamason Family Collection)

Although William's family background was Church of England he had in adulthood joined the Open Brethren Church and became an Elder. This was to have repercussions on Phil's family life.

William was a strict disciplinarian, his methods demonstrated by soft speech and a big stick. Whilst being a tolerant parent to the other siblings he was hard on the young Phil, who clearly was showing early signs of the fighting spirit that was to characterise his life. An insight into the Brethren Church of the time, with its uncompromising principles, shines some light on what today might be regarded as undue toughness. In this God-fearing, scripture-driven household 'The Word,' and obeying God's will, was paramount and a lack of control could not be tolerated. William and Violet have been described by Pat Magill, a long-time family friend and member of a Brethren household, as a "Brethren couple driven by faith." To lose control was "seen to be losing faith and therefore to be a failure," so when Phil showed his high-spirited side his father considered there was no other recourse than to beat him. On one such occasion, bewilderment and alarm rapidly spread through this church congregation, reverently gathered for a Baptism celebration. Minutes before the start of this solemn event, the sizeable pool, central to this total immersion ritual, was discovered to have been mysteriously emptied. Phil and his accomplices had apparently engaged in a covert act of youthful, sacrilegious sabotage. Wrath was doubtlessly vented! Pat Magill also speaks of Phil's much later life and recalls their times together when he would drive south to Dannevirke to visit Phil to share a beer and some old memories. "We would discuss how we had both managed to break the 'shackles of control,' and have a laugh."

Phil and his siblings grew up in the Depression. The economic repercussions of this period for New Zealand, still a predominantly rural society, were profound. Known as 'The Sugar Bag Years,' labour camps, abandoned land, and vagrancy were among the obvious signs of hardship that characterised the social landscape. Directly or indirectly no one could have escaped the consequences, although the Lamasons were fortunate as William's professional skills ensured that he was in continuous employment.

The family lived in Napier, a coastal city in the sunny Hawke's Bay region with a stunning seascape that once earned it the title of the 'Nice of the Pacific.' Its other notable feature, Bluff Hill is an impressive landmass which dominates the city and surrounds. The Lamason's large family home at 32 Morris Street however was on the flat in the McLean Park area. In the light of subsequent events this may have been fortuitous. Within a five year period the family was to be affected by two very distinct upheavals, the first widespread, the second not.

The Napier earthquake struck at 10.47am on February 3, 1931. Registering 7.8 on the Richter Scale, this shake still stands as New Zealand's deadliest, lasting for two and a half minutes and killing 256 people. The cities of Napier and neighbouring Hastings 20 kilometres to the south were devastated and damage was widespread. Water and sewage systems were cut and bridges demolished. Buildings toppled like flies. Fires raged uncontrollably through the business district of the city. Coastal areas around Napier were lifted by two metres, dramatically and instantly changing the landscape.

Phil, aged 13 years, was a pupil at Nelson Park School. When the 'quake subsided family members recall he was sent off on his bike around the neighbourhood to check out friends and deliver an "all's well" message from the Lamasons. School kids would have been outside for their mid-morning break on the first day of the school year at the time the shaking began. Phil's wife Joan remembered hanging onto a tennis net and jumping the 'waves' of tarmac as it rose and fell beneath her. Along with many children who were moved out of the area for a while, the young Lamasons were sent over to Taranaki to stay with relatives for a time. William was fully engaged in using his skills to help in the rebuild of Napier.

The CBD of Napier immediately after the earthquake of February 3, 1931. (Photograph courtesy of National Library of New Zealand)

Nothing however could have prepared the family for the impact of the second upheaval, which was life-long. Like the earthquake, circumstances intervened without warning. On the evening of March 3, 1936, William was killed in a car accident. With characteristic zeal he and four Brethren elders were attending to a church matter of some urgency. A locomotive hit the car on Napier's Awatoto railway crossing, shunting the vehicle along the railway line and killing William and his friend Mr John Garrett. Conscientious to the last William was upholding his responsibility to the church.

William's untimely death would have had a profound impact on the family.

Phil was eighteen and at university in Palmerston North when his father was killed. How would he have reacted to his father's death? Given their relationship, would he have felt deep sadness? Resignation? Forgiveness? Or a combination of all three? No doubt he would have supported his mother and younger siblings however he was able. In order to attend his father's funeral Phil first had to sell his bicycle to afford to buy a train ticket back to Napier.

William's offspring did him proud. All six were high achievers and of formidable intelligence. Nelly, the eldest – who stepped up to support their mother after the accident – was matron of the Napier Hospital. Sister Dorothy's achievements were impressive. She served with distinction with the WAAC's (Women's Army Auxiliary Corps) in the Second Expeditionary Force in World War II. In later married life, as Dot McNab, she received an Order of the British Empire Award from the NZ Government for her services to party politics and broadcasting. Noeline, a highly-regarded chemist, worked alongside her husband at the Waikato Hospital for many years. David, described as a "self-made man who was highly regarded in the farming industry," was a long-time manager of the Allied Farmers business in North Auckland. Phil held his siblings in high esteem and throughout his life continued to speak proudly of their achievements.

But it was with his brother Bill, number two in the family, that Phil forged his strongest bond in his early years. Phil talked of how, as teenaged boys, Bill and he were regularly woken early in their sleep-out batch across the yard from the house, by the 'snapping of willow!' Their father, William, eager to ensure his sons in the hard Depression years weren't succumbing to the jeopardies of an indolent lifestyle, would break a branch from the drooping willow tree beside the boys' bedroom window. For Bill and Phil, this unmistakable 'snap' was the cue to be out of bed, dressed and ready to face the day … thus avoiding the 'sting of the willow branch!' Sleeping-in was seen by William as a symptom of a creeping slothfulness.

In their growing up years Bill encouraged his younger sibling's high school sporting activities and was there to cheer him on during rugby or boxing fixtures. Later, as a Napier plumber and health inspector, Bill named his own son after Phil; and Phil was to name his third son after his brother Bill.

Phil with his larrikin ways had already felt the weight of his father's authority, so it would seem that these traits of determination combined with being 'a bit of a ratbag' were already embedded within the young Lamason. From early on he was a keen boxer with obvious ability. But when his Napier coach suggested to William that his "boy had potential" and wanted to take him further, William refused the offer. William's disciplinary measures were already setting Phil up to withstand pain and not to buckle under pressure. These were early survival skills in the making. What is certain is that on moving to secondary school, Phil's

Phil (right) with his older brother and mentor, Bill Lamason (circa 1936). (Photograph courtesy of Lamason Family Collection)

temperament combined with his childhood experiences stood him in good stead.

Napier Boys' High School has a proud history that dates back to 1873. The school curriculum was wide ranging and aimed to equip its students to be future leaders in their chosen professions. Old boys achieved prominence in the armed forces, church, public service, the arts and academics, legal profession, business and sports.

Following the earthquake which toppled the 'once majestic Assembly Hall like a pack of cards,' the school added a farm from reclaimed land and quickly built up a reputation for agricultural achievement. Although farming was Phil's number one interest and agriculture was part of the curriculum he obviously chose not to 'achieve prominence' and do the study at school. As it was, Phil quickly earned some status of a more questionable kind. Difficult as this is to believe, he claims to have endured caning – six of the best – on a daily basis during his school career. At the conclusion of this ritual – and unflinchingly endured – public humiliation, Phil would turn the tables with a cheeky "thank you Sir," to the master. Unsurprisingly he gained hero status among his school mates. But galling as this public display of grit would have been to the authorities one wonders how they would have viewed him in private. With grudging respect maybe?

Little is known of Phil's 1932 and 1933 school career other than rugby and his boxing achievements. The boundless energy and fighting spirit had found an outlet at school and he trained hard. In 1932 he was the Flyweight champion. An account of the school's annual boxing

24

tournament records, "Lamason had a great advantage in height and reach and through using it scored frequently." Up close his opponent had an advantage but in the end "it was Lamason's fight all the way and he secured the verdict."

Searching through class records many years later the school archivist Phillip Rankin writes that the only mention of Phil was in the class rolls – he was in Form 3C in 1932 and the following year studied Form 4E Agricultural and Engineering. However, despite his time at Napier Boys' High School not being the happiest days of his life

Phil (seated left, middle row) as a member of the Napier Boys' High School Boxing Team, 1932. (Photograph courtesy of the Archives, Napier Boys' High School)

the school was "honoured to name him as an old boy." Again, records of him as a World War II Old Boy are scant. He is mentioned in the "missing" section but with no other detail, and in the final list of Old Boys at War compiled in 1947, his DFC and Bar and being "Mentioned in Despatches" are recorded. Years later when acts of his heroism began to emerge he was invited by the school to attend ANZAC services. The answer was always declined. "No thanks, not happy years."

In hindsight it's interesting to read the principal Mr WT Foster's 'Message For 1933' published in the 1932 Diamond Jubilee edition of the school magazine at the conclusion of Phil's first year at school. The boys are exhorted to, "Not, as I have recently heard, regret the years spent on your secondary education. Real education cannot be assessed in pounds, shillings and pence. If you have learned well, you have a treasure trove that no thief, no slump can filch from you. If you have played well, you have acquired the team spirit; you have imbibed the truth that co-operation is essential to success. You have learned to stand up to difficulties 'with courage never to submit or yield'..." Was Phil in assembly to hear those words from his headmaster? As history has demonstrated, they could have been written for him.

Phil's facetious attitude followed him through his young life and set him up to be a 'tough cookie.' His willingness to stand up to authority was now well established and would stand him in good stead for future events. At age 15 Phil was ready for the wider world. He continued to be a dogged pugilist and at various times sustained the inevitable broken nose. Not once, but six times. The 'nose' was to have repercussions later.

But for now, Phil's next and enduring passion awaited him. His ambition to be on the land had fuelled a determination to become a farm cadet and for Phil there was only one option. This was Smedley Station at Tikokino in Central Hawke's Bay, south of Napier, and a prestigious training establishment for aspiring shepherds. It was founded by the late owner Josiah Howard who, on his death in 1919, bequeathed the property to His Majesty The King, 'in the confidence that the Government of New Zealand' would use it as a 'foundation or endowment for the purposes of agricultural education.'

The property is a 4000 hectare farm set in the foothills of the Ruahine Ranges. With iconic scenery encompassing bush-dotted hills that become steeper towards the mountains, this is country that captures a New Zealand stockman's spirit.

In this environment Phil would acquire his stock farming skills. Skills that involved learning to muster, to shear sheep, work dogs, tackle a lambing beat and learn to ride. This was horsemanship of the rural kind. Add in the association with likeminded young men doubtless from different backgrounds but with a common aim of their love of the land.

So now Phil's first test awaited him, the selection process for the Smedley cadetship. Here was a young lad with nothing but determination to back him. He was a 'townie' preparing to step outside the family mould and set a new direction. Fresh from school and undeterred by being on his own Phil presented himself for the interview. At stake a precious scholarship with long odds. Eighty applicants for just six places. Success would be hard earned. Unsurprisingly the characteristic determination and panache duly prevailed. Phil was enrolled into the cadet school to embark on a two year course combining practical skills with study. With the cadet training only beginning in 1931, his was just the fourth Smedley intake. Here, aged 16, Phil

Lamason became an early trainee in an institution that has continued on to command respect in the New Zealand farming industry.

In 1935 Phil demonstrated his learning ability and farming skills by passing out of Smedley as the top cadet. This achievement earned him a scholarship to help towards his further tertiary level studies. Much later Phil was to return as a Board member and then chairman of the Smedley Trust for over 20 years from 1962 to 1982.

Following Smedley Phil enrolled in a Diploma of Agriculture course at Massey Agricultural College in Palmerston North (late to become Massey University). To help finance his studies Phil had singlehandedly cleared 100 acres of unwanted bush (scrub), at the back of Smedley by hand using a 'slasher.' Scrub cutting by hand was commonplace among farming practises of that era. Phil wore through the metal blades of two 'heads' in the process. It's also said that he shot and ate rabbit. Later on in his life the circumstances of eating rabbit would come back to haunt him.

Meanwhile, in the family tradition of excellence Phil achieved top honours in Sheep Husbandry, completing his Diploma at the end of the 1937 year. His subjects were Physics, Chemistry, Physiology, Pathology, Farming, Surveying and Botany. But nor were his sporting interests overlooked. Phil was a member of the college rugby 1st XV, a long distance running champion and also played cricket and tennis.

Church was not forgotten either. Phil wrote to his mother, Violet, soon after his father's death "Dear Mum, Just home from the meeting so thought I would let you know how Phillip John is progressing." He had been to three Saturday lectures and then visited an old friend from the church. "Called on Eric Gilding who was very pleased to see me, but was very upset as he was very fond of Dad and Mr Garrett... Today (Sunday) I went to the morning meeting, Bible Class in the afternoon and the meeting at night..." Phil was obviously looked after. "The people of Palmerston North are very good and I have been invited out to several places. In fact, I don't think I'll ever have a Sunday dinner or tea at Massey." He signs off early "Your loving son, Phil," and apologises for his writing as "I'm feeling particularly lazy tonight." Phil was at home in his learning environment.

Graduation over, Phil moved back to his home town and took on a job with his old school, Napier Boys' High, undertaking the dual responsibilities of Farm Manager and Housemaster. It was during this time that a life-long friendship blossomed into romance. The lovely lady

Smedley Training Farm cadets, 1934. Phil is standing, second from left. (Photograph courtesy of Lamason Family Collection)

Trainee cadet accommodation huts at Smedley Training Farm (circa 1930's). (Photograph courtesy of Smedley Training Farm Archives)

Smedley Training Farm Honours Board. (Photograph courtesy of Mike Harold)

Massey Agricultural College, Diploma of Agriculture staff and students 1937. Phil Lamason is 3rd from left in the seated front row. (Photograph courtesy of Lamason Family Collection)

29

Phil Lamason (standing sixth from right) in the New Plymouth Old Boys Rugby Team, circa 1939) (Photograph courtesy of Lamason Family Collection)

was Joan Hopkins. Small, with dark curly hair, a pretty face and ready smile, Joan had been Phil's childhood sweetheart.

The Hopkins family were of English descent, Joan's grandfather Edward having migrated to New Zealand and undertaken a career as a merchant and grocer. Joan, born in November 1919, was the eldest in the family of four children of William Hopkins and his wife Jeanne Junk.

The Hopkins and Lamason families had been long-time friends in Napier and lived within 100 yards of each other. To both families Phil and Joan's prospective marriage was an ideal partnership – one 'made in heaven.' They had known each other since childhood and it is easy to imagine their friendship blossoming into a mutual attraction. Little is known of their courtship but photos of picnics and a happy group of young people suggests that their church group provided the catalyst for social contact.

Then in November 1938 Phil took on a new challenge, a position with the New Zealand Department of Agriculture in New Plymouth as a livestock inspector. Phil could now put his abilities to the test, hone his skills in Animal Husbandry and earn a reputation as an astute stock picker. It was an action-packed time. Tennis, along with senior grade rugby with the New Plymouth Old Boys' Club kept him fit. There were family contacts too – aunts and uncles – in nearby Stratford and Hawera.

Long distance contact with Joan would have proved challenging at this time. However on one occasion luck intervened. Phil had recently begun to pursue a growing interest in flying with the New Plymouth Aero Club and was able to persuade an instructor to take him on a Sunday flight across the rugged North Island to Napier. Here he was able to spend some unscheduled time with his beloved Joan. From there the story is told of how the Tiger Moth ran low on fuel during the return journey, prompting an unscheduled stopover at a farm, where the willing landowner provided a top-up. This farm fuel mix proved satisfactory and the mission was successfully accomplished.

Joan Hopkins (circa 1940) (Photograph courtesy of Lamason Family Collection)

But Joan Hopkins was definitely her 'own person.' She was active, social, sports-loving and strong-minded. These qualities would serve her well in the years immediately ahead. Her daughter Cherry proudly recounts her mother's initiative in becoming the first female bank-teller in Napier. Joan, who had an aptitude for figures, noticed an advertisement in the local paper and applied for the vacancy, only to be told that it was a position reserved for men. Undeterred, she was eventually given the job due, she was told, to "a lack of available men."

Maybe they were signing up for the war, but it is likely Joan was employed on her own merits. Prior to this change in career, Joan was employed at Steven's Bike Shop. A keen cyclist, she saved up to buy the latest pushbike with skinny tyres to ride all over Napier. She was also part of a strong Marching Girl presence in the town and adept at 'swinging the baton.' During the War when it was feared that a Japanese invasion of New Zealand was imminent, Joan learnt to fire a revolver. Just in case.

Phil and Joan picture beside the Tiger Moth aircraft in Napier 1940. (Photograph courtesy of Lamason Family Collection)

Joan Hopkins (back second left) and Phil (back third left) on a social outing with friends and family in Napier. Phil's brother Bill is centre of the front row. (Photograph courtesy of Lamason Family Collection)

Of her childhood years, Cherry Lamason writes of her mother Joan: "I have seen Mum hit a bullseye every time using an air pistol. A friend once bought a gun, set up a target and asked Mum to have a go. She was making scones at the time, so dusted off the flour, went into a crouching position you see the American cops use, and proceeded to hit the target every time. 'Glad I haven't lost my touch,' she said and returned to the kitchen." Small wonder that the Lamason marriage was built – mutually – on such strong stuff.

Volunteering for Military Service

Second only to Joan, Phil's other passion was flying. "I had been interested in flying and had joined the Territorial Air Force but only actually started training when war broke out," he recalled in an interview with Charles G. Rowland MD in 1985. This was "not out of any sense of patriotism but for the hell of it, and a love of flying." On September 20, 1939, just two days after his 21st birthday, Phil completed his Short Service Application, volunteering to become a Reserve with the Royal New Zealand Air Force (RNZAF). Only 17 days earlier Great Britain had declared war on Germany. Phil stated that he had "flown 15 hours as a passenger and intended to learn … the majority of the flying being done with the New Plymouth Club." Highlighting a mechanical disposition Phil also noted in his application that "I have owned both motor cycles and cars during the past two years and do my own repairs etc. I always have been a keen amateur mechanic."

Phil had also run into a problem when he signed up. The boyhood boxing injuries that had left him with the multi-times broken nose required attention. "I had a medical within about two or three weeks of the war breaking out but had to have a minor operation on my nose, which prevented me entering the service until about the middle of 1940," he once recalled. The nose became a defining feature. Once described as a "tall, handsome New Zealander with blue eyes and a broken nose," a later truncated version became "the broken-nosed Kiwi." In another high profile account written in a renowned war story 'The White Rabbit,' (published 1952) Phil is described as "a New Zealander with the battered nose of a boxer." This injury had slowed his breathing but if Phil was to be a pilot he had to be able to breathe through his nose while wearing a flying mask. He underwent the surgery and with characteristic haste immediately discharged himself from hospital.

Phil during his training time at RNZAF New Plymouth in late 1940. (Photograph courtesy of Lamason Family Collection)

Consequently it was some nine months later, and soon after signing his Attestation for Service as a Reserve in the RNZAF Ground Training Course (GTS) that Phil was called up for basic training. He entered the recently developed RNZAF Levin (Weraroa) on September 30, 1940. Weraroa was a local airfield which had previously been a New Zealand Government Training Farm. In October 1939 the Initial Training School from RNZAF Station, Rongotai in the city of Wellington was transferred to this Levin base. Most of the RNZAF and WAAF trainees for the first half of WWII underwent their basic training at Weraroa, Levin. The GTS course comprised six weeks of lectures, drills, routines and procedures which instilled into trainees the essential disciplines of military life – disciplines which for Phil were to become a life-line in the grim days of Buchenwald. Phil's test results showed that he graduated from this introduction into 'military ways' with above average results.

Progressing to the 'learning to fly' phase of training, Phil returned to New Plymouth to enter RNZAF No 2 Elementary Flying Training School (EFTS) which had been set up on the hastily transformed New Plymouth municipal aerodrome at Bell Block. Reflecting New Zealand's overall unpreparedness for war, this RNZAF Station when Phil arrived on November 23, 1940, was conducting flying training in an 'assortment of machines.' These planes had been taken over or 'impressed' into service from aero clubs around the North Island.

Elementary pilot training comprised an eight-week course during which equal time was spent in ground studies including map reading

RNZAF Station, Weraroa, Levin, 1941. (Photograph courtesy of Airforce of New Zealand Archives.)

Above: RNZAF New Plymouth at Bell Block, (circa 1940). (Photograph courtesy of Air Force of New Zealand Archives.) Below left: De Havilland Tiger Moth (Photograph courtesy of Mike Harold). Below right: Miles Hawk.

RNZAF Airspeed Oxford aircraft. (Photograph courtesy of Airforce of New Zealand Archives.)

and basic navigational skills plus learning to fly. The flying training routines, in the summer skies with Taranaki's Mount Egmont in the background, included stages of dual tuition with the support of a staff instructor, followed by segments when the trainees flew in pairs, 'practising their patter on one another.' During the Elementary Training phase at RNZAF New Plymouth, Phil's record shows he completed 25 hours of dual control and 25 hours solo flying in DH60 and DH82 Tiger Moths and also in Miles Hawk aircraft.

Successful graduation from Elementary Training promoted Phil to Service Flying Training School, commencing on January 18, 1941, at the No 3 Flying School at RNZAF Station, Ohakea. This base, newly created on the sweeping river plains of the Manawatu/Rangitikei region of the North Island, was where Phil undertook his eight weeks of Intermediate and Advanced Training.

These phases were designed to introduce and equip trainees with the more complex skills required to fly service-type, multi-engine aircraft. The RNZAF Ohakea Station at this time comprised a handful of available Airspeed Oxford twin engine aircraft for the training of airmen. 'Oxfords' were well suited for this purpose with the normal three crew seating set-up being adaptable for pilot, navigator, bomb aimer, wireless operator, air gunner, or camera operator training. During his Intermediate training time Phil completed 25 hours dual and 25 hours solo in the Oxfords. He then added a further nine hours dual and 46 hours solo flying in the same aircraft at the Advanced stage. This higher level training covered all aspects of flying including aerobatics, low-level and night flying, along with testing that extended to skills in stationary target bombing, bomb aiming and gunnery.

Phil Lamason pictured during his Intermediate and Advanced Flying Training at RNZAF Ohakea, 1940. (Photograph courtesy of Lamason Family Collection)

Phil was awarded his Flying Badge, his "wings" on March 10, 1941. At the completion of Advanced Training on April 12, 1941 and with an overall grading of 75% Phil was pronounced by his instructors to be "a sound, keen type, and good all round pupil with average ability." Most significantly they noted his leadership potential, commenting that he was a graduate that "merits commission with some more service experience."

Successful Kiwi trainee airmen like Phil Lamason who graduated with very good grades from the Advanced Training School courses in New Zealand were, at this stage of the War, posted directly on to the Royal Air Force (RAF).

Amidst this frenetic aviation focus Phil and Joan were married. Their wedding took place at the Gospel Hall, Carlyle St, in Napier on March 29, 1941. Whilst being a very happy occasion for the newly-weds it was also to be a brief time together. The shadow of War loomed on the horizon. Just four short weeks later Phil bid his beloved wife 'farewell.'

As part of a contingent of 218 Kiwi airmen, Phil departed Auckland on April 29, 1941 on a regular scheduled sailing on the ocean liner 'Awatea' destined for Canada.

Some of this group of airmen were assigned to further wartime preparation in Canada as part of the unfolding Empire Air Training Scheme, colloquially known as 'EATS' and better known later as the highly regarded British Commonwealth Air Training Plan (BCATP). This was not so for Phil. On arrival in Vancouver on May 14, 1941, he

Phil Lamason and Joan Hopkins, wedding day, Napier, March 29, 1941. (Photograph courtesy of Lamason Family Collection)

along with some others in the group exchanged the idyllic comforts of the ocean liner for a more austere travel experience – the 5-6 day train journey across the huge early summer panorama of the North American continent. Phil registered at his assigned Manning Depot on May 20, 1941 to await his designated ocean convoy and transportation across the North Atlantic Ocean to Britain. During this waiting stage, which could vary in time between a few days to a few weeks, airmen were engaged in some military activity to maintain fitness and readiness. However they also enjoyed short periods of leave, day travel and especially the warm hospitality offered by local people.

Tight security surrounded the arrival, formation and departures of ships in wartime Atlantic convoys. Phil's voyage across the North Atlantic was aboard a Merchant Navy ship as part of a larger convoy. Because of the heavy U-boat presence in the area the convoy required destroyer protection. Progress was slow, a factor that slightly unnerved the captain of Phil's vessel. He put on a fast pace, to the point where the naval escort was in danger of being overtaken. In an exchange of signals by Aldis lamp, an order to slow down was met by refusal from the merchant captain. Phil had read the exchange of signals and was amused at this show of defiance. The ship he was on made landfall at Scapa Flow on June 28, 1941.

Phil pictured at the conclusion of his pilot training with RNZAF, 1941. (Photograph courtesy of Lamason Family Collection)

Convoy records for Atlantic crossings show that the convoy code named HX132 and comprising 34 ships, including escorts, left Halifax, Nova Scotia on June 10, 1941. Log notes from leaders of this convoy concur with Phil's account, describing one vessel as a "ship always 4-8 miles astern of station," and how "no amount of signals to her had any effect at all." One other day there was consternation and the convoy ceased sailing altogether, when one of the ship's captains reported that he believed his vessel had struck a submarine. His concern proved to be unfounded and normal sailing was resumed. Records confirm that on June 28, 1941, ships from this convoy arrived at different ports in the northern parts of the United Kingdom.

Relieved to have finally arrived at the theatre of war and with the RAF in his sights Phil Lamason was ready for action. He was just 22 years old.

Phil Lamason, on arrival in England and the RAF, July 1941. (Photograph courtesy of Lamason Family Collection)

War and New Horizons

Background to Phil Lamason's War

The outbreak of World War II in Europe came as a result of Germany's invasion of Poland on September 1, 1939. Earlier the German Fuhrer, Adolf Hitler, had reached an agreement with the Soviet Union that the two powers would divide Poland between them. A month beforehand Great Britain and France, in an effort to forestall Hitler's plans, had signed a treaty of promised mutual assistance with Poland. Left with no other option, Great Britain and France honoured their guarantee of support for Poland. At 11.00am on September 3, the British Prime Minister Neville Chamberlain declared war on Germany.

On Phil's arrival in the United Kingdom, history suggests that the strong and commanding Lamason presence, combined with his good looks, made an immediate impact. The story goes that when asked at the RAF Personnel Reception Centre in Bournemouth as to what type of aircraft he wanted to fly, the response was immediate. "Spitfires." As the Spitfire was widely regarded as the 'glamour machine,' this is unsurprising. "So you want to fly Spitfires?" the interviewing officer persisted. "Yes," insisted Phil, determined to have his way. The answer to Phil's assertion was a resounding 'No,' along with a couple of nights in the 'lock-up' for insubordination. The RAF was looking at Phil's steady, reliable character and his leadership potential. It seems that once these qualities were ascertained the pilot in question was immediately siphoned off into heavy bombers. "We're not wasting you on a fighter," he was told. Within a few days he was off to No 23 Operational Training Unit (OTU) at RAF Pershore in the picturesque Worcestershire countryside to commence training for entry into Bomber Command.

The events preceding Phil's arrival undoubtedly had some bearing on his wish to fly Spitfires. Just 12 months previously Britain had her back to the wall. The feisty little Spitfire – along with the dependable Hurricane – stood between defence and defeat. Confronted by the continuing Nazi threats and aggression, and unsuccessful in his efforts to form a cross-party government, Chamberlain resigned as British premier on May 10, 1940. This ushered in the ultimate embodiment of the British Bulldog spirit, Prime Minister Winston Churchill.

Then, on June 9, 1940, German and British forces clashed in the skies over the United Kingdom in the opening salvo of the Battle of Britain.

Hitler's aim was to force Britain to agree to a negotiated peace settlement by implementing Operation Sea Lion, a sea and air blockade of the English Channel and the British Isles. The enemy would be starved of resources and blown out of the sky. From July to September of 1940 both sides were locked in what proved to be a defining time in the War and the first ever military campaign in history to be fought entirely in the air. Early on, as the Battle of Britain was gaining momentum, RAF Fighter Command had fared extremely well. But at best this was a lopsided contest. Whilst countering the German assault with every resource at its disposal, Fighter Command was desperately outnumbered by the Luftwaffe ratio of four to one. As time progressed the Luftwaffe pressed home its 'take no prisoners' advantage with increasing confidence. Inevitably the sheer weight of enemy numbers began to tell on the RAF as daily tallies revealed the glaring lack of replacement pilots and fighter aircraft on the front line. Resources were in short supply and, as September approached, RAF fighter squadrons, pilots and ground crews were rapidly reaching exhaustion point. Fighter Command needed a miracle if it was to continue.

Unbelievably it was the Germans themselves that provided it. Flying over England with night coming on and unable to locate his target, one lone, lost German pilot dumped his bomb load on London. Churchill's retaliation was swift. Berlin was bombed the following night. Enraged, Hitler switched tactics, removing the emphasis on the annihilation of British air bases to destroying London. Thus, on September 7, 1940, began Hitler's revenge, the Blitz. Hitler's decision was a gift to the RAF. In this moment he had unwittingly handed Fighter Command the respite that was so badly needed. During the ensuing seven days of reprieve from Luftwaffe attacks, British airfields were repaired and Fighter Command was able to rebuild its squadrons back to sufficient strength for the desperate battle of the skies eight days later.

On Sunday, September 15, 1940, as both sides were engaged in the all-out aerial combat of their lives, and their nationhood, Winston Churchill chose to drop in on Fighter Command's Control HQ at No. 11 Group, Uxbridge. Seated above and overlooking the vast plotting table with live radio communication crackling in from the pilots, Churchill asked Group Commander Air Vice-Marshal Keith Park the vital question. "What are our reserves?" In an answer that defined to the core the essence of the British fighting spirit, the New Zealander replied, "There are none, they are all up."

In the desperate 13-hour battle high above England's green fields that day, the Spitfires and Hurricanes of RAF Fighter Command waged their war against the superior numbers of the Luftwaffe's Messerschmitts. Fighter Command stamped its authority over its skies. The Battle of Britain was won. And so was immortalised Churchill's historic utterance: "Never in the field of human conflict was so much owed by so many to so few." Within a few short days of losing this immense battle, Hitler cancelled Operation Sea Lion.

German hostilities continued through to May 1941 with bombing raids on British cities, ports and industrial areas. London endured 11 weeks of relentless nightly bombing from September into November 1940. But were the people demoralised? No. From April 16-19, 1941, when one third of London was decimated, and damage inflicted on iconic landmarks including Buckingham Palace and Westminster Abbey, the catch phrase "We can take it," sustained the British fighting spirit.

In the end both parties had suffered heavy losses. The Germans had 1600 aircraft knocked out of the skies while British losses were in excess of 1000 fighter planes. In the eight months of the Blitz, 18,629 men, 16,201 women and 5028 children had perished. A heavy toll for both sides.

With Hitler finally abandoning his invasion of England, the bombing war began to gather more momentum. England caught her breath and turned to RAF Bomber Command to take the battle into the heartland of Germany.

No 23 Operational Training Unit, RAF Pershore

At the start of July 1941, Sergeant Phillip John Lamason was ready and motivated to do his duty. Little could he foresee how events yet to unfold would test the very fibre of his being.

RAF Pershore and No 23 Operational Training Unit presented Phil with his first experience of flying an operational heavy bomber aircraft. The steadfast but aging Vickers Wellington was at this time the backbone of the Bomber Command training and operational flying. Flying daily 'circuits and bumps,' with the support of an instructor, ensured that recently-arrived trainee pilots quickly became familiar with the dependable, twin engine 'Wimpy' bomber. Then graduating to the command of the airplane, the pilots further acquainted themselves with the capabilities of the machine, clocking hours above the spectacular

43

Vickers Wellington bombers.

patchwork of the English countryside in summer. At the same time, other trainee airmen at the base below focussed in on the specialist skills particular to their forthcoming bomber crew positions. The Wellington bomber was generally flown on operations with a crew of six, comprising pilot, co-pilot/observer, navigator, radio operator and two air gunners, one at the front and one at the rear of the aircraft.

Phil completed his operational conversion to pilot heavy bombers on August 10, 1941.

Bringing these volunteer airmen together early in their bomber operational training was a key step in the somewhat random but generally effective 'crewing-up' process. This usually took the form of putting the trainees together in an airfield hangar and letting the pilots, as the aircraft 'skippers,' co-ordinate the process of forming their own crews from the talent available, ideally creating a compatible team to whom they would ultimately entrust their lives. The new crews then embarked on developing the teamwork needed to undertake operational flying and especially the skills of flying night missions. Long hours were spent on cross-country flights, bombing practices, air gunning, manoeuvring into formations, implementing evasive actions and especially the skills of safely negotiating emergencies caused by the vagaries of the English weather. Flying these training sorties continued on into the first weeks of Phil's first active service deployment to RAF No 218 Squadron.

Sergeant Phil Lamason (wearing the flying cap) with his 6-man Wellington Bomber crew pictured beside their aircraft at No218 Squadron, RAF Marham, in September 1941. Phil trained on and later flew the twin engine Wellingtons operationally at RAF Marham before the Squadron transitioned to heavier Stirling Bombers in January, 1942. Crew personnel changed regularly for Phil at 218 Squadron. Flying together and pictured this day, Left to Right were: Harry "Stubby" Stubbs, I.A. Campbell, W.B.Richardson, Phil, Dick Mendes, Tom McDonagh. Harry Stubbs (21 August) and Tom McDonagh (5 May) were killed on operations during 1942. (Photograph courtesy of Lamason Family Collection)

No 218 Squadron, RAF Marham

During the time of Sergeant P.J. Lamason's first operational posting at No 218 Squadron at RAF Marham, in Norfolk, East Anglia, a solid core crew flew together regularly on operations under his command. Flight Engineer, Sgt H.G. Stubbs; Wireless Operator, Sgt R.H. Poole; Air Observer, Sgt I.A. Campbell; Navigator, Sgt Willet; and the Air Gunners Sgt S.V. Reeve, Sgt W.B. Richardson and Sgt T.W. Dunk in the rear gunner's turret.

Three days before Phil arrived on base at No 218 Squadron, RAF Marham on August 21, 1941, Churchill's War Cabinet received the damning Butt Report, presenting the results of an inquiry into the effectiveness of Bomber Command's operational raids for the year to date. It was not good reading. Here was Phil, an airman new to operations, advancing into the frontline of a division of the RAF which was suddenly under the microscope. Although providing a welcome emotional boost to the battered British populace below, this well trained airborne echelon was now being challenged to address its inaccuracies. The report had shown that the impact of the RAF bombing raids on the German military machine was negligible. Despite the positive reports of returning aircrews, evidence showed otherwise. "Only a tiny fraction of bombs were falling within miles of their intended targets." This was happening at a disturbing cost in human lives.

No 218 Squadron, RAF Marham was at that time commanded by a New Zealander, Group Captain Andrew McKee, later to become Air Vice-Marshal Sir Andrew McKee. Known to his men as 'Square McKee.' He was interviewed shortly before his death in the 1980s and mentioned the young Lamason's "exceptional" flying skills along with other equally well-known Lamason attributes – his 'hard case,' or 'larrikin' ways. This behaviour would eventually cost Phil a rank.

Phil's second recorded operational flight was on the night of November 7/8, 1941. As the captain of one of 13 Wellington crews involved from No 218 Squadron, he joined with another 156 aircraft from other squadrons and bases to execute a bombing mission on the heavily defended German capital Berlin, the political stronghold and hub of the Nazi regime.

The Berlin mission, together with ancillary raids targeting the cities of Cologne and Mannheim, involved a total of 392 different Allied bombing aircraft and their crews. Sadly, as was the pattern to date, the bombs missed their specified targets. Even more tragically, 37 of the planes failed to return that night. This was more than twice the loss of aircraft previously experienced by Bomber Command in a single night. Things had to change. Sgt Lamason and his team flying in Wellington X9745, along with their fellow crews from RAF Marham, returned safely to base, having endured a baptism of fire. As a Squadron, they would seldom again be so lucky.

Recollecting this period of the War in later life, Phil Lamason recounted: "There was a moment when, for the first time, I distinctly remember feeling confident that we would definitely win the War...we were on a raid to Brest, in France, in a Wellington bomber. We were flying in formation towards the target, maintaining the mandatory radio silence, when suddenly our Wireless Operator blurted out, 'The Japs have just bombed Pearl Harbour!' It was the night of December 7, 1941.

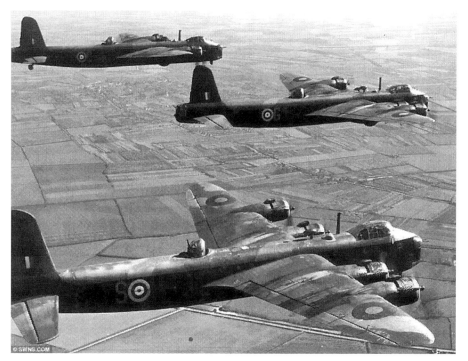
Short Stirling Bombers in flight.

I remember shouting back to the crew through the intercom, 'Now we're gonna win the War!' I just knew in my heart that once the Americans joined the War, with all their industrial might, that the Nazis would be doomed!"

The mid-winter months ushered in change at RAF Marham. In February 1942 a process started in December, was completed, the conversion of No 218 Squadron from the slower, older, Wellington bombers to the newer, heavier, four engine Short Stirlings. These lofty, Jurassic-like monsters were the largest of the British built wartime bombers of that time. Stirlings required additional crew members to those needed to fly the Wellingtons. Added to the existing mix were a mid-upper air gunner, and a flight engineer whose job it was to manage the four engines and, in most cases, act as the back-up pilot. Once airborne these giant aircraft with their strongly built wings were surprisingly manoeuvrable, and a joy to fly. Phil quickly adjusted to the challenges of the Stirling and was later deployed into a pilot-training role on this aircraft.

Many years later Phil outlined the vagaries of the Stirling to his aviator son-in-law, Graeme Simmonds: "Nasty on take-off. No steering to keep it straight until it reached about 20 knots below lift-off speed. Problem!! Not enough bite in the rudder to force the aircraft to stay on the centre line of the runway. It had to be controlled by handling each individual engine's thrust to keep it straight. The accidents were catastrophic due to this design fault. Simply, there was not sufficient rudder force from the single tail fin above to look like it would work… Think of the Lancaster bomber… it had two tail fins, each in line with the central thrust of the pair of engines on the wing ahead which equated to CONTROL!"

Early on, Phil and his training crew experienced first-hand another vulnerability of the Stirling. After a training flight on February 13, 1942, the undercarriage of Stirling N3713 collapsed on touch-down at nearby RAF Lakenheath. No one was hurt and Sgt Lamason and crew quickly returned to the fray, flying an operation to Le Havre the following night – this time in a different Stirling.

If Phil's ability to handle the Stirling was ever in doubt, the following will bear testimony to his expertise and his penchant for finding himself in uncommon situations. Graeme Simmonds shares an anecdote: Soon after the first Stirling bombers were delivered to the RAF, Phil received a "somewhat unusual command" delivered by an Air Vice-Marshal that the King, HM George VI, was "rather eager to see one in action." He had contacted the RAF with a simple request, to "please fly one over Windsor Castle." Three aircraft, one with Phil at the helm, were despatched in an impromptu formation fly-past. Phil was then instructed to send the other two aircraft back to base, before putting on a "damn good display" for His Majesty. "I know he did that," says Graeme, whose recollections come 'straight from the horse's mouth.' "And with an empty bomber, light in weight, four engines at full power, it was as near a fighter-like display as possible." According to Phil's daughter Trish Simmonds, the King was so impressed with the display that he issued an invitation to join the family at Buckingham Palace. Here Phil met the young Princess Elizabeth. King George commented to Phil that he was very pleased to meet with "people who are in the front line of the action." This was the first of several visits.

In a later sequel added by Lamason family friend Glenys Scott, Phil again met the King on his return to Britain from Buchenwald and was requested to do a repeat flight over Windsor Castle for "old time's sake."

Flight Sergeant Phil Lamason and four regular crewmen in front of another of the newly arrived Stirling bombers, at No218 Squadron, RAF Marham, November, 1941. Left to Right: "Stubby", Phil, Sid, Rich, and Doug. (Photograph courtesy of Lamason Family Collection)

The words from the King that have been passed down are, "If I can arrange an aircraft would you do a 'beat up' over Windsor Castle once more."

Darkest January 1942 also had heralded change at the very top. Anxious to address the issues of operational ineffectiveness and wastage, the War Cabinet appointed Sir Arthur Harris as Air Chief Marshal and head of Bomber Command. Harris, known in RAF history as 'Bomber Harris,' was at the forefront of an uncompromising strategy, to 'bomb the hell' out of Germany in the belief that national morale would collapse in the teeth of prolonged and sustained attack. The result was an unrelenting series of night attacks on German cities and the industrial zones outside of them. It did not take long for his strategies to be implemented.

For Phil at No 218 Squadron the Bomber Harris tactics began to take effect over the month of March. Among other missions and training sorties, the Lamason crew flew as part of three night bombing missions on the industrial city of Essen, attacking the home of the Krupp armament empire in the heavily defended Ruhr Valley, the geographical and industrial heartland of Nazi Germany. While these operations showed marginal improvements on the impact made by past raids, the arrival of Bomber Harris was most dramatically announced to the Nazis on the night of March 28/29, 1942. Harris had been looking for a chance to test his 'bomber streaming' plan, whereby a first wave of bombers over a city target, aided by the newly implemented Gee radio navigational system, could create a conflagration – uncontrollable fires which would work as a giant beacon to accurately guide successive waves of bombers to their mark.

For his purpose he chose the old, almost medieval styled city of Lübeck on the German Baltic coast. With its narrow streets and wooden buildings Lübeck was a soft target, but one Harris justified by linking to the important port facility and a nearby U-boat training school. Nine Stirlings from No 218 Squadron flew as part of the 234-strong bomber operation to Lübeck that cloudless night. For Sgt Lamason's crew the Lübeck operation was their second mission in Stirling N3725, an aircraft which was to become a familiar mount for Phil during his time at RAF Marham. The No 218 Squadron operational record for the raid states that: "Many fires were started by the time our aircraft arrived; bombs were straddled over the town railway lines near the main station. Never before had the crews seen so many fires – to put it in their own words, it was 'just one big party.'" Over two consecutive nights, 400 tons of incendiaries and explosives rained down onto the hapless city and at least half of the buildings were destroyed in the firestorm which ensued. For Harris this was vindication.

On April 25 each year New Zealand commemorates ANZAC Day, the day when the nation pauses to honour the memory of its war dead. But the newly commissioned Kiwi Pilot Officer Phil Lamason would have little thought for commemorations on that day in 1942. Here, at RAF Marham he and his crew were focussed on the mandatory pre-operational aircraft testing and mission briefing and planning in preparation for that night's operation. While Bomber Harris was intent on again 'unleashing the whirlwind' this time for a second successive night on the city of Rostock, Phil's and five other Stirling crews from No 218 Squadron at RAF Marham were to undertake a special mission to bomb targets in the city of Pilsen, home to the Skoda armaments plant in Nazi occupied Czechoslovakia. Planned as a smaller, diversionary raid to distract the German defences, these Stirlings, lacking the protection afforded by the greater numbers of aircraft in a bomber stream, were rendered most vulnerable. Airborne by 2130 hours, Pilot

Flight Sergeant (F/S) Phil Lamason alongside the undercarriage of one of the newly arrived Stirling heavy bombers at RAF Marham in November 1941.(Photograph courtesy of Lamason Family Collection)

Four of 218 Squadrons most distinguished pilots throughout 1942. Left to right F/Lt Roy Spear DFC RNZAF, F/Lt Geoff Corser DFC RAAF, F/Sgt Henderson, S/Ldr Phil Lamason DFC RNZAF and F/O Don Thomson DFC RNZAF.

(Photograph courtesy of Lamason Family Collection)

Officer Lamason and his crew Sgt Poole, Sgt Campbell, Sgt Willett, Sgt Davis, Sgt Richardson, Sgt Reeves and Sgt Stubbs began their planned eight and a half hour return mission across enemy-occupied territory. Dense, cloudy conditions over the target area meant that just one of the raiding aircraft was able to pinpoint the aiming point and no conclusive evidence was gathered to determine the success of the mission. Nonetheless, grimmer events were already unfolding for this operation. Stirling W7506 captained by flying colleague Pilot Officer Millichamp was not heard from after take-off, disappearing without trace – still lost to this very day.

For Phil and his crew, unluckily, some superstitious airmen would suggest, flying Stirling N3721 for the first time on operation, the real action was about to begin. After they turned for the long trek home their aircraft suddenly drew the attention of an enemy night fighter. What followed is best described in the citation given to Phil on May 15, 1942,

Stirling N3725 became a familiar 'mount' for Phil Lamason during his time at No 218 Squadron, RAF Marham. Phil skippered this bomber on 13 operations, including the contentious first raid on Lübeck and the First Thousand Bomber Raid on Cologne. Stirling N3725 completed a total of 31 bombing operations before crashing dramatically in Norfolk – the result of catastrophic engine failure as she returned from a night bombing mission in September, 1942. F/O John Frankcomb and five of his crew died in that crash. (Photograph courtesy of Lamason Family Collection)

when he was awarded the Distinguished Flying Cross (DFC) for his courageous actions and leadership that night:

"Pilot Officer Phillip John LAMASON, (NZ 403460), Royal New Zealand Air Force, No 218 Squadron. 'One night in April, 1942, this officer was the captain of an aircraft which attacked Pilsen. During the return flight his aircraft was attacked by an enemy fighter and sustained damage; the hydraulics were shot away and the turret rendered unserviceable, while a fire broke out in the fuselage. Displaying great presence of mind, Pilot Officer Lamason coolly directed his crew in the emergency and while two of them dealt with the fire, he skilfully outmanoeuvred his attacker and finally shook him off. By his fine airmanship and great devotion to duty, Pilot Officer Lamason was undoubtedly responsible for the safe return of the aircraft and its crew.

This officer has completed 21 sorties and he has at all times displayed courage and ability.'"

A tour of duty in Bomber Command in World War II usually comprised 30 completed operations. This tour at No 218 Squadron took a full 12 months for Phil Lamason. In that time he completed further sorties to places which are synonymous in the annals of World War II history – on Dusseldorf, Essen (four times), Mannheim, Berlin and on the industrial town of Bremen twice, including returning home once with the bombs still aboard, the bomb doors had failed to open over the target. On the night of May 30/31, 1942, he flew Stirling N3725 to Cologne as part of Bomber Harris's grand Operation Millennium, the first Thousand Bomber Raid. He flew missions on Dortmund, Saarbrücken, Duisburg, Osnabrück, and on Warnemünde and its nearby Heinkel armament factory. He went gardening, 'planting vegetables' (mines) off the island of Baltrum in the North Sea, he dropped 'nickels' (propaganda leaflets) over the North East of Paris and in the early months he flew two unsuccessful Wimpy missions on 'the toads of Brest' when the German navy, the Kriegsmarine, were using this French port as safe harbour for three key warships.

It was often a lottery. As Phil once said, "You were always frightened." Cloud, ice and wind conditions affected the accuracy. Flak (exploding shells) and night fighters...mechanical failures, so critical at the moment of touch-down. There was always attrition... the failure of planes to return to base... "aircraft not heard from after take-off"... the empty beds. There were also the lucky stories... like the crew of the Squadron's Wellington X9810 that was hit by flak one night in September, 1941, and was ditched off the Belgian coast and whose crew paddled their dinghy for three days in the English Channel, before eventually coming ashore near Margate in Kent. Events which had colleagues living to fly in another bombing mission on another night...

In his tour at No 218 Squadron between August 21, 1941, and August 28, 1942, Flight Lieutenant Phillip John Lamason (NZ 403460), Royal New Zealand Air Force, had flown 30 operations. He had clocked-up 150 hours in training and in operations in Wellingtons, plus the same amount in Stirling bomber aircraft. Phil had earned his break from operations.

Flight Sergeant Phil Lamason pictured at the controls of a Stirling Bomber aircraft, RAF Marham, early 1942. (Photograph courtesy of Lamason Family Collection)

In the early spring of 1942 Phil had been appointed to set up a Stirling bomber training flight at the RAF Marham base. During July No 218 Squadron had relocated to RAF Downham Market, a satellite airfield for RAF Marham, so making way for the establishment of training units and in April, 1943, the setting up of a Pathfinder Force. The rapid expansion of Bomber Command along with the continuing high loss of crews created the need for a better training regime. Specialist units were being established to bridge the gap which had become very evident between the Operational Training Units and the actual flying of missions over enemy-held territory. Bomber Harris had decided that the only successful way to train new aircrews was to make use of operationally experienced airmen as instructors. Phil was the 'go-to' person at RAF Marham and No 218 Squadron Conversion Flight was dutifully established on the base. However, because of the demand this plan placed on Squadron personnel it soon became necessary for the smaller squadron flights to be combined into larger training units. In Phil's case, No 218 Squadron Conversion Flight combined with three others to become No 1657 Conversion Unit (CU) at RAF Stradishall which became effective in October, 1942, for the fine tuning of trainee Stirling bomber crews.

The psychological impact of long distance raids on Bomber Command crews, who faced almost nightly the uncertainty of life and death, would have taken its personal toll on fortitude and stress levels. This was "the enemy within." It's easy to imagine then the therapeutic value of a few days leave. Phil's 'therapy' was to visit the Cadzow family on their farm near Edinburgh in Scotland. Here he formed a lasting friendship with John Cadzow – always referred to by Phil as "old Mr Cadzow." Here also, was a farmer whose major interest was in cattle. It seems the pair "talked cattle endlessly." Graeme Simmonds recalls being told that Mr Cadzow was fascinated by New Zealand tools for stock management and Phil's eye for stock. Drafting gates, for example, were an innovation to his host so Phil designed and helped build him a set. At the time these were said to be the first drafting gates in the region. Phil's host once invited him to a cattle sale in Ireland, remarking that "you have a better eye for stock than me so just go ahead and buy them." Such was John Cadzow's esteem for the Kiwi pilot that he offered to bankroll Phil if he would return and continue farming. Later, when Phil eventually acquired his own land in New Zealand, he named the farm 'Glen Devon' after his friend's property in Scotland. Happily the family connection has passed into the second generation with a visit to New Zealand by John Cadzow junior who formed his own friendship with Phil's son John Lamason.

No 1657 Heavy Conversion Unit (No 1657 CU), RAF Stradishall

After a period of leave, it was on October 3, 1942, that newly-promoted Squadron Leader Phil Lamason began his posting with No 1657 Heavy Conversion Unit (No 1657 CU) at RAF Stradishall in Suffolk. Here he was to spend the next 14 months and complete 1000 flying hours instructing and training new Stirling crews.

On the face of it the Lamason stories that follow could give the impression that life on the RAF Stradishall base was one long laugh. This was not the case, but as well as demonstrating his highly regarded flying skills Phil did manage to write himself into the annals of station history. An extreme example of high spiritedness that has come from many sources, including the family, will be explained later. It must be said that although the Lamason stories have been narrated in many different forums over the years, the RAF Stradishall era was the genesis.

Phil Lamason (4th from left in front row) pictured with the group of Conversion Unit instructors at 1657CU based at RAF Stradishall in 1943. Phil had been commissioned Acting Squadron Leader to organise the establishment of a heavy bomber (Stirlings) Conversion Unit at No 218 Squadron at RAF Marham in May 1942. This unit later in the same year merged with other similar squadron-based training units to create 1657 CU at Stradishall where Phil was posted as a flying instructor. (Photograph courtesy of Lamason Family Collection)

Recently promoted Pilot-Officer Phil Lamason, DFC, (second from right), photographed with a group of New Zealand Officers and Sergeants in 1942. Also in the group (fifth from left) is Group Captain Andrew 'Square' McKee, DFC, AFC. McKee, who served a long and distinguished career in the RAF on into the late 1950's, held a senior command position at No 218 Squadron then at No 15 Squadron during the months that Phil Lamason served at RAF Marham and RAF Mildenhall. (Photograph courtesy of Weekly News and Lamason Family Collection)

The writer wishes to acknowledge the RAF Stradishall Memorial Trust for recording these escapades in such an entertaining fashion at source.

The Commanding Officer of No 1657 CU was Squadron Leader BR Ker. He had been OC of No 218 Conversion Flight at RAF Marham and had Phil and some others of his old squadron join him at RAF Stradishall. It is stated that Phil, along with fellow Kiwi, Roy Spear, brought "a wealth of experience of heavy bomber operations," including the first Thousand Bomber Raid. Ker was reportedly of a somewhat strict disposition. This made for some resistance from his unit, many of whom were of the more free-spirited 'Commonwealth variety,' Phil included. It seems that one snowy evening, whilst the CO and Lamason were doing the rounds visiting the Flights, the authoritarian Ker was incensed to find the ground crew huddled around a roaring fire in one of the dispersal huts. To Phil's dismay, all the men were put on charge. This was too much for a fair-minded Kiwi who once complained that he seemed to spend a lot of his time "emptying the cooler of disgruntled wrong doers."

The construction and repair required at RAF Stradishall was a feature of the airfield due to mishaps and pieces of hazardous machinery that were often around. This could result in Stirlings being bent by their inexperienced pilots, who tended to damage tails and wings, particularly whilst turning. These events were liable to result in a 'telling off' from the instructor. On one occasion however the instructor had 'egg on his face.' Phil, who had always insisted to his pilots that they "take care when taxiing," was deep in conversation with his fellow pilot and neglected to properly check out the pathway ahead of the aircraft. Meanwhile a bowser (fuel truck) driver who was happily making his way along a perimeter track of the base at regulation speed and minding his own business, was somewhat dismayed to be suddenly 'passed over' by a fast-closing Stirling. For the bowser driver acceleration was fruitless, leaving him no option but to 'abandon ship.' Given that one of the Stirling's 'props' carved a path straight through the vehicle, this was a wise choice. Meanwhile back in the cockpit, expensive crunching noises indicated that all was not as it should be at ground level. The result was a shaken but fortunately unhurt driver, a mangled bowser and a red-faced instructor. Phil Lamason took some time to live down that incident.

"Take care when taxiing." (Painting by Mike Harold. Photograph courtesy of Mike Harold)

Phil recalled from this time an occasion when a Stirling bomber got stuck in the grassy verge of the airfield and how they resourcefully used another Stirling with all four props wound out to take-off speed, as a towing vehicle to pull the bogged aircraft clear. He also recalled to Glenys Scott how during this time he and his friend Wally Runciman once dropped their Stirlings down almost to ground level in a contest to see who could successfully take the heads of off the stalks of a cornfield using the rotating propeller blades as a harvester. Phil never disclosed who was deemed the winner of that event.

In another 'low level' incident there is a story about Phil and an air traffic controller and their ongoing wager about whose turn it was to 'shout' when they were in the bar. The arrangement was that Phil would fly at very low level towards the tower, which was the equivalent to about three storeys high, and his colleague would face him at the window. In effect they were eye balling each other as the plane approached. This required great nerve on the part of the controller. His challenge was to not signal a retreat by a previously agreed wave of his hand before the aircraft crossed a certain point of very close proximity

The Control Tower Wager. {Painting by Mike Harold) (Photograph courtesy of Mike Harold)

before lifting over the top of the tower. If the controller's nerve failed him and he signalled before the agreed mark, then he had to buy the round. The story goes that Phil never had to 'shout.' When the commander enquired from the tower as to the identity of the transgressing aircraft the control tower staff pleaded ignorance. The plane must definitely have belonged to some other base.

Mishaps inevitably went hand in hand with the instructional and training process. The skies in this part of England were constantly dotted with aircraft coming and going and the hazards of congestion were very real. On occasions these incidents were very serious as was the case on November 6, 1943, when a Stirling (R9192) on a night training flight out of No 1657 CU at RAF Stradishall and flying in cloud over Cambridge at 7000 feet, accidentally collided with the tail section of a Wellington bomber (X3637). The impact sent the latter's crew of seven Australian airmen corkscrewing to sudden death. The pilot (Flying Officer D.W. Thompson RNZAF) and crew of the irreparably damaged Stirling were somehow able to wrestle their aircraft to a safe landing nearby. During the WWII years, more than 3000 volunteer Allied

The irreparably damaged front end of the Stirling bomber R9192 from No 1657CU, RAF Stradishall. This aircraft and crew miraculously survived a mid-air (7000ft) collision with the tail end of a Wellington bomber (X3637) during a night training flight on November 6, 1943. Incredibly the crew of the Stirling were able to retain sufficient control to battle the aircraft to a safe lending. All seven crew members aboard the ill-fated and disabled Wellington bomber, died in this accident. (Photograph courtesy of Lamason Family Collection)

airmen were to die in training mishaps and crashes, many of these men perishing without having ever flown on an operational mission.

Phil too had moments of emergency on these training flights. One time an aircraft malfunctioning required that the training crew he was with land at the nearest available airfield which happened to be RAF Polebrook.

In the summer of 1942 this base had been turned over to the United States Army Air Force (USAAF) for their heavy bomber group. In what can again best be described as yet another Phil Lamason serendipity moment, among the first people to approach and shake his hand after making safe touch-down was a familiar face. Congratulating him on the "great job in getting that kite down," was none other than Clark Gable. The iconic movie actor was serving as an air gunner with the US 351st Bomber Group for a year. Phil commented to Gable that he "recognised him from 'Gone with the Wind' when he and Joan had seen the film before the war back home in Napier." Phil's lasting memory of the unexpected encounter was that Gable "seemed a good sort of a bloke."

The local landscape around RAF Stradishall in Suffolk was characterised by flat marshlands and long straight canals with adjacent grassed flood-banks, and provided ample scope for Phil's off-limits low-flying skills. Together with his mate Wally Runciman, the pair would occasionally drop their bombers down to the water level of the canals, the Bedford canal in particular, and play follow the leader. This meant that on-looking farmers could only see the top of the aircraft's rudder above the stop-banks. While these 'beat ups' were huge fun for the pilots they were less so for the 'locals.' Complicating this were the various footbridges along the canal. Every time the pilots came upon one the aeroplane had to be lifted to gain clearance. This was a deft manoeuvre. Lift too steeply and the tail gunner took a dunking, too low and the plane collected the bridge. Inevitably there was an incident. In the version related many years later, Runciman was in the lead and just managed to clear a suddenly looming bridge. Lamason however was less fortunate. Slower to lift in time he collected the bridge and crunched in the front of the aircraft's underside. When called before the Station Commander the culprits concocted a yarn about hitting the one and only tree on the marshland. Their only difficulty was that the incident had been reported numerous times by concerned locals. The frustrated commander told Lamason to go away and stop causing grief.

The RAF Stradishall version differs however. Here, Lamason was in the lead and Runciman clipped the bridge. "The story hatched, that the second pilot had 'clipped some trees' on his landing approach, failed to hold water owing to the aircraft having been identified during the incident. The perpetrators duly came clean, were reprimanded by 'the Groupie' and calm returned for the locals of Bedford Canal. Apparently the locals had been zealous in their written complaints to officialdom as Runciman and Lamason discovered when the Groupie fished in his pocket and handed over a sizeable sheaf of letters." Many years later Phil would tell these stories to willing listeners including Graeme Simmonds. "Phil always regarded the Bedford Canal 'beat up' as one of his best escapades," Graeme recalls. He once asked how much space there had been between the wingtips and the sides of the canal. The reply was nonchalant. "A good yard."

Dunking the Tail-gunner. (Painting by Mike Harold)

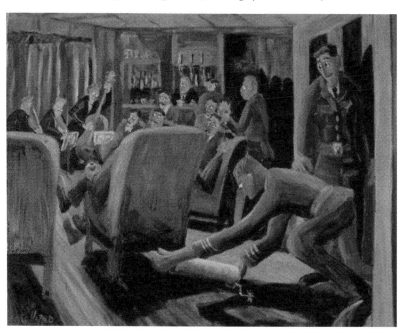

The Incendiary into The Mess. (Painting by Mike Harold) (Photographs courtesy of Mike Harold)

63

But time now for the ultimate pièce de résistance and a story that still lives on. This version belongs to RAF Stradishall although typically, there are others. The spacious Officer's Mess at RAF Stradishall provided ideal facilities for many activities and functions, and in addition to the residential and dining rooms, it contained a dance hall, snooker room, lounge and ante-rooms. The standard décor had been embellished by several superb murals mostly of village scenes, and also a well-stocked bar. During one fairly restrained drinking session the gentle strains of an Entertainments National Service Association (ENSA) string ensemble could be heard coming from the ante-room. Not being 'string quartet men' several officers had declined the invitation of the Base Commander to attend their recital, and as their drinking became more serious it was decided to 'liven up the concert a little.' Who actually suggested making a bomb remains 'classified' but the ring leaders were represented by members from the Dominions! The experts were soon able to convert a cardboard tube, some cordite and a simple fuse into live ordinance. With no thoughts of retreat, the fuse was lit, the door of the ante-room opened (by a supposedly reasonable staff officer) and the bomb rolled in. One vivid recollection is of the back of the Air Commodore who was sitting close to the door. Although the potential force of the device was never calculated, it was certainly effective, the soothing sounds of the viola, violin, bass and cello being obliterated by an ear-splitting explosion, followed by silence – and then bedlam! The immediate response came when the officers, now rapidly sobering up, were faced by their livid soot-streaked Commander, and at that moment several future careers looked decidedly precarious. Punishment was unexpectedly severe for, although nothing was said, the bar was permanently closed. After two days, and in anticipation of worse to come, it was agreed that an apology was needed. Phil Lamason, Art Nicholl and one other presented themselves to the Air Commodore to apologise and to explain their views on chamber music. Maybe they suggested that the Andrews Sisters would have been a better choice. It was in vain. Phil was demoted a rank, but he was also on the move to another squadron. He was however twice Mentioned in Despatches for "bravery and distinguished service" during his time at RAF Stradishall.

Phil pictured with a group of fellow Instructors at RAF Stradishall, 1943. Left to Right: "Ging" Howarth, Phil, "Tubby" Neilson, Ricky Witney and Hank Tilson. (Photograph courtesy of Lamason Family Collection).

No 15 Squadron, RAF Mildenhall

No 15 Squadron at RAF Mildenhall, in Suffolk, proved to be Phil's final posting. On arrival came a welcome sequel to the bomb incident. Phil was again under the command of Group Captain Andrew McKee from his time with No 218 Squadron. Dismissing the recent demotion at RAF Stradishall the CO immediately restored Phil to his rank of Squadron Leader ordering him to "put your ring back up as 15 Squadron wants a new Flight Commander." Together with the rank restoration came the CO's firm warning that no such stunts were even to be considered on his Base. For the record Art Nicholl also ended up at Mildenhall but this time on No 622 Squadron.

"Necessity" the proverb says, "is the mother of invention." This was especially so at the operational frontline that Phil was re-entering on December 1, 1943. Whilst the tide of the War was slowly ebbing in the Allies' favour, improvements in the strategies and mechanisms of engagement on both sides had continued apace. At the time of Phil's arrival at RAF Mildenhall, No 15 Squadron was transitioning from Stirlings to the more 'state of the art' Avro Lancaster. Stirlings with their limited 'ceiling' had become 'sitting ducks' to the improvements in the enemy's use of radar, searchlights, flak and night fighter attacks. The Lancaster had been designed by Roy Chadwick as a refinement of his earlier smaller Avro Manchester bomber. At the start of 1944 'Lancs' were being rolled out on mass production lines from factories around Britain at the rate of around 230 aircraft per month to meet Bomber Harris's demands.

With its gracefully wide wingspan and four resonating Rolls Royce Merlin engines, this bomber could carry a load of fuel and bombs equivalent to the weight of the aircraft itself. The Lanc could operate at a higher ceiling of 23,500 ft. when needed and comfortably flew the greater range in distances now required for the successful accomplishment of bombing missions. It was the quintessentially functional and clinically efficient bomber aircraft of its time. Not built for comfort, the Lancaster was about power and the effective delivery of destruction. It became an icon, a significant point of difference in determining the outcome of the War but also came in for some light-hearted 'flak.' An anecdote from No 15 Squadron titled 'A Brief Encounter': "Try telling some survivors that Lancasters were a delight to fly, they were queens of the sky, and they will cast you a quizzical glance. For them there are memories of clapped-out kites at Heavy Conversion Unit, or Lancaster Finishing School, even their squadron. They were never to know a factory-fresh Lanc, still smelling of paint and dope, still a little stiff on the controls.

"All through Operational Training Unit on Wimpys or Whitleys, then Heavy Conversion Unit on Halifaxes, or Stirlings, or Lancasters – even Manchesters – they had grappled with worn-out crates well past their prime. As if they did not have enough to do – learning their trade, moulding together as a fighting team – there were the frustrations and dangers presented by tyre creep and buckling undercarts, gycol leaks, or coring, engine fires and twisted fuselages to contend with. And there was the ever-changing weather to battle with!

"Always there was the prospect of their very own spanking-new Lanc when they began their tour. And invariably they were disappointed to find that, as new boys, they had to take the oldest kites, until the flight commander was satisfied they 'had the makings,' had served their apprenticeship, were deserving of a new one. Too many crew failed to come through the so-called apprenticeship...

"One Flight Lieutenant, Bill Blott, who was posted to No 15 Squadron at RAF Mildenhall found himself allocated Lanc W4355

The Lamason Lancaster Bomber crew pictured in January 1944 at the start of their operational time together at No 15 Squadron, based at RAF Mildenhall. These seven air crewmen flew unchanged as a unit on 15 bombing operations, including that fateful final mission together on 8 June 1944. Left to Right (with RAF ranks at the time of the photograph): Navigator, Flying Officer (F/O) Ken Chapman; Bomb Aimer, Pilot Officer (P/O) Gerry Musgrove; Wireless Operator, F/O Lionel George; Flight Engineer, Flight Lieutenant (F/Ltn) John Marpole; Pilot, Squadron Leader (Sq/Ldr) Phil Lamason; Rear Gunner, P/O Tommy Dunk; Mid-Upper Gunner, Sergeant (Sgt) Robbie Aitkin. By the time of the crew's final operation together, Tommy Dunk and Gerry Musgrove had been promoted to the commission of Flying Officer while Robbie Aitken had by that time been promoted to the rank of (W/O) Warrant Officer. (Photograph courtesy of Lamason Family Collection)

described as a 'real banger,' whose F700 was itself tattered and oil-stained, ready for the rubbish heap. She rattled... she leaked ... she was a sluggish climber... Blott went to the top and 'bitched' to his 'A' Flight Commander, none other than Squadron Leader Phil Lamason. The New Zealander however was unmoved and Bill Blott's bitch fell on deaf ears."

Many airmen were by now into their second tour of operational duty. As a consequence of this, the newly appointed Squadron Leader Phil Lamason was able to surround himself with a hand-picked, mission-hardened aircrew, well prepared for the challenge of flying at the forefront of bombing raids. Phil would have known his team well. These seven men were to fly as an unchanged unit for 15 operations over the next six months, clocking some 200 Lancaster flying hours in training and on operations. These were to be their final months of wartime flying action and the pathway for each to his wartime destiny.

So aboard the Phil Lamason Lanc, how did this crew line up?

Fresh from a year of 'rest' at No 1657 CU at RAF Stradishall, perched on the 'dicky-seat' beside Phil and beneath the perspex cockpit canopy was Flight Engineer, Flying Officer John (Ginger) Marpole, 139292. John's key responsibilities were to monitor everything mechanical on the aircraft, especially the performance of each engine, the management of fuel flow and the hydraulics, and to communicate this information to his skipper. In the worst event of the Captain becoming incapacitated, the Flight Engineer would be next to pilot the plane.

For a man just 22 years of age, John Marpole, from Shepperton, Middlesex, England had experienced a lot of war. Enrolling with the Royal Air Force Volunteer Reserve (RAFVR) in October 1939, he had already completed 30 operations with No 218 Squadron, at RAF Marham, as a member of crews flying the Wellington and Stirling. During that time he had quickly shown that he was good at his job, having been seconded in the later part of his first operational tour into the crew of Squadron Leader Arthur Oldroyd. Although they had never flown in the same crew, John Marpole, like Phil Lamason, had flown on the hard missions at No 218 Squadron. The Oldroyd crew had been another of the select six aircraft from RAF Marham dispatched to Pilsen on that ANZAC night when Phil was greatly tested and consequently awarded his DFC. Having survived that raid unscathed, John Marpole's crew had been re-directed to the same target just eight nights later on May 4, 1942. This second raid was their turn to 'cop-it.' Their initial flak battering happened when they were caught in the cone of searchlights over the target, on the way home it was followed by even more flak action over the Ruhr, and an attack from a Junkers 88 night fighter aircraft over Brussels.

Only skilled and resourceful work by the crew nursed the haemorrhaging Stirling W7469 safely to an emergency landing at Manston. It was not surprising that in May, 1945, John Marpole was awarded a DFC for performing his wartime duties "with merit and distinction, gaining the confidence of his Commanding Officer by his efficiency. By his zeal, determination and consistent devotion to duty, he has set a very fine example, which will be an incentive for others to follow."

In the nose of the Lancaster, Flying Officer Gerald Albert (Gerry) Musgrove, J/17952 (RCAF), multi-tasked as Bomb Aimer, Observer and Front Air Gunner. Throughout the flight he provided a flow of locational information to assist the Navigator. On the run in to the target Gerry lay prostrate using the bomb sights to accurately direct the Captain to pinpoint the spot; and he was then responsible for releasing the bombs at the right moment. When the Lanc was under air attack he stood up to operate the twin .303inch guns in the front turret to help defend the aircraft. Born and raised in Calgary, Gerry Musgrove aged 28 and serving in Bomber Command with the Royal Canadian Air Force (RCAF), had already logged considerable operational flying time at No 15 Squadron from the middle of 1942. He too had survived the terror moments. In the early hours of the morning of July 29, 1942, Gerry's aircrew under its captain, Pilot Officer Meredith, had limped their badly battered Stirling N7588 to a crash-landing at RAF Coltishall after it experienced a night-fighter attack and suffered serious flak damage while returning from a raid on Hamburg. Gerry was to complete his 30 operations while flying with Phil Lamason and his crew over the next few months and was to be awarded a DFC for his courage, duty and service, after returning to his homeland at war's end.

Shielded by his blackout curtain and crouched over his map on the tiny chart table tucked-in behind the pilot, was the aircraft's Navigator, Flying Officer Kenneth Walter Chapman, 138136, from Reading, near London. To 25 year old 'Chappy' went the responsibility of plotting and then monitoring the flight path of the aircraft. His challenge throughout the operation was to co-ordinate data from the very basic altitude and airspeed instruments on his display panel with the observations and information being fed to him by other members of the crew. Accuracy was paramount. In darkness, often cold and cloudy weather and in variable wind conditions, he drew on all his mathematical strengths and scientific knowledge to correctly guide the aircraft to and from the target. If instruments failed, then the ancient maritime art of plotting the course by the stars became a last resort. Navigation done poorly meant the aircraft was lost.

Reflecting late in life on Chappy's skills, Phil recalled the night of March 23, 1944, when on a raid to Berlin, higher than forecast winds caused havoc for many aircraft. The prevailing conditions required navigators to quickly make dramatic changes to the planned flight paths. Because these required adjustments sounded so extreme, many of the navigators and skippers failed to make the corrections early enough, as the bomber stream headed out from England. Phil's navigator Ken

Chapman was exceptional. Not long after setting the heading for the outbound long haul to Germany, Chappy called his Skipper, "Turn left 55 degrees to stay on course." This was more than double the normal correction required when turning into a cross wind to stay on track. Phil said he trusted his navigator's word and Chappy's calculation of the wind proved to be correct. Unfortunately however, in such a freak powerful cross wind, many aircraft navigators could not cope with the possibility that such an alteration to heading could possibly be true. By not applying that extreme correction into the cross wind, over half the aircraft were swept away off course, never found their target and became lost somewhere over Germany in the night's black sky. As a consequence, a very high loss of aircraft occurred.

Chappy had earlier served time at No 15 Squadron before his return to RAF Mildenhall at the same time as Phil Lamason's arrival. He too had previously flown some tough missions – like the trilogy of night operations to Essen over just five days at the start of June 1942, flying Stirling N3758 with Sgt Steel and his crew. Chappy and Phil had become close mates, a friendship formed in their time together at No 1657 CU at RAF Stradishall over the previous year. Their very survival of the war would see their paths inextricably joined as together they would be immersed in the hellish depths of human wartime depravity.

Deeper into the fuselage seated above the bomb bay of the Lanc but still close to the Navigator, Wireless Operator, Flying Officer Lionel Henry James George, 138213, sat at his table beneath the perspex bubble and beside his tiny, lateral observational window. The Wireless Operator's role was to listen for and transmit any command instructions or important updates from outside the aircraft and communicate these to the captain – not an easy task against the constant rhythmical drumming of the four Merlins. Lionel George had also completed an earlier operational tour of 30 missions on Wellingtons and Stirlings through 1941-42 at No 218 Squadron at RAF Marham, during which time he had occasionally flown operations in the same crew as John Marpole. He had also been involved with Phil in the formation of No 218 Squadron Conversion Flight in the spring months of 1942, and had transferred to No 15 Squadron in December of 1943 from the short lived No 623 Squadron based at RAF Downham Market. On May 15, 1944, Lionel George was awarded the DFC with his citation reading: "This officer has completed numerous sorties on his second tour of operations. In the course of his activities he has participated in attacks on a wide range of targets including four attacks on Berlin and seven attacks on Essen. He is a wireless operator of high merit and his skill has contributed materially to the success of the operations in which he has taken part. He has displayed great courage and devotion to duty." Lionel George was clearly a man with significant wartime flying experience.

In this typically cross-section British Commonwealth WWII aircrew, Scotland was represented by Glasgow's 22-year-old Warrant Officer Robertson Brown (Robbie) Aitken, 1001191, who manned the exposed mid upper turret.

Bomb Aimer Gerry Musgrove standing alongside Tommy Dunk in the tail gunner's turret of the Lamason Lancaster in 1944. (Photograph courtesy of Lamason Family Collection)

The gunners' duties were essentially as observers and defenders – a job which Robbie executed with a sense of duty and courage to the very end. Having also come into Bomber Command from the ranks of the RAFVR, Robbie Aitken had previously served in crews flying similar missions as Phil Lamason's crew at No 218 Squadron through the first six months of 1942. Usually occupying the mid-upper turret but occasionally at the front of the Stirling, Robbie Aitken had flown some challenging raids in the crew of Sgt Boyd.

In later years Phil Lamason was to say of Robbie Aitken at No 15 Squadron, "He was the only crew member who was not a commissioned officer…I had tried to persuade him to apply for a commission. I thought he was worth it. He was a superb gunner…but he said he preferred to stay with his mates in the NCOs' mess." In recent times Robbie Aitken has become immortalised in the amazing digital wartime imagery 'The Last Defender' by Polish artist Piotr Forkasiewicz and his name preserved in the French village of Jouars-Pontchartrain, where a road close to Robbie's final resting place was in 1994 renamed by the local people as "Chemin de l'Aviateur Aitken" to "honour him and other Allied servicemen who fell on French soil."

The Commissioned Officers in the Lamason Lancaster crew at No15 Squadron, RAF Mildenhall, pictured probably in January 1944. Pictured (Left to Right): Flying Officer (F/O) Lionel George, Flight Lieutenant (F/Lt) John "Ginger" Marpole, Squadron Leader (Sq/Ldr) Phil Lamason, F/O Ken "Chappy" Chapman, and newly commissioned F/O Gerry Musgrove. (Photograph courtesy of Lamason Family Collection)

The rear gunner, "Tail-end Charlie" to the crew, was Flying Officer Thomas William (Tommy) Dunk, 160014, from Bulawayo, Southern Rhodesia, (nowadays Zimbabwe). Aged 32 years, Tommy had also arrived in Bomber Command via the RAFVR and had flown as a member of Phil Lamason's crew from the very beginning at No 218 Squadron. Together they had transitioned from the work-horse Wimpys through the lumbering Stirlings into the irrepressible Lancasters at No 15 Squadron. In this time Tommy had already flown some big raids with Phil Lamason's crew. There would have been a strong trust in mutually held specialist knowledge, judgement and skills between these two experienced officers. Isolated in the freezing cold of the tail of the Lancaster, the rear gunner had the primary responsibility of alerting the crew of any pending attacks from the aft quarter. Like his skipper he had to be very good at recognising distant aircraft by their silhouetted shapes. He then had to defend courageously in the face of attacks, often launched by night fighters stealthily approaching from behind and beneath the Lancaster. The rear gunner was invariably in the front line. Statistically Tommy's was the most vulnerable of all WWII aircrew positions. He too rests this day in French soil, his supreme sacrifice commemorated in a street name – "Rue du Lieutenant Dunk" in the French town of Plaisir.

So Squadron Leader Lamason at RAF Mildenhall was supported by some of the very best.

RAF Mildenhall was a larger RAF base and home to several squadrons in the course of the war. In 1944 No 622 Squadron shared the base with No 15 Squadron. Consequently there were always larger numbers of bombers coming and going as Bomber Harris directed.

'Archie' Hall, a WAAF (Women's Auxiliary Air Force) and friend of Phil's worked in the 'Ops Room' at RAF Mildenhall, the 'Holy of Holies.' In her book 'We Also Were There,' Archie offers an insight into her time on the station. She was assigned to the 'nerve centre' from which all secret information was issued. It was a "fairly large room containing nothing superfluous to the job." She writes of the 'sacred' desk and how "Facing this desk on the opposite wall and covering its entirety was the operations board. Upon this was chalked, when the time came, all the coming night's operation 'gen.'

"At a smaller desk manning the telephone and noting down all necessary information, sat the sergeant watch keeper. The watch keeper's other important role was to record the details of aircraft on operation on a huge board that took up the whole of one of the walls in the 'Ops Room.' Duty on an operational night was a long period of tension.

"As each aircraft took off, the sergeant watch keeper chalked up the details on the board – call sign and letter, aircraft number, captain's name, time of take-off and estimated time of arrival back at base – whilst leaving columns for time landed and other relevant details. During the long wait for the return there could be no relaxation. We were ever on the alert for early returns (with engine failures etc) and for the chance 'Intruder' – enemy fighter aircraft sneaking in to await the return of our bombers.

"Then as soon as the first aircraft was heard overhead (mission completed) all were alerted. At that time there was no radio transmission – silence prevailed over base and the entire landing procedure could be heard. In fact a great deal of chat came over the air to ground radio – the faint whistling of a certain signature tune could be heard signalling that my 'special' crew was overhead." For Archie, to have all the crews returning was wonderful, but "the long wait for those overdue, and the final acceptance that they would not return was hard." In the midst of tension there were parties. These were much needed 'to break the strain.' Part of Archie's work was the 'little tasks.' These were the very personal one of handing round the canvas bags, one to each crew, for the collection and safe keeping of each man's private possessions, papers etc. As she recalls, this could be a rather 'chokey' task. There were times when someone would say, 'If I don't come back Archie, you can have this,' and pick some treasured article.

"And then was the much-awaited homecoming. Gradually, in would troop the aircrew looking tired and emotionally spent. They then had to sit patiently while they answered a load of questions when all they wanted was their fried eggs and bed. The questions required by Intelligence were, of necessity, many and detailed. They included dinghy sightings, distress signals, enemy shipping, the target attacked, how it was identified and the weather. Then there were the all-important bombing details. The time, height, magnetic heading, the bomb aimer's description of results, aircraft damage if any and then finally would come the pilot's personal report. Only then could they head for the eagerly-anticipated bacon and eggs."

WAAFs learnt their first lesson immediately they set foot on an operational station. This was a 'must.' No matter what the circumstances one must 'keep a stiff upper lip at all times.' As she recalls this was, "not always easy due to the many tragedies in this small world of mine." Professional to the core, Archie's account also reveals the lesser-known, more human side of warfare on a daily basis.

In the 14 months since Phil's last operational time at No 218 Squadron, improvements in bombing raid effectiveness had been greatly facilitated not only by the ascendance of the Lancaster, but also by the development of the Oboe radio navigation system and the use of flares placed by Pathfinders or Master Bomber aircraft which refined the aim point for the other bombers.

When Phil and his new No 15 Squadron Lancaster crew flew their first operation together, a raid on the German city of Brunswick, on the night of January 14/15, 1944, they were again joining many other crews in continuing Bomber Harris's latest campaign initiative to overwhelm the enemy with numbers. The plan to bomb Berlin and other German cities, Harris believed, would "break German resistance." He further believed that if the RAF and USAAF combined in the campaign, "It will cost us 400 to 500 aircraft. It will cost Germany the war." This was proven to be prophetic. For the enemy too had made significant strides especially in the use of radar to guide night fighter aircraft, and in adopting a new strategy of attacking the Lancaster from behind and

Lancaster bomber being prepared for operation. (Crown copyright)

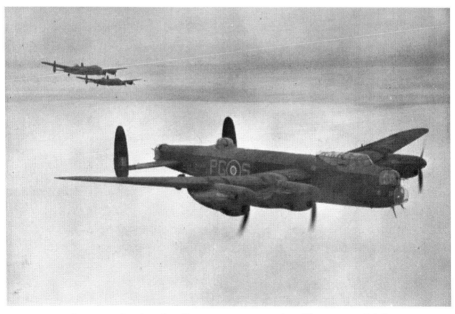

Lancaster bombers heading out on an operation (Crown copyright).

beneath the vulnerable under-belly. The toll was to become catastrophic. Statistics show that of the 7337 Lancaster aircraft built, 3932 were lost in action. The human impact of that for crews, friends, families and colleagues was enormous.

While the Americans bombed in day-time, the RAF Squadrons pounded relentlessly away at night. Harris was determined to have up to 800 bombers at his disposal for any single night raid. Over the next two months the Lamason crew were to fly some big operations in these massed bomber streams: two seven hour return raiding flights to Berlin; Leipzig, six and three quarter hours; Stuttgart, seven and a half hours; and Frankfurt, six hours. These times are daunting to modern travellers in the comfort of today's giant airliners. Consider too that it was always at night and in the late European winter and early spring months. Add to that the altitude. It was cold! Intensely cold! The leather/wool lined flying suits, boots, gloves and helmets were undoubtedly helpful and Lancasters did have a crude heating system of sorts which ducted warmer air from the inner engines. But this would have been little help for the Lamason crew as Phil and rear gunner Tommy Dunk routinely removed a perspex sheet or two of cockpit canopy or rear turret when over enemy lines to improve visibility and help in the earlier detection of approaching night fighters. This Arctic-like flying environment was not a place for the faint hearted.

Flying raids down 'Happy Valley' (Germany's Ruhr industrial heartland) at any time was scary. The Nazis had concentrated huge defences into this area. The combination of radar, searchlights and anti-aircraft ground fire meant that exploding flak could disable or, with a direct hit, destroy an Allied bomber. Given that aircraft in a massed bomber stream to the target could not deviate from the set path, the danger was all pervasive. Raw courage and focus on duty was paramount as crews ran the gauntlet through these flak barrages. Frightening – yes! But nonetheless these bursting shells made for a spectacular light show in the night. Phil Lamason once laconically commented how, "You knew it (the flak explosion) was close to you when you actually heard a 'bang' above the noise of the aircraft engines...it spoiled Guy Fawkes Night for me forever!"

After dropping the heavy bomb load, the Lancaster rose dramatically in altitude "like you were riding an elevator." It was at these times the aircraft was most vulnerable to enemy night fighter aircraft attack. Such attacks required the Lancaster pilots to take immediate evasive action.

76

Many relied on the corkscrew manoeuvre, "a sharp diving turn to port followed by a climbing turn to starboard." No doubt Phil practised and used that ploy to good effect.

On the night of April 29, 1944, on setting its homeward journey after successfully bombing a target in the city of Essen, the Lamason Lanc suddenly found itself 'coned' in the German searchlights. Phil's crew spent a harrowing 22 minutes in this predicament. Their repertoire of evasive tactics would be hugely tested. It is not recorded whether Phil adopted a defensive tactic that night which he often proudly enjoyed reminiscing about – a 'power dive.'

The detail of a 'power dive' as explained by Graeme Simmonds, again provides insight into the Phil Lamason character and skill… "A power dive is an extremely dangerous manoeuvre in a Lancaster bomber. It takes a cool head and a lot of nerve to perform this unbelievable feat in flying. It was a strategy used if an aeroplane was 'coned' or lit up by three or more searchlights to escape becoming a super bright-as-day target to be shot down by heavily concentrated anti-aircraft flak battery defences on the ground. You needed a lot of altitude to perform this move in an air battle. The nose of the plane is sharply forced over into a vertical dive with the air speed rapidly building, as the power of gravity and four V12 Merlin engines at1400 HP each accelerate the plane like a large bomb downwards towards the earth. The speed is beyond the manufacturer's design limits for the plane and beyond the maximum stress levels demanded of it. Nevertheless, the Lanc could take it!

"Virtually, nearly every second of power plunging speed is 1000 feet in descent! Now you MUST get this plane out of this dive! Even if the pilot braces himself with both feet on the flying panel in front of him with all of his strength to pull the aircraft out of the dive, the controls remain rigid, like concrete. You now must use the only way out of this crazy kamikaze-like dive. The incredibly powerful 'trim' device located on the extreme rear edge of the elevator (horizontal tail fin of the plane) will force the airplane out of its vertical dive by the very, very, oh so careful, cool as, slow winding of that elevator's trim handle. If you are too fast and panic, raising the nose sharply, a sudden massive shock-stall will stall the aircraft, way too low in altitude to ever recover flight. An aircraft stalls when its wing loses lift from its beautiful smooth laminar air flow over the top of its wings. This has nothing to do with any engine stalling or losing engine power. Any wing stalled plane is no

longer flying, just dead weight in the sky! It will then naturally pitch forward, nose down due to its basic built-in weight balance, slightly forward to cause the nose to drop in case of a stall. Think of an arrow losing forward momentum. Its nose, the heavy end, must drop. You must have flying speed for the wings to fly at all. The pilot's aim is to come out of the dive at such speed that his aircraft escapes the searchlights to hide once again in the safety of the black night, cutting off those fatal search lights. He is now safe, escaping the lights and anti-aircraft gun batteries trained on him."

Oberstleutnant (Lieutenant Colonel) Walter Borchers.

These Bomber Harris missions, known collectively as the Battle of Berlin, reached crisis point on the night of March 30/31, 1944, with the raid on the city of Nuremberg. The low level operation on a clear night, without the support of any diversionary alternate raids, was intercepted early by German night fighters. The attackers wrought carnage, carving up and scattering the streamed RAF bomber formations. Phil Lamason, at briefing, had spoken strongly and critically against the planned path for this particular raid. The Lamason crew flying their familiar Lancaster ED473 successfully made target and, despite the devastation unfolding in the sky around them, survived what for them was a seven and a half hour mission. That night 795 aircraft flew in what historically became known as the infamous Nuremberg Raid. Ninety-five bombers were shot down or crashed, an almost 12 per cent loss of aircraft in a single raid. This was far and away the biggest Bomber Command loss of aircraft in a single raid for the whole of the War. It "effectively ended the Battle of Berlin."

78

Map of UK and Central Europe showing RAF Bases and operational targets featured in Phil Lamason's War story. (Map Courtesy of Mike Harold)

Throughout this time Oberstleutnant (Lieutenant Colonel) Walter Borchers was emerging as a star in the German Luftwaffe. Aged 28 years, this veteran fighter pilot sporting successes from the early German air offensives, the Battle of France and the Battle of Britain, was now refining his defensive flying skills as a leader in the Nachtjagdgeschwader (Night Fighter Wing). As a night time defender of 'The Motherland,' Borchers was rapidly building his total of aircraft 'kills' as his Wing honed in on Allied bombing missions. He and Phil Lamason would cross paths one night.

Fourteen operations in six months at No 15 Squadron meant much time was also spent in training flights and 'local flying.' As part of the latter, Phil is recorded as having experienced flying the speedy Mosquito fighter bomber and also the United States Liberator bomber – all contributing to his grand total of almost 1700 military flying hours.

In later years Phil reflected to family friend Glenys Scott on the key elements which he believed contributed to his crews' successful completion and survival of 44 bombing operations over Occupied Europe. He talked of the strong connections of friendship, trust and camaraderie which helped them bond as a tight group, as was the case

79

with so many of the other bomber crews. He spoke especially of the adherence to discipline by all crew members and their immediate acceptance and reaction to his commands as the captain of the aircraft. He highlighted the vigilance of the crew – their ability as a group to quickly identify other aircraft in the night sky, a skill which he prided himself on having executed particularly well. He drilled his crew on the importance of getting five seconds warning of an incoming enemy night fighter – five seconds before it attacked meant he could successfully take evasive action.

Phil also described to Glenys how the crew would purposefully and regularly practice their emergency response routines in training flights, right down to the evasive flying tactics and procedures to follow in the event of a 'bale-out.' There was also the attention to detail – for example the air gunners would routinely polish the bullets in the ammunition belts prior to missions, to minimise the likelihood of the cannons jamming should the aircraft come under enemy fighter attack. They all favoured carrying the smaller navigator-type parachutes which could be easily attached and worn on the chest. He also felt that instinct played an important role for himself as the pilot, especially the ability to decide quickly on options and 'fly by the seat of your pants' as occasions so often demanded. Needless to say, there was always a big element of good luck thrown into this mix.

Phil's crew were to fly three more targeted city raids, to Aachen, Cologne and Duisberg before the changes in Bomber Harris's plans were implemented. The new emphasis for Bomber Command was to begin the softening-up of German coastal defences for the imminent Operation Overlord, and to strategically disrupt communication systems necessary for the German reorganisation of defences to combat the Allied invasion which was expected to follow the pending D-day landing. For this purpose the Lamason crew had flown three short missions to targets at Le Mans, Boulogne and Calais over the last two weeks of May.

Then, on the night of June 7/8, 1944, 17 Lancasters from No 15 Squadron were detailed for operations targeting the large railyards at Massy-Palaiseau near Paris. It was to be the most fateful night for the Squadron.

Soon after midnight Squadron Leader Phillip John Lamason, NZ403460, DFC, and his crew, cranked Lancaster MkIII LM575-H to life and taxied out, awaiting the clearance to take off for this strategic railyard raid. It was to be their 15th mission together but just their second riding LM575-H. The clearance was given and the four reverberating Merlins clawed the Lancaster into the air at 0041 hours. Soon the Lamason crew were climbing into formation and winging their way out over the choppy waters of the English Channel. This moonlit, mid-summer night mission, was on course for the hinterland of the German occupied French capital city of Paris. It was just another 'milk-run.' Another routine night mission.

Into Darkness: Bloody Bloody Buchenwald

"No! No! I can honestly say I never once took a step backwards, never!" - Phil Lamason.

In the words of a New Zealand journalist writing many years later, Phil Lamason was "a reluctant hero." With the exception of his flying exploits he rarely spoke of his Buchenwald experiences and, when he did, the information consistently erred on the side of understatement. So it has been left to others to tell his story. The writer therefore is indebted to multiple sources. Some are authors who have been captivated by the story of 'The Lost Airmen of Buchenwald' and felt the urge to make it available to the world, while others are fellow prisoners who have written their stories.

In particular, mention must be made of Australian writer Colin Burgess and his book 'Destination Buchenwald.' In April 2016, when asked for permission to include material as recounted by Phil Lamason concerning his evasion, betrayal and capture, for the purpose of this work, Burgess generously responded: "I would be more than happy to support this tribute to a wonderful man who should have received far more recognition in his lifetime. I only got to meet Phil Lamason the one time, when he was in Australia and gave a presentation on the Buchenwald experience at a western Sydney club, although we were in touch by telephone and by air mail (before emails came along). I would be delighted if you used anything you wish from 'Destination Buchenwald' in this new project." A significant part of the narrative through this section is taken directly from this source.

Alongside, as key sources, stand the work of fellow Buchenwald inmates Art Kinnis and Stanley Booker's '168 Jump Into Hell,' Joe Moser's 'A Fighter Pilot in Buchenwald' and the diary kept by Phil's navigator, Ken Chapman. These 'on the scene' accounts offer descriptive and personal insights into their shared experience. Chapman is also quoted by Colin Burgess during his own interview process. Together with these are further sources: New Zealander Max Lambert's 'Night After Night' and Mike Dorsey's documentary film, 'The Lost

Airmen of Buchenwald.' With such information at hand, the Phil Lamason story, his role in the events to come, and the esteem in which he was held, can be much better understood.

Therefore if the following information seems piecemeal this is due to the differing accounts and styles available, along with the writer's wish that the words and style of each individual be presented in the context of a multi-layered tapestry. Finally, in order to avoid reader distraction with constant author attributions, let us now gratefully acknowledge en masse, their contribution to the whole.

Raid on Massy-Palaiseau

The Phil Lamason story continues. It is the night of June 7, 1944.

"There was some low cloud and we flew in as the first wave of aircraft to attack at 8000 to 9000 feet... Unfortunately, we arrived over the target area about half a minute early, before the Mosquitoes (Pathfinders) had dropped their flares, and I throttled back, not wanting to over-run the objective. It was a bad mistake..." Phil told Max Lambert. It is the prelude to the life-changing terror-filled minutes which are to follow. It has been a little over one hour of flying since take-off at RAF Mildenhall and Lancaster MkIII LM 575 LS-H approaches the target for the night on the outskirts of Paris, the strategically important road bridge over the railway yards at Massy-Palaiseau close to the Château de Versailles.

Prowling in the moonlit silvery wisps of cloud below are twin engine Messerschmitt Bf 110 and Junkers Ju88 aircraft of a Luftwaffe night fighter wing, the 'Nachtjagdgeschwader.' These hi-tech formidable defenders have been airborne from their base at Athies-Laon, just north of Paris, for a little over one hour, patrolling at around 4000 feet awaiting confirmation from ground radar of incoming Allied bomber formations above. In the lead Messerschmitt with its deadly upward pointing dorsal 'Shräge Musik' cannons, ace Pilot Major Walter Borchers and his air gunner are charged for action. On edge, they await directions from their third crewman, the navigator and radar operator who is critically monitoring for arrivals overhead... Suddenly the Lichtenstein radar array locks in on the decelerating Lamason bomber above... the tantalising Achilles underbelly of a Lancaster. Time to strike! Metaphorically styled in the words of Canadian aviation writer Dave O'Malley, "Like a shark rising from the depths of the abyss, the night fighter emerges from the cloud, vectored towards its prey."

Messerschmitt 110f night-fighter aircraft similar to that flown on operation by William Borchers on the night of 8 June, 1944.

And then through the inter-com, in what were to be his last words, the voice of tail gunner Tommy Dunk crackles an alert to Phil Lamason, "There's an aircraft behind us…I think it's another Lanc."

Phil is not so sure. He immediately drops the nose of LM 575 LS-H into an evasive dive. At that very moment the night fighter opens fire. The shuddering cannon shells rake the plunging Lancaster from wingtip to wingtip. The battle-hardened Borchers dives his Messerschmitt to hammer home the engagement. He knows what it takes to bag his quarry. This is the second of three Lancaster aircraft that will fall victim to this German ace in a devastating 10 minutes of action this very night.

Courageously, mid upper gunner Robbie Aitken, 'The Last Defender,' has his twin machine guns chattering frantically into the face of this uncompromising attacker. But the Lanc's rear turret is strangely silent. Tommy Dunk, Phil's long-serving tail gunner has been mortally wounded in the initial flurry of fire with a shell wound to his neck.

"I thought I'd beaten him as I rolled out of the dive," Phil recounted to Max Lambert. "But I looked out and there was a little fire burning in the middle of the starboard wing. It spread rapidly and next thing the whole wing was on fire." An incendiary shell from the night fighter has ruptured one of the Lancaster's fuel tanks. Time is up for this Lamason

Above: 'Under Attack.' The harrowing moments of the attack on the Lamason Lancaster, LM 575 LS-H recaptured in the amazing digital art of Piotr Forkasiewicz. (Photo courtesy of Piotr Forkasiewicz and Lamason Family Collection.) Below: Detail of 'The Last Defender' by Piotr Forkasiewicz captures the heroic actions of mid-upper gunner Robbie Aitken in the crippled Lancaster, LM 575 LS-H. (Photo courtesy of Piotr Forkasiewicz.)

Lancaster team. With no more defensive options, the devastated Squadron Leader yells the fateful skipper's command, "Out! Out! Bale out!"

Phil struggles to control the stricken aircraft for maybe another minute or so as bomb aimer Gerry Musgrove pops the lower front escape hatch, and squeezes himself through the awkwardly narrow gap into the tormented torrent of night air. Wireless operator Lionel George is close on his tail. Flight engineer Ginger Marpole has taken a moment before he bales to unfasten Phil Lamason's seat straps and clip a parachute to his skipper's harness – Phil had always preferred not to have the discomfort of sitting on an attached pilot's parachute during missions. Meanwhile he battles on trying to hold the dying aircraft for just a few more seconds...

Dave O'Malley graphically captures this moment: "The big bomber is dying, her lifeblood streaming in angry, high octane sheets from her starboard wing fuel tanks...Beneath the Lancaster the escape hatch opens and crew members, abandoning the dying aircraft while they can, tumble out into the slipstream like rag dolls. On the top side of the Lancaster however, the mid-upper gunner, Robbie Aitken, with his back to the approaching French farmland, empties his ammunition boxes into the German, giving time for his crew to get out of the mortally wounded aircraft. The searing muzzle flashes of his twin Brownings stab the night like dragons, likely blinding the young gunner. Hot brass shell casings tumble unseen in the darkness to thud heavily into fields and villages below, while oily grey smoke, ghosted by the streaming funeral pyres, wafts behind from two of her engines...The sound is the sound of hell: four thundering Merlin engines; the foundry shriek and snap of wind-whipped flame; the rip-saw burp of Aitken's .303 Brownings; the heavy thump of the night fighter's cannons. And perhaps above it all, the angry scream of Aitken as he fights to the end of his ammunition."

Years later, Phil still expressed amazement at the intensity of the heat coming from the burning aircraft and how he thought it would consume them. "I really thought I was going to die in that aircraft that night," Phil told his friend and keeper of his story, Glenys Scott, many years later. Three men have safely baled. And finally, Phil made his own exit as described to Lambert..."The next moment I was flung from the cockpit down the steps and into the nose as the starboard wing fell off and the plane started to spin, going down in a ball of fire, bombs still aboard. Chappy – Ken Chapman the navigator – was down there, stuck…so I had to get him up and push him out. It's a funny thing the strength you have sometimes." In fact, in the act of pushing the navigator out through the hatch, Phil smashed Chappy's head causing him to bleed profusely. They got out at low altitude – 1000 feet, perhaps 2000. Lamason remembers saying to his navigator "My God, Chappy, you're making it short for me." He jumped a second after Chapman…

To Glenys, Phil also recalled the relief of feeling the blast of rushing cold air on exiting, and the sharp jolt felt soon after as his parachute canopy opened. He remembered just "a handful of pendulum swings" before his feet crunched at speed into the fresh, French farmland below. It was 'hang-time' enough for him to witness the plummeting Lancaster slam, a fireball, into the wooded grounds of a French château (Forêt de Sainte-Apolline) between the village of Jouars-Pontchartrain and the town of Plaisir. More poignantly Phil remembered watching the partially opened parachute of Robbie Aitken streaming earthwards – the dreaded 'candle in the wind' – the heroic gunner having given his all, leaving his own baling-out too late to secure his own survival.

The devastation is complete. It is 0200 hours on Thursday June 8, 1944, and Phil Lamason has dramatically descended into a sleepy French countryside. Nineteen other Lancasters have succumbed to a similar fate in this one operation.

On June 24, 1944, unbeknown to either Phil Lamason or any of his crew, Phil was awarded a Bar to his Distinguished Flying Cross, the citation stating "Since the award of the DFC this officer has continued to operate with courage and devotion to duty of a high order. He has completed a large number of operational missions including several attacks on Berlin and other heavily defended German targets and has always pressed home his attacks with vigorous determination. His gallantry, leadership and enthusiasm have been extremely praiseworthy." It seemed an appropriate recognition for the actions of a brave leader. One can also appreciate a certain irony in that the decision makers for this award were, at that point in time, completely unaware of any details of this courageous 'main event' which had unfolded in skies above France in the early hours of June 8, 1944.

Spare a thought for Joan Lamason, back home in Napier, New Zealand. Like so many, she is a war-time wife. She is getting on with her own life whilst living in the constant shadow of her husband's absence and the knowledge that with every mission he undertakes, he is but a hair's breadth away from death. It is sometime later that Joan receives an official letter dated June 8, 1944:

"Dear Mrs Lamason, You will now have been informed that your husband, N.Z. 403460 Squadron Leader Phillip John Lamason, failed to return from an operational flight on the night of June 7/8, 1944. I am writing to express my deepest sympathy with you in your anxiety and also to encourage you to hope that he is safe.

"He was the captain of an aircraft engaged on an important bombing mission over enemy occupied territory and after take-off nothing further was heard. It appears likely that the aircraft was forced down and if this was the case, there is some chance that he may be safe, and a prisoner of war.

"In this event it may be two or three months before any certain information is received through the International Red Cross, but I hope that the news will soon come through.

"I would be grateful if you would inform me should you receive a prisoner of war card from your husband. My reason for making this request is that a Squadron Prisoner of War fund arranges a monthly despatch of comforts, and I am most anxious to include your husband's name on the list at the earliest possible moment.

"During your husband's service with this Squadron he had won the respect and esteem of all whose privilege it has been to serve under him and he earned the fullest confidence of those with whom he co-operated in organisation and command. In addition to his 45 operational flights, he has done extremely valuable work in the Squadron as Flight Commander. There are few men whose work and enthusiasm I have admired more, and if there were more like your husband this war would not be so long finishing. His loss is a heavy blow to the Squadron where he will be greatly missed by his many friends.

"His personal effects have been safeguarded and will be dealt with by the Committee of Adjustment Officer, R.A.F. Station Mildenhall as soon as possible, who will write to you in the near future.

"May I on behalf of the whole Squadron express to you our most sincere sympathy and the hope that you will soon receive good news.

"Yours sincerely,

Signed. W.D. Watkins."

Evasion and Capture

Lamason had landed in a field near the village of Trappes..."I hid my parachute and Mae West – the yellow inflatable life-raft the airmen wore around their neck and chest – in the bushes. I had sprained my ankle badly on landing and was pleased to come across my navigator, Ken Chapman, a few moments later. We remained together from then on. We walked across country for about two kilometres until we heard some voices. We dropped to our bellies and crawled towards the voices until we recognised the French language..."

Chapman: "At approx. 2.05am I discover I'm not going back to England. No! I'm floating to French soil by parachute, a nice sensation. My nose is bleeding profusely. Lucky me? Yes I'm still alive. I see two other parachutes coming down. French soil is fairly hard to drop onto from 2-3000 feet. My 'chute' hidden etc. I contact Phil the Skipper who is doing likewise. After handshakes and a brief spell of cursing our rotten luck we decide to walk in 'this' direction. I tripped over barbed wire! Phil notices a blockhouse – no it wasn't. He notices other parachutes in the field – no they weren't, they were black and white cows lying down. We hear voices, first thoughts may be Germans courting. We crawl nearer on our tummies. Foolish, we both go up to the group. I ask various questions in my rusty French..."

But as Phil recalls, "they didn't appear to be at all keen to assist us, and pointed us in another direction where they said we might find some help. Soon after, we heard more voices coming from the courtyard of a house. The two of us approached the small group of two or three families who had also been watching and listening to the raid. We declared our identity and were at once taken to a nearby house where we were given first aid for our injuries, which were minor, a strong alcoholic drink, and a light meal." They were provided with food and taken a mile or so to some woods where they were told to stay until daybreak when help would arrive.

"Early the next morning a boy aged about 16 years brought some food and told the two men that members of the Resistance would come and arrange to give them some shelter," Burgess records. "A little later two French women arrived, one of whom spoke reasonable English..." Ken Chapman remembered their first day as evaders as being a combination of confusion and uneasiness, but recalled with fondness the people who risked their lives to help.

Phil: "The woman who could speak English welcomed us and gave us a great deal of encouragement by telling us of the work of the French people as a whole against the Germans. She went away and returned later with the local postman, a member of the Resistance. Evidently he just wanted to look at us, but could speak no English; again they left and we found a clearing in the wood and lay and rested in the sun. About 11.00am the English speaking woman returned with the French boy, carrying a sack of civilian clothes. We gave up our battle dress for these, and although we looked a couple of tramps we could reasonably pass as a couple of French labourers to a dim Jerry."

Chapman wrote: "Morning, day break arrives and we eagerly await the whistling tune, 'I'm a Yankee Doodle Dandy.' To our surprise we first hear on the path through the wood a whistle, 'It's foolish but it's Jim.' This was an hour before our friends arrived. Was it one of our 'cobbas'? We daren't go and look."

Chapman then describes their walk to a rendezvous, "where a car would be waiting for us. Phil, who had sprained his ankle, had great difficulty in walking the two or so kilometres through the wood. After cautiously avoiding two German soldiers repairing telegraph wires we reached the car containing the driver and his pal, who had been searching for us. The 'car' was a contraption with an engine of sorts, with a cab built of wood and numerous holes in the floor. I was to curl up in the back and cover myself with sacking. Phil, donning a beret, sat beside the driver.

"The ride was anything but comfortable, and in my position I could see nothing of the countryside. We dodged a couple of German motorcyclists who threw suspicious looks at the car, and arrived at a farmhouse. Here we were taken inside to a good meal. I produced a packet of Players (cigarettes) and our French friends went into raptures. Towards the end of the meal the son, spying at the gate, ran in to announce a car of German soldiers approaching and we had to make a hurried exit through a window, across the garden, and scale an eight-foot gate, which Phil found some difficulty climbing. We ran across a ploughed field, jumped into a running stream, and hid under the stump of a fallen tree. Soon our friends came to say that the Germans had called for water for their car!"

"The two men were taken to a barn near the house until it was considered safe for them to be driven to their first lodgings," Burgess continues. "They were covered with sacking in the back of the car, and eventually pulled up in a side street in a small town of Montfort L'Amaury. Here they were welcomed by Roger Cuillerier, the town locksmith, and his wife Yvonne. Inside the comfortable house a pleasant surprise awaited them in the shape of George Scott, an American airman. Yvonne produced some more respectable clothing and hid their personal belongings for them while they changed.

"Well we settled down. It was now nearly 1600 hours and I looked a sight with my face all plaster etc so Yvonne sought a doctor, an Indo-Chinaman," Chapman remembers... "We drank their wine, were visited by numerous friends in the evening and finally, very tired, retired to a good warm bed." The men stayed with the Cuilleriers for five days, never leaving the house except to use the outside toilet, and only then with extreme caution. To pass the time Phil enjoyed playing chess and ping pong with their young son, Francis.

Chapman's version mentions an eight days' stay and the generosity of their hosts. "It was a bit cramped. We eagerly listened to the BBC, played Patience, or slept. We had a few French cigarettes, 'Gauloise,' and we enjoyed these. I had a little 'Three Hums' left so also enjoyed my pipe. Cigarette butts we kept and rolled again... Many were the visits of friends, all members of the local Resistance. Here they didn't come empty-handed. One of them brought a couple of bottles of wine, another one cigarettes, another one some milk, another eggs, another joints of meat (a farmer of course) and so on. We lived and ate well. The common Frenchman didn't, food was scarce. With a bit of money the Black Market was useful though its produce was very expensive...

Chapman wrote: "We saw our first German after a day, a dim looking fellow with specs on... inwardly laughing at him to think we were avoiding capture."

"One sad event during their stay was the occasion on which the entire village turned out to bury the RAF crewmen killed during the recent raid," writes Burgess. Among these were Lamason's crewmen, Tommy Dunk, buried in the Plaisir Cemetery, and Rob Aitken, buried in the nearby Jouars-Pontchartrain Churchyard. "The villagers accorded these men a solemn ceremony and reverently laid wreaths of red, white and blue flowers on the fresh graves in a gesture of respect."

Unknown to Phil and Chappy, fellow crew members Gerry Musgrove with the help of Resistance members Marcel Steinmetz and Rene Didier, along with John Marpole and around 150 other Allied airmen ended up being hidden in the 'Forêt de Freteval.' This camp had

Anne Marie Errembault (alias Antionette) who as a member of the Comet Line played an important role in the evasion of of Phil Lamason and Ken Chapman. (Photograph courtesy of Geraldine Cerf du Dudzeele and Francois Ydier)

been set up by the French Resistance in the Freteval Forest where the evaders were safe from becoming entangled in the Allied ground advance and the German retreat. The successful evaders' escape route the Comet Line, and other escape pathways, had become threatened by these same changing events. Gerry Musgrove is recorded as having been liberated by the advancing US troops on August 13, 1944, and flown back to England five days later. Lionel George was also successful as an evader, but there are no details of his experiences of that time on the run.

Soon after the arrival of Phil and Chappy at Cuillerier's home George Scott was moved on to another safe place, and the day after his departure "...amid great commotion a badly burned American fighter pilot was brought to the house, suffering from shock and exposure. Yvonne fussed over the young pilot (whom they knew only as Jack and who was later identified as James Irving Lindquist), applying jelly to his burns and placing him in their double bed. Ken Chapman felt bad about taking up their only other bed. "We implored Yvonne and Roger to take our bed, but they wouldn't hear of it. Yvonne slept on the divan, Roger on the floor. Next day Roger made a steel arch affair to raise the clothes off Jack's badly burned legs."

On June 18 an attractive blonde-haired Belgian girl named Marie (later identified as Anne Marie Errembault of Dudzeele, alias "Antoinette") accompanied by two men, picked up Phil and Chappy, now disguised as house-painting tradesmen, in the now familiar

Phil Lamason (left) and Ken Chapman (right) at the home of Madame Christiane Lefebvre (centre) in Rambouillet. (Photo courtesy of Antione Poliet and the Lefebvre Family)

motorised vehicle. She spoke excellent English and told Phil that arrangements were under way to have them taken out of France, either by aircraft or by train to Spain. "With luck," she said, "they would be back in England within a fortnight."

Chapman wrote: "I donned a beret, a white jacket, a pair of white trousers imitating a painter. We piled into a car amid paint pots and off we went. This time we could view the countryside and the lines of German tanks and transport in the woods."

They finally arrived at the village of Rambouillet and the house of Monsieur Plumsard, whose genial wife gave the airmen a cup of black-market tea and a large bowl of strawberries. That evening they were handed over to Madame Christiane Lefebvre and her son Georges Claude Lefebvre, their next benefactors in Rambouillet. Madame Lefebvre's husband, a commandant in the French army, had already been captured and was in a German Prisoner of War camp. A little later they were joined by a third airman, Flight Sergeant Dick Rowe, who had been shot down a few days earlier.

The three airmen remained with the Lefebvre family until the morning of July 5, when they were told to prepare for another move. They gave their sincere thanks to Madame and were escorted into the country by Monsieur Plumsard to await their conveyance. Not long after, the local fire engine pulled up beside them and the three men were instructed to don fire helmets and coats. Feeling terribly conspicuous, but pleased to be on the move again, the three men chatted, noting with some alarm a few bullet holes in the canvas cab of the tender, which Monsieur explained were the result of a fighter attack.

Just outside the village of Chevreuse, on the side of a hill, the fire engine chugged to a halt by the wayside, where they were met once again by Marie, together with Monsieur Maurice Cherbonnier, the village librarian. They removed the firemen outfits and, trying to appear nonchalant, the party of five strolled into the quaint little village. After walking down the cobbled street they reached the library and paper shop, where they were greeted by Madame Cherbonnier and her daughter Janine. Upstairs they were introduced to a couple of RAF airmen – later identified as Flight Sergeant Robert Davidson and Sergeant A. Hunter – and Lieutenant Phelps of the US Army Air Force.

Conditions in the small flat were crowded, although generally amiable, but it was with a certain amount of relief that Marie arrived on July 9 and said she had to take two men to another house. Phil and Chappy elected to go, and wished the others good luck.

A brisk ten minute walk soon had them at the large elegant house of Madame Kalmanson and her two daughters, Denise and Colette. After formal introductions they were taken upstairs to their room, which contained two beds. Even here they had to exercise caution. According to Chapman, "Denise and Colette spoke English fluently, easing matters considerably. Our stay here was very pleasant and we enjoyed it. An unusual thing – Monsieur Kalmanson was 78 years old, and they didn't inform him of our presence in the house. This procedure provided us with endless amusement, and we kept up a regular game of hide and seek. On many occasions Mr. Kalmanson came to the kitchen after meals to speak to his daughters, and this created panic as we had to recede into a far nook without being seen. The girls usually held him at the door, by standing astride the threshold..." Chapman added, "For the men to visit the toilet, they first must inform Monsieur's daughters to ensure the coast was clear. Washing and shaving was even more difficult so we arranged to shave on alternate days to take up less room in the bathroom." Phil and Chappy also had to borrow their unknowing host's razor blades. These blades, Chappy recalled, "were often blunt."

Phil Lamason (left) and Ken Chapman pictured with sisters Colette (standing) and Denise Kalmanson while evading at the Chateau of the Kalmanson family in Chevreuse. (Photograph courtesy of the Kalmanson Family)

Chapman described how "On Bastille Day, July 14, Denise and Colette produced Union Jacks and numerous flags and we had a little party in the attic, celebrating with two bottles of champagne..."

But eventually the game was up... while en route to the toilet, Chapman came face to face with 'Pop.' However after an initial alarm and several 'Bon Jours' and 'Ca Va's,' Chappy was able to explain their position. "He came into our room to see Phil eating his breakfast." Fortunately 'Pop' was able to accept the situation and hesitantly agreed that the men could stay. The family gathered and "after much laughter we went downstairs and joined them for lunch for the first time."

In total, the two men spent an idyllic fortnight at the house, eating breakfast in bed, reading, playing ping-pong and chess, sunbaking and generally helping out in the extensive vegetable garden at the rear. However time was soon up for the fugitives and "we were told to move on. The girls ironed and pressed our clothes and, after an early lunch with special wine, many 'Bon Chances,' tears and handshaking, off we went."

Looking back, their time with members of the French Resistance and the Kalmanson family in particular must have seemed like a mirage: An oasis in the desert of misery which was to come.

Of their departure Burgess writes: "The Kalmansons were genuinely sorry to see their guests leave, but understood their desire to return to England." They set off from Chevreuse on foot in the company of Monsieur Cherbonnier and Janine. They walked three kilometres until they reached the station, where Janine bought the tickets. Marie was at the station and told Lamason and Chapman that she would take over and escort them to a 'safe house' in Paris. It was July 22 and Phil and Chappy had now been on the run for six weeks.

The train was crowded, particularly with poor folk from Paris who had come to the country to buy, beg or steal vegetables from the farmers. Lamason and Chapman stood patiently in the crowded carriage as the train moved slowly from the platform. The passengers had to disembark at Massy-Palaiseau and walk to another train three kilometres away. Phil caught Chappy's eye and winked. Only weeks earlier they had been above the same place, trying to blow the bridge to pieces, and now they had to suffer the inconvenience inflicted by the RAF bombers. Another train was waiting at a bomb-damaged station and they clambered aboard with Marie.

Hours later the train arrived at Gare Université and the two airmen caught their first sight of the elegant, ancient city of Paris. Liberation they felt, was now near at hand.

On their arrival in Paris the Belgian girl, Marie, guided Phil and Chappy to a two-storey house at 66 Rue d'Assas, overlooking a school by the magnificent Luxembourg Gardens. Here she handed them on to their next hosts, the Werths (later identified as Suzanne Josephine Canart, wife of Léon Werth and their son Jean Louis). Despite the acute shortage of food in Paris, Madame Werth provided them with good nourishing meals.

After a pleasant weekend, Madame Werth guided the two men to their next rendezvous. She rode her bicycle a cautious 100 metres ahead of the airmen, who strode after her until she arrived at a small bench where she indicated they should wait while she watched from a discreet distance for the next link in the Underground chain to appear.

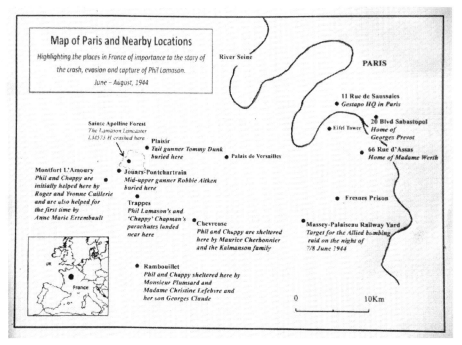

Map showing key locations relating to the crash of Lancaster LM 575 LS-H on June 8, 1944 and the ensuing evasion and capture of Phil Lamason and Ken Chapman. (Map courtesy of Mike Harold)

It was Monday July 24, 1944. The air-raid sirens began wailing as Phil Lamason and Ken Chapman sat uneasily on a wooden bench in the heart of occupied Paris, waiting to be picked up by their next contact on the escape line. They looked up, hoping to see some Allied aircraft, but none seemed interested in flying over the French capital that day. Parisians largely ignored the sirens and scampered about on their daily business. A few metres from the bench stood a nervous Frenchwoman, the helper who had brought them to this spot. She waited and watched as well, but she was observing the pedestrian traffic, looking for her contact or any signs of trouble.

The air-raid sirens were still sounding when a portly Frenchman strolled over to Madame Werth. They talked for a few moments and then she beckoned the two airmen over. Then with obvious relief but tears in her eyes, she wished them a safe journey and indicated they should go with the man named Georges Prevot. As they watched Madame Werth remount her bicycle she smiled, crossed her fingers as a sign of good luck, and pedalled away.

The routine was the same as before. They followed Georges Prevot at a safe distance as he walked towards yet another place of hiding. They crossed the Seine at the Île de France, enjoying their first sight of the magnificent Notre Dame Cathedral in spite of their precarious position. Next they passed the Prefecture, the Place of Justice, and entered the Blvd de Sebastopol. A few brisk strides took them to an apartment opposite Demoy's Restaurant, and they followed Georges up a narrow flight of stairs to the top flat. Here they were greeted by a young, short and fair-haired man wearing thick-lensed glasses, who introduced himself as Captain Jacques. Phil Lamason, in his debrief in July, 1945, remembered this man "… we met a regular visitor to the house who claimed he was working for the British Secret Service. He spoke fluent English and French. He was known as 'Jack' (surname unknown). His description is 5ft 7ins in height, grey eyes, wore moderately thick lensed glasses, medium fair hair, fair complexion, gold in front teeth, aged about 28 and very well dressed."

Jack assured Phil and Chappy they were now on the final stage of their journey and would soon arrive back in England. As Lamason recalls, the contact's words were quite heartening: "This man claimed to be working for the chief organiser of the escape route to Spain (the Comet Line). He had a detailed story of how the journey would be accomplished, and claimed to have made the journey seven times."

Findings by French researcher Franck Signorile, in 2017, confirm that Ken Chapman and Phil Lamason were now under the 'care' of the multi-lingual double-agent, Guy Glebe d'Eu, Count of Marcheret. Guy Glebe d'Eu, or "Captain Jack" ("Captain Jacques") as he sometimes called himself, was posing as a British Intelligence Officer. He was in fact a member of the Nazi-run counter-evasion service in Paris and had been successfully infiltrated into the the Comet Line using the 'funkspiel' technique…the sending of false messages to British Intelligence using captured Resistance radios. At this time, Guy Glebe d'Eu's point of infiltration into the evasion network was at the home of Georges Prevot, at 20 Blvd Sebastopol.

The two airmen were completely taken in by this man's alleged credentials. Chapman wrote: "I'm afraid Jack completely deceived us and we believed his spectacular tales too lengthy to add here… We were in extremely high spirits and did not exercise sufficient caution."

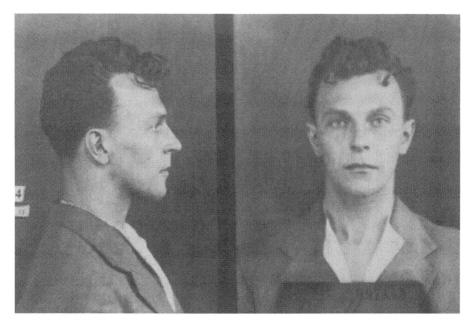

Guy Glebe d'Eu, Count of Marcheret, who as a member of the Nazi counter-evasion service successfully infiltrated the Comet Line network and betrayed Phil Lamason and Ken Chapmen into the hands of the Gestapo. (Photograph courtesy of Franck Signorile)

Colin Burgess continues, "The two men relaxed and were all smiles as they were introduced to Georges' sister Genevieve." Ken Chapman felt quite at ease and remembers every effort being made to ensure their comfort and make them feel that they were safe and among friends. "We had good meals here and had a comfortable double bed to sleep in. We were given clothes to wear so that our own could get pressed, and we could go out onto the balcony overlooking the Rue de Sevastopol to watch the throngs of people go by. Georges and Jacques provided us with tobacco, so we were fairly well supplied. That night Georges and Genevieve came in with two bottles of champagne, which we soon disposed of!"

The following day Jacques returned to the flat with a young RAF evader identified only as Bob (now identified as F/O Ralph Taylor from 10 Squadron). Later, while conducting a questioning session, Jacques asked the three airmen for the names of those who had helped them in their journey across France. Immediately all three became suspicious, and Lamason asked Jacques why he needed such delicate information. "Many of these people are poor and need money," he explained. "If you prefer not to tell me their names it is all the same to me, but it is usual

99

for us to show our gratitude by rewarding such patriotism with an amount of 200 francs for each day you were with them."

"It all seemed perfectly reasonable. Jacques' credentials and authority seemed to be in order," so the three men divulged the names and locations of their past helpers. The following day Lamason and Chapman left the apartment building with Georges and Jacques and were handed over to Jacques' assistant, an unpleasant looking woman with copper-coloured hair and spectacles. Jacques would not divulge her name, but recent research identifies her as Yvonne Lallier. She took over responsibility for the 'welfare' of the two airmen and guided them along the banks of the Seine, through the beautiful gardens of the Louvre, and onto the Place de la Concorde. Here they waited for an hour until they were picked up by two men in a black Citroen. Both spoke perfect English with strong American accents.

The passenger in the front seat, who reminded Lamason of a Hollywood movie gangster, introduced himself as Jacques' chief in the Resistance work. He was a tall man of 80 or more kilos with brown hair and blue-grey eyes. Lamason's first impressions were actually borne out when he told them something of his background. In response to a question about being picked up by agents who seemed to be Americans, he claimed to have lived in Chicago for 12 years, and to have known Al Capone!

His driver was an even taller fellow in his mid-twenties. A ruggedly good-looking man, he had fair hair, blue eyes and a faint scar along his forehead, just below the hairline. He told the men he had been born in California and had joined the French Air Force in 1939. It what appeared to be an easy conversational manner he tried to cajole Lamason into a discussion about the comparative air defences of Britain and Germany, but the New Zealand Squadron Leader was non-committal and would not be drawn into talk on such a provocative subject.

They drove past the Eiffel Tower and pulled up in front of a block of flats near La Forte Boulogne. Here the two airmen were temporarily separated, Lamason in one room and Chapman in a small children's bedroom. On the surface, things seemed to be going smoothly.

But Chapman was beginning to feel somewhat ill at ease with their situation. "I felt terribly lonely and I had plenty of time to think. Swastikas were scrawled on the walls and to me this seemed strange. However, the tall American came in and reassured me." That night the two evaders shared an uninspiring meal before retiring, although the

100

news that they would be on their way home the following day brightened their outlook. Both spent an uneasy night wondering what the morning would bring, and the hours crept by until it was time for breakfast. Chappy made his way downstairs, where he found Phil already chatting away with six other airmen, who were moving in prior to departure for Spain and freedom. The hours now passed quickly.

It was not until lunch was over that their move was fully organised. Chapman was to ride on the back pillion of a Frenchman's two-stroke motorcycle to the prearranged rendezvous near the Champs Elysees. Both men were dubious about the wisdom of this move, as they now found themselves directly in front of a German barracks, and the area was swarming with enemy guards. Chapman takes up the story:

"We were left in the company of my escort. We crossed the road to a café and ordered some beer. Meantime we watched the passers-by. Many German troops were passing but no private vehicles. All the French people used cycles, of which there were a multitude. At 1500 hours I paid the bill and I returned to our rendezvous point across the road. A quarter of an hour passed and no one had arrived, and I was uneasy – there were too many Germans about who might recognise us for what we were.

"Soon two strangers came up, shook hands with our guide and with us, and led us to a car. We got in and at last thought we were on our way. We drove some five minutes then suddenly entered what later proved to be Gestapo headquarters (on Rue des Saussaies) with two guards outside."

Years later, recalling his efforts to resist captivity, Phil told Canadian documentary-maker and writer of this book's foreword, Mike Dorsey, "I tried to grab hold of one of them and eventually they shook us off and I realised I was 'gonna get myself shot very quickly'…and that was it. They gave me a couple of dongs on the head with the butt of a revolver and I found that subdued me a bit." In Phil's view 'the guy at the house' had proved to be 'the rotten apple we hoped would not spoil our cooking.' They were so close and yet so far. Advising Chappy to 'play it close and sit tight because we are POWs now so it's routine,' he asked, 'so what's the worst they can do to us now? Shoot us?" Unconvinced, Chappy persisted, "What if they get rough, demand information, ask strategic questions?" "Hold on, just hold on," was the reply.

Chapman records being taken to a yard where a large number of French people had congregated, having handcuffs removed and then being bundled into a Black Maria, three to a very small compartment. "So dark and dreary with the females lined in the middle. We were driven out and after 20 minutes arrived at Fresnes Prison." Here they were put "solitary in cells, our belongings taken and left outside the door. What a climax… I looked around me at the bare horrid walls and the barred window…Here I thought of home, my darling wife Muriel who was expecting our first baby. At last I fell asleep. The fleas really went to town." It was July 27.

From this time on the ensuing events will mark the descent into a layer of human behaviour that falls far beyond even the lowest level of social acceptability. For the victims who experienced the degradation, humiliation and suffering on a daily basis and overcame, theirs was the ultimate triumph of fortitude and the spirit. For those who succumbed, theirs was the ultimate sacrifice.

Fresnes Prison

So to Fresnes Prison. Nearly 20 kilometres south of Paris, this was the largest criminal penitentiary in the country. At this time it was being filled with political prisoners. "Entrance to the prison was gained through a set of heavy gates off the main road to Paris, then driving down a cobbled private road through an avenue of magnificent poplars until reaching the main gate," writes Burgess. "Here twin statues of the Sisters of Mercy were positioned either side of the huge iron gates. However many of the men and women despatched to Fresnes were only too well aware that mercy had very little place in the SS doctrine, unless it was the swift mercy of a bullet." The majority of prisoners were French and were gaoled for sedition and non-cooperation. Among the agents held there at different times were the famous Odette Sansom, and Wing Commander F.F.E. Yeo-Thomas, of whom more is recounted later.

The cells, measuring four by two and a half metres, had stone walls partially covered by crumbling plaster, into which were scratched dozens of messages proclaiming both hope and despair. A large, frosted glass window, through which thick bars could be seen, was set high in the wall opposite the steel door. Beside this door sat a lavatory, a tap, and a small enamel basin secured to the wall, as well as a wooden shelf and pegs to hang clothing. A single bed frame lay folded against a wall. When this was lowered a shapeless palliasse served as a mattress. The

Fresnes Prison, Paris, undated.

prisoners were inspected through a small oblong slit and spy hole set into each door. The majority of cells had no lighting, and prisoners were checked by guards shining a torch through the inspection slit. In those cells which had lights supplied, they were kept on all night.

The men were shepherded into a series of small wooden cubicles from which they were eventually taken, one at a time, made to strip naked, and thoroughly searched. It was here that most of the men had their 'dogtags' ripped from their necks by guards shouting abuse and calling them 'terrorfliegers' (terror fliers). Any signs of disobedience or defiance brought a savage blow to the head, or a swift kick to the shins with a heavy jackboot.

Such was the environment into which Phil Lamason, Ken Chapman and many other airmen were bundled. Expectations of a return to England were fast receding.

After a short interrogation, Phil was slung into a cell where he found a young girl unconscious from being repeatedly drowned in a barrel of water. The officers were using their favourite method of torture and were relishing it, laughing and screaming questions at her.

Phil and Chappy were held in Paris by the Gestapo for 18 days until they were transported on the morning of August 15.

In their statements made to Mike Dorsey for his documentary 'The Lost Men of Buchenwald' 60 years later, other prisoners offer an explanation of how they were categorised as spies, saboteurs and 'terrorfliegers' by the Gestapo. This mistaken assumption, from which their captors consistently refused to budge, changed the airmen's status from POWs to police prisoners. It was also to have a profound effect on the post-war reception the airmen encountered with their various governments. Put simply, their story was later met with disbelief..

The airmen talked about the Gestapo being a law unto themselves, with no adherence to the protocols of the International Laws of the Geneva Convention. "They were cruel, barbaric sadistic people… they showed no mercy towards us."

Dorsey commented on how "The men were put in trucks and transferred from Gestapo HQ in the centre of Paris to Fresnes Prison on the outskirts. The prison had about 1200 cells most of which were occupied by French Resistance captives. They were confined to small cells with two or three fellow inmates. They could hear the moans and groans of people being tortured. 'You could hear shots echoing in the prison and through the grapevine we found out people were being shot as well as tortured.'"

Phil's aim was to get out as fast as possible. "I was thinking about escaping all the time… thinking about what to do and the Germans were pretty well aware of that too… and I always had what I thought was an extraordinarily heavy guard around me… I needed three or four people and probably I was pretty cranky and I thought that if I could have grabbed a revolver or something, I would have.

"As soon as they got full-up (the prison cells) they shot a few people. I had that in my mind and then they came along with a dozen or so soldiers and I thought 'My God they're going to shoot me!'" he told Dorsey.

"I was being pushed along and I couldn't think what the devil to do… and when we got to the bottom floor I looked and there was a door open and in there was a German officer working at a desk. I jumped in through the open doorway and he got a surprise and a hell of a fright, and was reaching for his revolver… he didn't know me or anything about the guards who were guarding me and who were trying to push me out… he spoke perfect English and I told him who I was and that I objected strongly to the treatment.

"'I am a senior British Officer. The Geneva Convention states that all POWs have the right to care and protection until their return to their respective countries. My fellow RAF captives deserve to be given their rights.' I then demanded to see the senior officer." The English-speaking German Officer told Phil to stand at ease before enquiring the circumstances from the soldiers. "This is not an ordinary situation and I will need more information."

Phil: "He barked out an order and I went back to my cell again. I had a feeling that maybe I had done the right thing by jumping into his office." Returned to his cell Phil heard tapping on the water pipes. He figured out the Morse Code and replied, learning there were over 160 other RAF prisoners in Fresnes. Then, at mealtime he had an altercation with the guard who screamed at him in German to stand at the back of his cell and to put his hands up until the meal was deposited through the hatch. Phil yelled back and threatened to "wring his scrawny Fascist neck." Intimidated, the guard backed away.

The testimony of other inmates reveals that, "Very few of the airmen who entered Fresnes Prison escaped brutal physical beatings, and the constant threat of death. The living conditions were totally degrading while the food was both appalling and irregular." The cells were tiny, there were no facilities for exercise or outside contact and men were obliged to wear the same clothes through their confinement... "Fleas, lice and other bugs thriving on filth were a constant aggravation..." In addition the men lived in fear of "the trip up to Paris and the notorious Gestapo headquarters." There was also a "much-feared torture chamber... the terrifying sounds of men and women screaming and sobbing rent the air at all hours."

Malcolm Cullen from Maungataroto, New Zealand, was also betrayed to the Gestapo and taken to Fresnes Prison. Cullen was a fighter pilot and had flown Typhoons with No. 257 (Burma) Fighter Squadron. Like Chapman he had kept a diary and was interviewed by Burgess. Like many others, Cullen gleaned news of the outside world from Frenchmen who went out on working parties and then "conveyed their findings to all and sundry by the heating system which ran up the inside wall of the cell. Each had an opening into this pipe, about seven feet up the wall, and by climbing onto our one and only stool we could shout into this primitive means of communication and receive our replies. The cry of 'Avez vous du nouvelle'? (have you any news) could be heard every morning... Morse Code was also used and with a spoon in one hand to make the 'dits' and a small piece of iron in the other hand for the heavier 'dashes,' news was passed along the whole floor."

"Over several weeks captured airmen were being delivered to the prison, transported there in company with French prisoners and

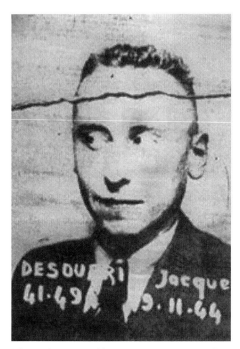

The infamous infiltrator Jacques Desoubrie who was responsible for the betrayal of more than 80 of the Allied airmen in Buchenwald into the hands of the Gestapo.

sometimes one or two fellow aircrew," writes Burgess. They were not to know for some time the actual number of airmen sent there or the enormity of the deception that saw so many picked up through the actions of double agents and traitors such as Guy Glebe d'Eu and the infamous Jacques Desoubrie."

Guy Glebe d'Eu is now deemed to have been responsible for the betrayal into the hands of the Gestapo, of more than 40 of the group of 166 Allied airmen who ended up in Buchenwald with Phil and Chappy. His traitorous notoriety is still especially remembered in France for the role he played in the betrayal of 35 young French partisans who were executed by the Gestapo in the Bois de Boulogne, Paris, in August 1944.

It is now established that Jacques Desoubrie was responsible for the betrayal of more than 80 of the captive Allied airmen in Buchenwald. He was described variously by his victims as an anaemic, weak and 'bug-eyed' person, and was reputed to have received payment of 10, 000 French francs from the Germans for each airman he handed over to them.

Desoubrie's favourite ruse in gaining confidence with unsuspecting Resistance workers was to pass himself off as a British agent and he was reported as having been responsible for the arrest of some 50 French and Belgian Resistance workers, almost all of whom were executed. Many an evader was taken in by his oily charms, excellent English and smooth reassurances. He would interview evaders and try to learn as much as he could of their activities, backgrounds and the names of those who helped them.

Researcher Franck Signorile explains that these two traitors fled Paris before the city was liberated by the Allies on 25 August, 1944.

Guy Glebe d'Eu, Count de Marcheret, was arrested in Denmark, in August 1945, and Jacques Desoubrie was eventually arrested in Germany, in March, 1947. Both men were returned to France and trialed in 1949. They were held accountable for their acts of treachery, found guilty, and executed by firing squad.

Canadian Stanley Booker, a 10 Squadron air observer on Halifax bombers, adds his own 'take' on Fresnes Prison. "Each day was the same – the soup trolley on its noisy track made the same noise as it approached your cell down the long metal corridors... having overcome the initial shock of being shot down and established a new pattern of life as an evader, it came as a profound shock to be caught, given a thorough beating up... and thrust into a dark, bare cell, confused, angry and wondering what was going to happen next."

Meanwhile after D Day, "things began to get a little hectic in Paris" and pressure on the Gestapo grew as the Allies approached the city... And as August progressed news of the approaching Allied armies raced through the prison grapevine...The prisoners "began to allow themselves a little hope," as reports filtered through of the advancing American Third Army said to be approaching Versailles and the Free French forces under General Leclerc who were nearing Paris. While much had to be "rejected as hopeful exaggeration, one thing was abundantly clear – Paris would soon be liberated..."

Cattle Truck Journey

It was Tuesday, August 15: the final day of evacuation from Fresnes. The day in Paris was hot, sticky and hazy...The men were called out and as they met on the ground floor it became apparent how many Allied airmen had been imprisoned. Writes Burgess: "The surprised shouting and conversation swelled as men recognised friends and fellow crewmen and realised how many had been in the same predicament..." Finally 168 airmen, not one in uniform, were assembled under a guard of 70 armed Germans. Gathered in the covered quadrangle, the men were told they were to be taken across Paris by bus and placed on a train for their next, unspecified destination. They were instructed that anyone who attempted to escape would be shot and a hand grenade thrown into the back of the bus that he came from. A few minutes later vats of thick soup were delivered and ladled into bowls. It was a welcome meal. Successive busloads of men were shuttled in batches to the Gare de L'Est station, but instead of entering the station itself the buses pulled

Cattle wagon or boxcar similar to that used for the transportation of the Allied airmen from Paris to Buchenwald, 1944.

up alongside a long train of French cattle trucks... "Hundreds of prisoners were milling about and the guards were kept busy shoving them into the dank trucks. More than 30 of the cattle trucks were linked together and with some carriages and guard vans, this formed a train of 400 metres long."

Art Kinnis recalled, "The goons gave us bread, one box of 'knackerbrod,' margarine and a tin of horsemeat between six of us. We were told that this was to last us from 2-7 days. A little later the French brought us Red Cross parcels one to three men. This parcel contained jam, biscuits, sardines and sugar. A small container 5-7 gallons for water, and a similar lidded can for use as a latrine were to be our next luxuries. Hypos were given to some of the serious heat cases and a few aspirins for those with headaches."

Inmates were to learn later that the trainload was the last to leave Paris. It contained 1650 men and 803 women. Fewer than 300 would return to Paris. As many as 100 were crammed into each car into what quickly became deplorable conditions. Burgess paints a grim picture: "It was the dog days of August. Even before the doors were slid shut the padlocked conditions in the unlit, overcrowded cattle trucks were unbearable, with the sun beating down relentlessly on the black roof half a metre above the heads of the occupants. Conditions worsened once they were closed in, as the interior temperature rose and the air became stuffy and fetid." In the middle of each car was placed a 20 litre water pail, together with one of similar size intended as the toilet.

It was at this point that Phil first emerged as their leader, quickly demonstrating his ability to take 'the tough stuff.' Taking exception to the guards' behaviour towards some of the prisoners he protested at their treatment, receiving in reply a hard punch to the face. Later, in 1999, he described the circumstances to reporter Warren Barton. "There were 96 jammed in our carriage and it was hot as hell. I realised we wouldn't last very long. I didn't know I was the most senior officer. I just got up, I told them who I was and I said I would take command. I told them that if they started moving round, or started squabbling they were going to die. I told them that quite clearly."

In his own handwritten version Phil recounts "…After several weeks on very meagre rations I, along with other prisoners from Fresnes, was loaded onto box cars and proceeded to travel to Buchenwald concentration camp. The wagon was jammed with 96 men, a number which, in the height of summer and the only ventilation about 2 square feet window, appeared disastrous. But I managed to assert some authority and like a chess board arranged people so all could be near the windows for a spell…"

Time dragged on. The train remained stationary, whilst "the perspiring prisoners cursed the stuffiness and reached agreements as to how many could sit down at one time. The coming night and prospects of sleep were not discussed. Finally, a little before midnight the overladen convoy of cattle trucks wormed its way out of the freight yards. Although it was only moving slowly, some fresh air began to flow into the carriages through the small ventilator windows which had been laced with barbed wire." Everyone ate a portion of their food although no water was permitted, despite protestations of thirst. Conditions then worsened demonstrably. "Men and women alike, many suffering terribly from dysentery, had to endure the degradation of performing their toilet functions in the middle of the crowded boxcars. The stench, compounded by a lack of substantial ventilation, was appalling...As the train trundled slowly through the night, sleep, for the occupants, was virtually impossible..."

Later that day the train was hauled into a long tunnel 70 kilometres from Paris and screeched to a halt, unable to proceed, as a rail bridge and the exit to the tunnel had been destroyed by the Resistance. Unmoving, within the tunnel, and with the locomotive continuing to belch dark pungent smoke into the constricted surroundings, the smoke began to penetrate the darkened boxcars. "Panic set in as the occupants began to cough and choke on the thick fumes," recounts Burgess. The airmen and the women who were packed in towards the end of the train were "comparatively fortunate." Eventually the train was shunted backwards out of the tunnel and the evacuees were informed they were to change trains. For some, this would entail having to carry "all items of baggage, the guards' packs and other stores across the remains of the bridge to the other train waiting several kilometres beyond."

Again, the Lamason leadership was to the fore when he confronted a guard who began "lashing out indiscriminately with a long, thick baton. The men had to pass by this brute as hurriedly as possible but few avoided the stinging blows." The sight of this bully beating his men horrified Phil, particularly when one of the victims, a young Englishman named Philip Hemmens sustained a broken arm. Without hesitation Phil strode over to the young man, grasped him by his good arm and marched him out of the column. Confronting a somewhat disinterested senior guard Phil demanded: "You must tell that guard to stop beating my men. We are prisoners of war and cannot be beaten by rotten bastards like him." To his surprise the German replied in good English, "You are not prisoners of war, you are terrorfliegers – child murderers. No, you are not prisoners of war." Then, in a small ray of kindness he took a look at the Englishmen's injured arm and promised to have a word with his colleague. The man scowled but then lowered his baton.

Chas Bowen, another incarcerated airman, told Mike Dorsey, "Phil Lamason had got beaten up pretty bad because he objected to having to carry the equipment." Phil's own account to the same interviewer described "a German who was around the bend... he was bloody mad... he had a bit of wood about three feet long and he was just bashing the prisoners just standing by the railway lines and everyone was trying to run past him…But I wasn't gonna run, I sort of walked up to him and an English voice said to him, 'Shoot him!' I turned around and there was about half a dozen guards with rifles trained on me. He said, 'None of them are going to get within five yards of you… and if you get within five yards, they're gonna shoot you, so you make sure they don't.'"

In his own account of being trapped in the tunnel, Art Kinnis recalled the "grim thoughts those crowded smoke filled hours in the tunnel produced. To be able to see would have helped but we were gasping, bewildered, and could only listen to the guttural shouting that now seemed to be all around us."

However, as Malcolm Cullen describes, a "temporarily uplifting detour" followed when the by then foul smelling and unkempt group disembarked from the train and made their way on foot through a village to board the replacement train. The local residents "were very sympathetic and showed contempt for our guards at every chance they got. They threw us bread and fruit and some of our boys managed to get a drink of cider." Water pumps along the roadside were besieged causing the guards to become threatening. The walk, some six kilometres in fresh air, had raised spirits, if only for a very brief interlude…"

Repacked into the "all-too-familiar box cars… the journey was soon resumed and, contrary to expectations, the train made good progress." That was until the occupants of the truck in which Art Kinnis was travelling attempted an escape. Careful preparations had been made, including weakening a loose board… August 18 and the train pulled up for another snap inspection…by now more boards had been loosened, so during the night when the train began to chug slowly up an incline, men began 'slipping out.' Some Canadians – but not Kinnis – were among them and "six desperate Frenchmen," one of whom was spotted and gunned down by a "wildly spraying machine gun." The majority of the escapees were then rounded up and dragged back to the train.

"All the occupants of the damaged carriage were shoved to one end and counted. Their latrine pail was kicked over, potatoes and other food items squashed underfoot and there was heated talk of shooting."

Canadian airman Dave High commented, "I was beaten with a rubber hose. I was struck mostly on the head, shoulders and arms, and was able to move about only with great difficulty for three or four days. I was black and blue for weeks."

Reprisal was not immediate. The train resumed its night time journey until a little after dawn when it slowed and halted in the middle of the countryside. A scarlet-faced Prussian officer arrived, roared at a Dutch pilot whose bi-lingual skills had already been proven, and then ordered the increasingly pale-faced listener to deliver the message.

Kinnis records the following: "When the German finished he moved off and the Dutchman turned slowly to face the others, badly shaken. 'I've been instructed to tell you that to prevent further escapes, and by way of punishment, 35 RAF airmen and 20 Frenchmen from this carriage are to be shot.' Howls of protest went up and the guards stiffened themselves for action. The prisoners selected to die were quickly separated from the rest and ordered from the truck… Frenchmen cursed and shook their fists…A short distance away two machine guns were set up on tripods…Many of the men began to pray and a muttered revolt ran through the intended victims. The first line of 20 men were ordered to step forward, machine guns trained on them….Tense seconds and then a minute passed. As they waited for the guards to receive the order to fire, they shook involuntarily with fear and anticipation… waiting for death was agony." Then the release. Summoned by the German to deliver another message, the Dutchman told the men they would not be shot. Their lesson had been learnt, for now. Instead they were ordered to remove their clothing. It would be returned at the end of the journey. But August 18 was not over yet.

That same day the train pulled up for another snap inspection. In the cattle truck from which the escape had taken place a 14 year-old French boy, obviously forgetting the order to stay away from the windows, grasped the ledge of one of the small ventilation apertures, intending to pull himself up so he could see outside. As he hauled himself up to peep out, a guard opened fire with his Schmeiser. One of the bullets hit the youth across the knuckles, shattering his hand.

Clutching his bloodied hand against his chest, he fell to the floor screaming. Moments later the door of the boxcar was unlocked and flung open as the guards demanded to know which of the naked occupants had disobeyed their orders… The lad clambered unsteadily to his feet and moved over to the door where he was flung out onto the ground. Several others were ordered to get out.

The prisoners watching from the open boxcar, and those peering through knotholes and cracks in the other wagons, saw two grim-faced guards grasp the boy under the arms and haul him to his feet. They asked the tearful youth if he was English or French and he stammered that he was French, following which he was motioned to proceed down the slight incline by the truck. As he moved off a Feldwebel unclipped his Luger and shouted an order at the guards. They then lifted their Schmeisers and fired at point blank range into the boy's back. The youngster threw his arms wide and then slumped forward, face down onto the ground. Just for good measure the Feldwebel walked down the incline, stood over the prostrate form and fired two more shots into the back of the boy's head. The faces of the men were "a study in incredulity… as they stood in shock at what they had witnessed." Two more men were ordered to come forward, whereupon, in their nakedness, they were given "small field shovels to hack out a shallow grave."

Dragging the youth's body up to the grave they buried him as best they could… and then were ordered, silent and grey-faced, back to the truck. As the train pulled away the dead boy's hands and feet could be seen, protruding grotesquely from his shallow grave. Several of the men felt ill. They too had touched the lacing of barbed wire over the small window and had even emptied pails of excreta through it.

For Phil, this cold-blooded murder of the French youth was a pivotal moment. "I suddenly realised what we were up against… these guys were gun happy… we were in big trouble!"

Chastened, the prisoners seemed to abandon any further attempt to escape, grudgingly accepting that any attempt to put a 'head above the parapet' would only bring a swift and terrible retribution. By this time the train had apparently crossed into Germany, causing some easing of the tension, although no lack of vigilance, among the guards who seemed relieved to have left French soil behind them and the risk of attacks by the Resistance. Clothes were also returned to the naked men.

Meanwhile two more days and nights had passed. Art Kinnis' account mentions the odd stop at small villages where prisoners could get out and stretch themselves, and even obtained several pails of water to have a wash. Starved of food, some were fortunate to obtain meat, bread and biscuits. In contrast, the litany of misery related by Burgess makes for grim reading. "With every passing kilometre, the occupants of the cattle trucks grew dirtier, more despondent and miserable. Every wagon stank of human waste, vomit and body odour. The prisoners itched and perspired incessantly and were ravenously hungry and thirsty. Added to this, the burning need for sleep had sapped the last of

113

their energy." Appearing to be nearing their limit of endurance, conditions, surely, could not get much worse? Wrong.

But then, a small ray of light to cling to. Rumours began sweeping the cattle trucks that the train was heading to Frankfurt. Here on the outskirts, as all aircrew knew, lay the Dulag Luft – the Luftwaffe interrogation centre where captured airmen were taken for questioning, before their dispersal to a proper POW camp. This routine for a captured airman was the accepted order of things. But no. The train swept through, followed by another night of misery.

Then the fifth morning, a slowing train, Weimar Station, railway tracks switched 100 metres behind the last carriage. A locomotive backed up out of a siding, linked up to the end cattle truck. Five cars carrying a cargo of female passengers were uncoupled…They were taken to Ravensbruck concentration camp. It was their last journey.

Buchenwald

Another track switch, the second, shortened train backed up. It made its way onto a sidetrack and began to pick up speed. The occupants felt they were now close to their destination. The train braked, slowed to a stop. Its cargo were the male prisoners. Outside, emaciated men dressed in filthy clothes were working beside the tracks ….

Standing up to the window, the German-speaking Dutch pilot, Spierenburg, started to question their whereabouts. When he finally lowered himself the news was grim. "We're at a place called Buchenwald." The men muttered among themselves. The place was unknown to them. Spierenburg continues: "I'm afraid it's one of the worst concentration camps in Europe. Not a prisoner of war camp but a punishment camp. I rather fear we are all in big trouble." Silent and unmoving the men just stood there. Someone delivered a heartfelt expletive.

The spell broke as the train began to move. The men started to talk again and a buzz of conversation followed. Their plight brought mixed reactions: while the French were visibly nervous, the airmen expressed anger. Why were they not under the protection of the Geneva Convention and therefore being taken to a Luftwaffe prisoner of war camp? Phil Lamason would ask this question many times in the ensuing weeks. Life as a POW, which would once have been considered as the worst of luck by these young airmen, is no longer an option.

Looking back, Joe Moser would paint a Utopian vision of life as a POW: "We thought of course we were going to a Prisoner of War camp, that our life would be quiet and simple, with respectful wardens, and continual whispering plots of how we would escape and rejoin the fight." And, he muses wistfully, "We would be fed three decent meals a day." Down-to-earth Phil, on the other hand, would never have indulged in such fantasy. But, knowing nothing of concentration camps or death camps, none of the airmen had any reason to believe such a horrendous thing would happen to them.

Return now to reality. The train arrived at its destination. It backed slowly up a long hill, past many well cultivated fields. It entered a big gate with a 50-foot guard tower on either side before rolling into a temporary platform. The platform was surrounded by barbed wire. Machine guns and searchlights were alarmingly visible. Behind the fence, large buildings, which proved to be factories, had an air of permanence and efficiency. There was something unnerving about them.

If the faces of the new arrivals had a glazed resignation about them it was brief. Incredulous, horrified, confronted, they were forced to take in an unimaginable scene. Seemingly oblivious to onlookers, hundreds of shuffling, emaciated men and boys were wearily going about their appointed tasks behind the barbed wire. Clad in dirty, striped pyjama-like tunics and with close-cropped hair, they were stoically indifferent to anything but the frenzied shouts and unrestrained blows of the German guards. Their faces were vacant, bony and skeletal. There was no acknowledgement of the newcomers, only empty stares. Graphically, their expressions spoke only of the inhumanities they had already endured.

Among the reactions to these soon to be all too familiar surroundings, the heartfelt reaction from a young Canadian airman eloquently captured the moment. "Dear God in heaven, what is this place?" Moments earlier, the solid wooden door of the cattle truck had been dragged open and a sudden burst of daylight had flooded the crowded, stinking interior. As he stared out into the vista that lay beyond the train the young man's face seemed to sag. He shuddered and repeated to himself, this time in an awed whisper, "Dear God in heaven!'

Phil, with his devoutly Christian background, may have had similar thoughts. But what can be surmised by now is that this filth-encrusted, sweat-soaked, urine and faeces stinking group, with bearded faces and clothes hanging off shrinking bodies, were rapidly coming to terms with the stark reality of their destination.

The behaviour of the SS guards provided the next shock. Here brutality was the norm. The big Alsatians restrained by strong collars and leashes held by SS guards, were Joe Moser's first recollection as he got off the train: "If the guards could snarl with the frothy, spit-filled, teeth bared growl like the dogs, I'm sure they would have. There were two rows of dogs and guards with just enough room between them for us to walk without getting torn apart. This was the gauntlet we walked through when we arrived at Buchenwald." As the prisoners were dragged from the cattle trucks those who fell to the ground were brutally kicked until they got up. The dogs snapped viciously at the men's bodies and tore at those on the ground.

In one cattle truck the occupants were beset by three thick-set guards who appeared in the open doorway and hauled them out head first onto the concrete platform. "Raus, schwein! Raus!" they screamed, their faces red with exertion and anger. For anyone who hesitated before jumping off the train a heavy club crashing down on the body was their punishment. Once off the platform the men were assembled on what was bleakly known as the 'Caracho Way,' (The Blood Way).

In the midst of this chaos, Phil's innate sense of responsibility quickly came to the fore. "I knew no one other than my navigator," he recounted to Mike Dorsey. "This was the case for many in the group. People were looking for someone to tell them what to do. I was surprised how many there were. I kept on inquiring 'Who are you? What's your rank?' A lot of these fellows were in civilian clothes. So I started organising them right on the railway line."

Here they were quickly moved along, whilst continually harassed by the dogs and the whipping and beating of the guards. As a small example of what was to come, a German major kicked a walking stick from under the arm of an American Flight Sergeant whose parachute landing had left him with a badly sprained ankle. "There are no cripples in here," came the growled warning.

Finally they reached a set of large gates upon which the words 'Buchenwald Konzentrationlager' had been forged. If the men still needed confirmation of their whereabouts, they had it now. And as they moved through the gates and into the camp the beatings continued to rain down upon increasingly fragile bodies. How much more suffering could they stand? Time would tell.

Above: Aerial view of Buchenwald at the time of its liberation by the Allies in 1945. Below: Well-publicised photograph of prisoners in Buchenwald at the time of liberation (Crown copyright)..

117

The infamous gate into the Buchenwald Camp with its inscription: 'Jedem das Seine' ('To each what he deserves').

The definition of 'Buchenwald' is 'Forest of Beeches.' In the ultimate of ironies this peaceful place was once the seat of profound thought from some of Germany's most erudite minds. Philosophers including Goethe and Schiller had gathered beneath these imposing trees, their meditative thoughts nurtured amid the raw-scented beauty and lush tranquillity of their surroundings – or so local legend had it. Now it had become a symbol of man's depravity to man.

A massive oak in the camp had become famous as 'Goethe's Oak.' According to local legend the revered poet had meditated beneath its lofty branches. Later, during the forest clearances that took place to make way for the camp, the Germans spared the tree, felled others around it and left it to stand as a monument to the might of the Third Reich. If the tree fell, popular belief had it, so would the regime.

In more immediate history the site had been a rugged and well-wooded estate of 140 hectares covered in beech and pine forest. Previously uninhabited, it had been bequeathed to the SS by its 'allegiant' owner. The camp was opened on July 15, 1937 as KZ (Konzentrationlager) Ettersberg, and then underwent a name change two weeks later to the less austere Buchenwald.

The camp's first inmates were one thousand political prisoners and convicts, deemed by Gestapo Chief of Police Heinrich Himmler to be enemies of the state. Mainly Jews and Roma (known then as gypsies) sourced from the already established camps of Dachau and Sachsenhausen, their task was to undertake the mammoth and back-breaking task of clearing the woodland slopes of the estate. They were forced to work 14-hour days in very primitive conditions. Tools were few and harassment from the guards was constant. To maintain his punishing hate-filled routine, Himmler appointed Standartenfuhrer Karl Koch of the SS to be Buchenwald's first camp Kommandant. While Koch's legacy of brutality is well documented by Burgess, it will not be noted here as he and his infamous wife Ilse, had moved on by the period in which we are interested.

The main gates to the camp reinforced the overtones of evil. "By the beginning of the Second World War the concentration camp was fully functional," Burgess records. "Proudly mounted above the main gate to the camp was the Buchenwald motto, 'Recht oder unrecht – mein Vaterland' ('My Country – right or wrong'). Then, entering the main camp compound, an iron gate, its gatehouse straddled by a two storey brick and wooden guardhouse, bore the slogan, 'Jedem das Seine' ('To each what he deserves'). Surmounting this were a watch tower and a searchlight."

One image that haunted Phil from the moment of his arrival was related to reporter Warren Barton: "One of the first things Lamason saw (on arrival in Buchenwald) were emaciated men, harnessed like animals, pulling a wagon. 'There was a fellow working them with a whip just like a bullock team. I had never seen anything like it. It confirmed for me … what we'd heard on the train about the death camp. It was a pretty dangerous place.'"

On either side of the gatehouse were steel-doored cells known to the inmates as bunkers or punishment cells, and beyond it was the main roll call or 'Appell' area. The newly-arrived group were ushered, or rather shoved, through this area by the guards, passing the Kommandant's office and the Political Department where selected inmates would undergo interrogation by the Gestapo. They entered through 'Jedem das Seine' into a large compound, to the right of which was a large brick building. Here they were ordered to turn right, then halted and ordered to sit down in columns. This was a welcome opportunity to finish off any remaining food scraps and to pass round precious cigarettes. The French even managed to produce some chocolate. Standing to one side throughout this procedure an audience of ragged men in striped garb,

119

kept at a distance by the guards, watched every move with craving in their eyes.

"The dull greyness, dinginess and heaviness to the buildings filled me with a sense of dread," writes Joe Moser. "I felt it deep within my gut...at the faces staring at us... empty, vacant, bony skeletal faces... No empathy or pity. Just empty, dead stares... I wondered if I could be reduced to such a state? If this was a POW camp, it was far, far worse than anything I imagined when trying to prepare myself to be a prisoner."

As the sun scorched down upon them, the men were then ordered to stand. They watched as their French comrades were separated and roughly ushered into the brick block and told to remove and carry their clothing...To the concern of their fellow prisoners they did not emerge for some time.

Art Kinnis commented, "We were told to grab our possessions and get out and line up by tens. One American was hit for no apparent reason by a swaggering German officer. Our spirits were on the ebb."

On the far side of the barrack area stood a squat building. Thick smoke belched from its tall chimney and mingled with the pungent, sickly smell which pervaded the entire camp. The men assumed it to be an incinerator but their innocence was misplaced. Unbeknown at the time, this was the camp crematorium. Later, word went round the group that they would not leave the camp except as smoke from the chimney.

Joe Moser recalled: "I did not identify the nauseatingly sweet and burnt smell that dominated the entire camp. I did not identify it as the smell of human flesh burning. That smell has stayed with me all my life, leading to a lifelong hatred of the smell of fried bacon."

Phil Lamason steps up

Phil took control. "I couldn't find anyone senior to me and when I did there was an American roughly about the same rank, but they were in a bit of a 'tiz' too and said 'You look after us. Tell us what you want.' Within a couple of days it was established that I was the senior officer. I was giving the orders. I said to them 'We need to be a unit and get out of here,'" he recalled to Mike Dorsey.

To Warren Barton Phil had said of this moment: "I gave them a bit of a talking to and I told them that we had to establish ourselves as servicemen; that they must march and act in a disciplined way. They were prisoners of war, and not political or criminal prisoners. Military

120

decorum would be maintained at all times and, until representation could be made through the proper channels, the orders of superior officers would be obeyed."

These were heartening words for the despondent group. Morale lifted a little and heroic efforts were made to maintain more dignity and discipline. But in the face of the bullying SS guards, who made them stand to attention and remove their hats whenever they passed, this was a challenge.

This positive assertive action was effective, unsettling the SS guards, as American Chas Bowen remembered to Mike Dorsey: "If we went from one place to another we would kind of march in unison like we were still in the military. This upset the guards tremendously. They expected us to be running wild all over the place and we weren't."

To Mike Dorsey, Phil added his thoughts about his leadership role at that time: "There were so many people dying, so many people getting murdered, I think that it wasn't really too difficult to establish command. People were looking for someone to lead and so on..."

Meanwhile all personal belongings had been confiscated, including most importantly their military discs. This single experience was to bear the most consequences. According to the Germans these could be bought in France for just a few francs. Such was the determination to disbelieve the airmen's repeated protestations of their rightful identity. From information obtained later from 'International Red Cross Excerpts from Documents,' these men, in the eyes of officialdom, were classified as 'DIKAL (Darf in kein anderes Lager)' – not to be transferred to another camp. This then was an instruction that the airmen were never to leave Buchenwald. The following passage gleaned by Colin Burgess confirms their evil intent:

"Their arrival at the camp on August 20, 1944, is recorded in the Red Cross information and further authenticated by a document from the SS archives in the Buchenwald Museum. Dated August 28, 1944, and signed by the SS Haupsturmfuhrer, Camp Medical Officer, there is a complete breakdown by camp registration number of the entire intake of prisoners who 'arrived from Paris on August 20, 1944, and were placed in the 'Zetlager' (tented camp within the 'Little Camp').' Against the serial numbers 78266 to 78423 (some numbers were not allocated to the new arrivals) appears a heavy annotation: 'TERRORFLIEGER.' Fortunately for their mental and emotional wellbeing the airmen were unaware of this development."

121

Nor were they prepared for their next experience. Following on from the earlier departure of their French comrades carrying their clothes, they too entered the brick building and were ordered to strip. Phil immediately took exception and directed Spierenburg, the Dutch translator, to claim their rights as prisoners of war and object to this treatment. The appeal fell on deaf ears. The men were shoved into an ante room where pockets were emptied, the contents placed in an envelope and clothing checked into a name-tagged bag. They were then subjected to the removal of every hair on their body. This humiliating experience has been variously described in painful detail. Unsurprisingly however there is little comment from Phil, so the writer is indebted to others who were more forthcoming.

Canadian airman Ed Carter-Edwards: "They cut off all our hair, every strand from every part of our bodies. The fellows who clipped us were most unkind. These 'barbers,' 20 or 30 of them, were fellow prisoners, Russians, Poles, Czechs and French. They were political prisoners, soldiers, black-market agents, and any other category deemed a threat to the state. They used old-style clippers, cutting underneath our arms and between our legs. They were so rough they nicked us pretty badly; we were bleeding all over, and to finish off their pleasure they used a swab and stuck it in a pail of fluid and dipped it under our arms and between our legs. It was some kind of lye and oh, did it burn! Imagine nearly 170 airmen dancing around like stripped chickens. It was funny but painful at the same time."

"Our grubby, smelly, belligerent and very tired 168 were led towards some 20 Polish inmates that appeared ready to do some shearing and we appeared to be the sheep," recalls Art Kinnis. "Hair that was our pride and joy came off far too quickly. We couldn't help but grin when we saw a well-trimmed moustache disappear with two quick strokes, after those same clippers had so carefully removed all hair from the unwashed body of the chap in front. When you saw a billiard ball head topping a baby-smooth body of the person in front and had difficulty in recognising him, you knew your world had changed.

"A man holding a large calcimine brush sat above a liquid filled bucket. 'Lift up your arms,' a swipe of the brush in each armpit, a swabbing of the pubis. 'Turn around and bend over,' a swat of the brush, vigorously applied to the ass. BOY DID THAT STING!"

Joe Moser's version: "We stood in a line, as naked as the day of birth. Soon I saw what the line was for: a haircut. It will forever remain the rudest, nastiest, roughest haircut of my life. The uniformed 'barber' grunted at me and poked my arm. I raised both arms up and the hair under my armpits was similarly half ripped and half cut away. I knew my groin would receive the same painful treatment, which it did." Of the disinfectant process he recalls: "I was told to close my eyes. The big brush was dipped into the tub containing the disinfectant and then swabbed over my raw and bloody body. Underarms and crotch burned like I had been stuck with a thousand burning cigarettes or stung by a hundred angry bees. Try as I might to keep it inside, I too yelped out in excruciating pain. Every part of me felt raw, scraped and abused."

The showers came next. There was some agitation as they were ushered into the large adjoining shower block. Word had it that the Germans had a habit of frequently killing prisoners by placing them in a shower block which in fact was a gas chamber. But here, there was one ray of light. Buchenwald did not have gas chambers. Its inmates were generally worked to death or summarily executed. But as the naked prisoners stood beneath the sputtering ceiling fixtures and were rained down upon by steaming hot water their relief was profound. Half-metre rag squares doubling as towels were handed out – one between two men. These, Art Kinnis complained, "rapidly lost their efficiency."

The naked, groaning and terrorised group were then marched to a different store. The camp clothing store completed the transformation from grubby, stinking but once 'free' men into the captive clones they were now to become. Each was issued with their prison garb of cotton shirt, trousers and cap, already baked at high temperatures to kill off any lurking lice. No attempt was made to match the size to the wearer. In Joe Moser's case being given "a normal pants size but a shirt with all that extra fabric that came down nearly to my knees," was a bonus. The clothes were hand-me-downs from previous prisoners who, presumably, had already met their death. But no shoes were issued and from now on the men had to go barefoot. Completing the hand-outs was a tin bowl about the size of a cereal bowl. "We were told to keep it and all our so-called meals were served in it."

Their next 'step' was to the registry office. Here they were ordered by 'a battery of scriveners' – prisoners like themselves but sporting black berets and armbands – to give personal details for their camp registration forms. As the forms required information the airmen were not prepared to reveal, they gave only their name, rank and service number. Although orders for this display of mass obstinacy are not attributed to Phil, his previous instructions that they form and behave like a military unit at all times were now being demonstrated.

It transpired that the information required of them was not of military origin but in relation to their personal skills and abilities. Following camp practice the men would be put to work at tasks they were best suited to. As each prisoner in the long line stepped forward, explained their status to the interrogator and asked for POW status, they were asked to step aside. Thus, this group of 168 men collectively defying the authorities was already creating a bureaucratic nightmare. "This had the effect of uniting us," recalls one American airman. "It was only then we got a comprehensive picture of how many of us were in the same predicament and it was only then that we came to be dealt with as an entity."

Despite threats from the 'Kapos' (foremen prisoners), the men remained resolute. Finally the clerks were instructed by a visibly furious senior Kapo to take only minimum details and each man was issued with a small white cloth bearing his prison number. The men were then individually photographed, holding a slate on which had been chalked their five figure camp number.

Little Camp

Any feelings of satisfaction about their small victory over bureaucracy were short-lived. Assembled outside in the heavy night air smiles faded as they were quickly surrounded by a squad of SS guards armed with lumps of wood. Clubbed again and again by shouting Germans, the prisoners were made to run back through the gateway along a stony road. In their unshod feet they staggered along the path as the heavy blows rained down upon them. Finally, under watchful eyes they were assembled with the French prisoners in the parade area. Another head count and the by then dispirited group were lined up in columns of five and marched off to the 'Kleine Lager' or Little Camp. This was the place for new arrivals and was already overcrowded.

Art Kinnis recalled that, "we were all in shock and wondered what and how the future could be handled. We required time to think and knew our group must become very united. The authorities must realise that we are all aircrew of the Allies and that what is now happening to us is against the Geneva Convention."

As the men marched towards Little Camp, prisoners behind the barbed wire fence were calling out, asking their nationalities. Many of

The Little Camp in Buchenwald, 1944. (Photograph courtesy of the Buchenwald Concentration Camp Museum)

the men were elated to hear familiar Anglo-American voices and in a multitude of tongues the airmen were besieged with questions as the prisoners pleaded for news of the war. Weeping Frenchmen cried out to their countrymen that the war would soon end.

The bare-footed brigade hobbled on, passing row upon row of one or two storeyed dark green wood huts. Turning a corner they moved down a small incline at the foot of which they were counted through a gate and then, 100 metres on, through another gate. By then it was nine o'clock. Darkness had closed in and – unsurprisingly – they were surrounded by barbed wire.

Standing on the cobblestones, the final gate closed behind them, the dismayed men took stock of their surroundings. Other than two large trees, five marquee-sized tents for the very sick, and a small stone building in which lived the 'Lager Altester' (Camp Senior) and his assistants, the area was devoid of shelter. Otherwise, the place resembled a rock pile and worst of all, there was no place to sleep.

It was speedily apparent they would have to sleep out in the open. Blankets, which had not been distributed by numbers, were shared among them. Stretching out to sleep on unforgiving cobblestones, the exhausted men made themselves as comfortable as possible. To their surprise an urn of lukewarm soup was delivered and speedily consumed. For many it was their first meal since leaving Fresnes. And for all, it was their introduction to the hitherto unimagined horrors of bloody, bloody, Buchenwald.

Art Kinnis remembered their first night. "Fortunately the night was warm and we did not notice the cold. Our sound sleep would be mostly due to the fact that it was our first chance to stretch out, plus our exhausted condition, and the fact that we noticed little difference between the floorboards of the box car and this slightly pliable bed of rocks."

Joe Moser also recalled their arrival. "We were marched to an open area at the northeast corner of Little Camp. Little Camp was a section of barracks where the prisoners received the least food and the harshest treatment. We waited there in the darkening skies of that August evening expecting to be directed to a barracks. Instead we were handed a blanket. Or should I say a third of a blanket? We were puzzled. We're supposed to sleep here? Soon we all sat down. The ground was not soft clean dirt, but rocky with larger flat rocks interspersed with gravel. OK, we will wait here until they find some barracks. It was not to be. This was our barracks."

The following morning the Little Camp prisoners were roused for a "slow and tedious" early morning roll call. The Appell. Moser recalled "a grey, striped mass lying on open, rocky ground. A confused, fearful, angry, and terribly hungry grey mass."

Each prisoner was then issued with a litre of cold and bitter ersatz coffee, made from acorns. They were then free to 'case the joint,' to wander around, talk among themselves and generally get the lie of the land.

The Appell was a word – and a routine – that became a way of life. It was the name given to the camp roll call and could last from one hour to three or four. The men would line up ten deep to be checked by the Altesters and then it was the SS private's turn. At his approach prisoners were ordered to stand to attention and remove their hats whilst a head count was undertaken. It soon became apparent that 'The Goons' were extremely poor counters and the tally was seldom correct on the first attempt. Appells generally took place at 7am and 4pm. For the main camp they were held on the large compound where prisoners were assembled in their tens of thousands. If German guards needed to be addressed at these rollcalls it had to be from a distance of at least three metres. Many were the instances of cruelty and suffering that occurred during this longwinded, twice daily routine.

An example: An airman standing near the front of the ranks in the customary Air Force manner, hands tightly clenched and wrists pointing along the seams of his non-existent trousers, was suddenly bashed across the face with a Luger. The assault drew blood. The perpetrator was an 'unhinged' long term SS prison guard, who had a problem with the position of the airman's hands. Apparently prisoners were required to hold their hands flat by their sides thus indicating they were empty. Another airman suffered a similar experience the following day. The guard, eyes blazing, jaws champing and mouth drooling, was regarded as being as mad as a hatter. He customarily carried a heavy stick and had no hesitation in using it. He has been described by Kinnis as "our 6ft 2inch, Lager Altester, a strong, fiery-tempered German who had known no other life for the past 12 years."

On another occasion the men were appalled at the condition of "a whimpering Pole," who had been badly beaten, kicked in the stomach and left to lie on the ground. 'Blood' covered the whole of his face and seemed to be pouring over the whole of his body. The crime? He had been caught stealing strawberry jam and what appeared to be blood was the result of his head being forcibly immersed in the barrel of jam.

The interminably long time of trying to stand quietly without moving, was used as a time to communicate important messages. For this reason prisoners were lined up facing the whipping block. As an extra means of intimidation a gallows would sometimes be pushed into the square. All the while the nearby crematorium poured out its acrid smoky reminder of death. Floating ash was the ultimate reminder of this brutal regime.

Due to dysentery being rife in the camp the latrine, of necessity, was central to daily existence. Supposedly capable of meeting the needs of one thousand malnourished and desperate human beings in one 'sitting' this vile smelling place was in constant use. At the far end of the brick building in which it was housed, was a room used to dump the bodies of those who had died during the night. Here they were stacked for transportation to the camp crematorium. One airman recalled counting 17 corpses when he peered through a window.

To stave off the dysentery the men resorted to toasting their bread over small fires in the hope that by burning it the resultant carbon might prevent or alleviate the disease. They also learnt to boil water to prevent its onset. Ironically the latrine was the source of the water. It was obtained at a certain time of the day but even boiling could not remove the stink.

Art Kinnis wrote, "Unfortunately the water and black bread had had a very disastrous effect on our bowels and kidneys, which condition lasted our entire stay. The liquid diet made several night trips to the Abort a necessity. These places were a nightmare for we would stumble barefooted over soggy flagstones at all hours of the day or night. Some of the cases we saw were extremely pitiful."

Ken Chapman recalls the arrival. "We were shown our quarters for the night. There weren't any! We had to sleep on the cobbles, with no blankets, no nothing except our thin prison clothes. We had an issue of soup before night. The latter was terrible, gazing at the stars trying to keep warm. We spent our first eight days like this. The second night I was so cold I slept in the lavatory which was warm although reeking with an obnoxious odour. Dysentery was very prevalent due to the water."

In the airmen's section of the camp were about 3000 people, including Russians, Jews, Poles and Frenchmen, some of whom were known to the prisoners. Among them was Georges Prevot. Prevot had been one of Phil and Ken Chapman's helpers during their 'on the run and heading home' period. He was in a distraught state and had shed a lot of weight. A lengthy conversation with Phil may have helped him, but how long ago now those events must have seemed.

While the regular prisoners' garb was the standard blue and grey striped pyjama-style clothing, each prisoner category wore a different coloured triangle on their jacket or trousers. This denoted their race, allegiance or crime with an individual serial number on a white cloth patch below the triangle. A black letter embroidered on a red triangle indicated the origin of 'other nationalities.' Thus F stood for French, T for Czechs, R for Russians, P for Poles etc.

The class of prisoner was recognised by the colour of the triangle: Red without letters – German political prisoners; red with black letters – other nationalities; green – common law offenders; yellow – Jews; pink – homosexuals; violet – Jehovah's Witnesses or others imprisoned for religious beliefs.

Black was for gypsies, 'shiftless elements,' and work dodgers. A group of young gypsies were fellow inmates. It took only a short time for the airmen to become wise to their 'taking ways' and to remain vigilant when it came to looking after their meagre belongings. In spite of the pains he had taken to hide it, Art Kinnis' compass was stolen on the first night and others also lost items. The youngsters begged or stole whatever they could. Due to the desperate needs of those surrounding them the men took turns to guard their possessions. This remained a necessity for as long as they were in Buchenwald.

Although the men had expected their time at Little Camp to be short, they nevertheless set about getting the section to themselves. Here they had an advantage. Due to their location on a large cobbled mound alongside the Altester's hut, their squatters' rights were unchallenged, although at first the French "were a trifle obstinate." Their rectangular area was known colloquially as the Rock Pile, the flagstones in contrast to the black, clay-like soil elsewhere in the camp.

The men were able to guard their food and keep the surroundings fairly clean. Some even found the rocks very comfortable. At the noon hour they received a gamel of thick soup which was delivered in a large tin or wood tub. Due to a shortage of bowls this was a long job. "For the first day or so until we became organised this was quite a shambles," Kinnis remembers. "At this time we received our ration of other food which included ¼ to ½ of a small loaf of black bread and 1500 grams of margarine. In addition we might get strawberry jam, honey, cheese, salt, meat spread or blood sausage in very small amounts. These items however were mostly conspicuous by their absence. Every other day we received a litre of potatoes and on these days we received only half a litre of soup. We received a gamel of soy bean coffee or mint tea before or just after 7.00am Appell and the same at 4.00pm. Although not very tasty it was hot."

Burgess's account of the camp diet is somewhat less charitable. "The ersatz coffee was always cold on arrival and if so much as a drop was spilt out of the urn, the entire carrying detail was beaten by the guards. Also in urns for an 11.00am delivery came the bread, tough black knackerbrod, topped by a cursory wipe of a margarine substance and the soup. Barely worthy of the name, the soup was little more than grass or nettles soaked in hot water. Often bug and maggot-ridden, it occasionally contained a cube or two of meat." The source was unspecified.

Meanwhile they made efforts to get comfortable. Torn up sacks, padded with straw, were used as footwear. They started looking for blankets, and by the end of the tenth day, had two between three men. It was not until the third week that each man had an individual blanket.

Much more disturbing for the newcomers was the behaviour associated with the arrival of the rations. Beset by constant hunger, the other prisoners resorted to fighting and scratching to scrape the bottoms of the food urns once the issue had been handed out. The airmen were appalled. The strong beat the weak underfoot and the weak sometimes died.

Unwittingly they contributed to this 'standard' behaviour by the inmates during their first experience of dining amongst them. On receiving the daily small individual portions of dark grey bread, which "smelt vile and tasted even worse," several men threw it away in disgust. They then watched in horrified amazement as dozens of starving inmates rushed at it, fighting for the pathetic scraps like wild beasts, scratching, punching and elbowing in a free-for-all of irrational and uncontrollable hunger.

With a mixture of pity and disgust the other airmen tossed their bread into the rapidly growing melee. The following day they again tossed away their bread ration, this time to a group who had patiently waited nearby. Despite the men's well-meaning intentions, Phil quickly stopped this practice because he did not want his men to be responsible for any deaths or injuries. Furthermore, unlike the foul-smelling soup, the bread was their chief source of sustenance. Phil's intervention was a timely demonstration of his organisational skills and leadership.

He had already instructed the men to write down their details: country, name, rank, serial number, their 1944 home address and newly-designated Buchenwald number. As Senior Officer he then chose 17 officers, each in charge of a ten man unit, to assist him with maintaining discipline. The two leaders immediately subordinate to him were Flight Lieutenant Tom Blackham and Captain Merle Larson. This new system enabled better management of the daily tasks including distribution of rations, and helped leaders to each become familiar with a few men. The pilfering which had begun on their first night in camp was also addressed, with each leader required to mount a round the clock guard.

The following narrative which clearly epitomises the outstanding leadership skills Phil displayed is reproduced from Joe Moser's publication 'A Fighter Pilot in Buchenwald.' Among the various published references regarding the impact of his leadership during the airmen's time in Buchenwald, this account is the most detailed. The writer sincerely acknowledges his published.

"After our first meal, we gathered back together in the open area where we had slept. It was about this time that Colonel Phillip Lamason stepped forward. Col. Lamason was the senior officer among the 168 of us, a tall, good-looking Squadron Leader from the New Zealand Air Force. I consider it one of the greatest blessings of this challenging time to have Col. Lamason as our commander. His quiet, strong but aggressive leadership was a critical factor not only in holding us together but also in facilitating our eventual release.

"'Attention!' he said unexpectedly in his clipped New Zealand accent. We instinctively got up, tried to get ourselves in some semblance of order, and stood stiffly waiting.

"'Gentlemen, we have got ourselves in a very fine fix indeed,' he went on. 'The goons have completely violated the Geneva Convention and are treating us as common thieves and criminals. However we are soldiers! From this time on, we will also conduct ourselves as our training has taught us and as our countries would expect from us. We will march as a unit to roll call and we will follow all reasonable commands as a single unit.'

"Then he proceeded to organise us all by the country we were from. Over each group he made the senior officer our CO or Commanding Officer. From this moment we once again became soldiers, now in a tightly-knit group experiencing what very few Allied soldiers would experience. It boosted our morale and gave us hope. We might be in these awful prison uniforms and be in the dirtiest, filthiest, most degrading place on earth, but we were soldiers.

"Lamason didn't do this just to improve our morale but no doubt because he saw it also as his responsibility to carry on his war duties despite these circumstances. His mind was quickly running to ways how we could either escape or somehow overcome our captors and, if not overcome them, make things as difficult for them as possible. He also no doubt believed that if the right opportunity presented itself, we would be able to operate much more effectively if military discipline and operations were applied.

"I can say this with some certainty because the actions he took in the days ahead demonstrated clearly that he was not a leader to sit back and

131

accept the fate that seemed to have been prepared for us. He would lead us into the fight to the very end if that is the way it is to end.

"There was another very important value to this imposition of military discipline. Already hotheads in our group were agitating. Of course we were all bitterly angry and frustrated. We were all but certain that no one knew our whereabouts. Since it had become clear to us that this was not a Luftwaffe prison camp, we believed correctly that we had fallen out of the system. The Red Cross had no contact with us. The US military did not even know that such a place as Buchenwald existed, let alone that Allied soldiers could be sent there. That meant that our families had no idea where we were either.

"But to act out on these frustrations with aggressive action and angry words against the Kapos who were our most immediate guards and tormentors made no sense. It would just get us into trouble. So the military discipline that Col. Lamason and then Capt. Larson imposed was a great help to all of us."

Many of the Kapos were professional criminals and, of all the tormenters at Buchenwald, they were among the nastiest and cruellest. As they were largely responsible for running the prison, the Kapos had to work hard to retain, or to improve, their positions. This was demonstrated by showing the SS officers just how rough they could be on their fellow prisoners.

The airmen, dire though their situation was, did have one bit of bad luck in their favour. While desperate to make contact with the outside world, especially the Luftwaffe and the Red Cross, the fact that the world had no knowledge of their whereabouts, in some ways worked to the group's advantage. It meant that the camp administrators chose not to allocate them any work beyond the confines of the camp. This was due to their non-transfer (DIKAL) status and the fact that no one outside must know they were there. The men could not be presented with an opportunity to escape therefore they were assigned 'light' duties, so simple domestic tasks such as cleaning, carrying and interior road maintenance were their lot. The irony was they had all been declared fit for work by the SS doctor.

But before the airmen had reached this 'light duties' phase of their incarceration an incident had occurred that was to have a profound effect on their lives.

Bombing of the Factories

Joe Moser: "The first big test of us as a military unit under the control of our commanding officers came quickly. Within the first couple of days after arriving at Buchenwald Col. Lamason was informed by the SS guards that we would begin working in the nearby factories. We had seen the factory buildings when we first arrived at the train station before entering the camp. There was a very large factory to our left, or south as we marched down the railroad tracks to the gauntlet of dogs and guards, and another smaller factory inside the main fence to our right. The large factory south of the main camp area was the Gustloff Works built in 1943. It was a German industrial factory built adjacent to the camp in order to take advantage of the slave labour provided by the inmates. But the industrial firm had to pay the SS for the labour of the inmates. Where initially the machine shop in the German Armament Works was used to make a variety of items, including luxury items for the SS officers such as large chandeliers, by the time we were there in the latter part of the war, both factories were busy at work producing war materials. The German Armament Works was manufacturing cartridge cases, anti-tank shells and parts for Messerschmidtt aircraft while the Gustloff Works was producing cannons, rifles, pistols and motor vehicles.

"The factories together employed 9000 prisoners and Col. Lamason was informed that we would be instructed to join the work crews. Obviously here was a great dilemma. While the horrors of constant torture and execution was not well known to us at this time, we knew that refusing to obey our masters would be to put our lives at risk – as if they weren't at risk enough already. But working on the guns and equipment that would be used to kill our fellow soldiers was equally unacceptable. Col. Lamason, no doubt in consultation with Capt. Larson and the other senior officers, informed the guards that we were soldiers and could not and would not participate in war production. I do not know what reaction this caused among about 80,000 prisoners at this time. While we were very afraid of what this refusal might mean, we were not aware of any reprisals or punishments, because of this principled and courageous stance. What I knew and was shared by everyone I knew is that I was proud to be an American soldier and Col. Lamason and Capt. Larson were two great leaders who I would have been glad to follow anywhere they asked."

On the morning of August 24, 1944, three separate incidents interrupted daily life. After a special Appell on the concrete area of Little Camp, the 'terrorflieger' contingent was separated and each man given two 'very painful injections' of a green fluid in the chest. With some knowledge now of the tendency to administer lethal injections, there was understandably some anxiety about the jabs. Much later, after the War, Phil would describe his association with the camp sick bay and its practices.

The second experience came from above. At 11.00am prisoners gazed expectantly skywards as the camp's air-raid sirens wailed a warning and the "dull thudding sounds of bombing in the direction of Leipzig filled their hearts with satisfaction." While some inmates were shunted into their barracks the Allied prisoners opted to remain outside. Announcing the presence of the US Army Air Force, two large formations of Flying Fortress bombers – 129 in all – were heading straight for the camp. While the men were gladdened at the sight, excitement quickly turned to fear when a Very pistol was fired from the window of the leading aircraft with a puff of white smoke signalling a bomb attack. Covering the men with machine guns, terrified SS guards ordered an immediate drop to the ground. The targets however were the nearby factories outside the camp, known for assembling the essential gyro components for Hitler's V-1 buzz bombs. American bomb after bomb decimated the factories as many terrified workers began streaming out of the burning buildings, only to perish at the hands of the guards. Death and destruction was rife.

Art Kinnis remembered, "The Americans and bomb-aimers among us recognised 'the signal to drop the load.' In no time at all the shrill whistling noise of falling death could be heard coming our way. These bombs went several miles past us and hit the local airfield, but it really put the fear of the devil into us."

Then, when the mighty Fortresses wheeled for home, a fluttering cascade of white leaflets rained down upon the airmen, who plucked them from the air with eager hands. Here displayed were two small photographs showing groups of uniformed Germans. But more surprisingly, in bold Gothic print, were the words, 'These men are German prisoners of war in England. They are treated according to the rules of the Geneva Convention.' Speculation was rife as the airmen pondered the implications of the message behind the words.

The third incident that day arose from the above. Fires 'sparked' by the bombing broke out in the main camp and the airmen were quickly instructed to become fire fighters. Barefoot and dressed only in trousers, they began to beat out several of the smaller fires and clear away wood and rubble. Amongst the debris lay numerous unexploded incendiaries. The work was hot, dirty and dangerous compounded by cinders falling all around. The men sustained painful blisters on their feet and bodies.

Several who were assigned to moving food and clothing supplies were able to purloin welcome supplies but some went overboard. To Phil's horror, one of the men was spotted wearing a highly polished pair of boots he had yanked off a dead guard. Reaction was swift. Calling the man a "bloody fool," Phil hissed at him to "get those off before another guard shoots you on the spot." The offending footwear was rapidly discarded.

Strewn everywhere in and around the blazing huts were blackened and rigid corpses and the now familiar stench of burning flesh hung heavily in the air. The dead and injured were taken away on planks of wood and stretchers.

There was another, deeply symbolic fatality. Goethe's Oak, the icon of Hitler's supremacy in the Buchenwald forest, had been hit by an explosive incendiary. Longer term inmates stared at the sight in amazement. Goethe's tree was now just a blackened, shattered corpse. The despised symbol of the Third Reich's strength and supremacy had fallen.

Along with the factories, seven buildings in the concentration camp were destroyed. In all, 175 x 1000 pound bombs had been dropped, 583 x 500 pound bombs and 279 incendiaries. As well as 80 German fatalities and 300 wounded, there were 400 prisoners killed and 2000 casualties. The scene was utter chaos. Wounded were being carried on stretchers, planks, doors, any object that would serve, in a continuous moving body to join the milling suffering mass of humanity.

"During the end of this firefighting effort some of the Altesters invited us into their hut where they gave us hot coffee, white bread and jam. It certainly tasted ideal and it gave us a welcome breather from the heat of the fire and the extremely smoke laden atmosphere," Art Kinnis recalled.

Amid their uncertain existence of hovering between death and survival at the whim of the dreaded hierarchy, the airmen, following a tirade relating to the origins of the bomb attack, were then handed some small snippets of hope from the Commandant immediately after the fire.

Commandant Pister: "I am grateful for your co-operation in helping to clear the damage this morning. Your position here is under review." This was the first positive statement they had received since their arrival.

Then later an officer told them that some of the SS had called upon their services to assist with the clearing up because "they knew the airmen's integrity under pressure could be relied upon and that they would keep their heads under adverse conditions."

Refusal to Work

Glenys Scott recalled Phil saying that "they did give some help with the salvaging of the food...but nothing else!"

Also talking with Glenys about this event, Phil said that when the fires broke out, he was summoned by the senior guard and ordered that he put his men to work immediately. Phil refused, again citing the Geneva Convention and their POW status. He spoke of how he was then instructed to kneel down. The guard drew his Luger and shoved it into Phil's temple. Phil waited for the inevitable explosion.

There was a long pause before the guard repeated his question, "Will you work for us?" "No!" Phil replied, before demanding to see the senior officer. The stunned guard then ordered Phil back to his barracks. Phil's boldness was based on the fact that he had men organised to take his place and lead the group if he was killed. This extreme act of defiance is one of the defining examples of Lamason's heroism when his life was on the line.

This form of Gestapo intimidation, while not always recounted in some sources, occurred more than once with Phil while they were in Buchenwald. Phil told Glenys that it did happen to him "on more than one occasion. They were desperately trying to break us!" Joe Moser referred to a similar incident when, on an earlier occasion, Phil was summoned by the officer in charge and informed that his men would be put to work in the armaments factory. Such events were not always witnessed by other prisoners... did Phil, with his customary dislike for the limelight, simply choose to keep those terrifying moments to himself?

In the days following the bombing raid and the fire, the weather began to change. Overnight the sky turned black and it began to drizzle.

Sounds of distant thunder heralded the change, the skies opened up and the rain belted down. The cobbles the men were sleeping on became wet and slippery and their blankets, or what passed for them, were soaked. For the next two days in these utterly miserable conditions the men remained outside and bore the brunt of the weather change. Then when it seemed they would die from exposure they were moved to a wooden barracks block in the next compound.

As they marched up the hill in driving rain with blankets over their heads, some took off their shirts and tried to keep them dry by holding them in their arms. Finally they made their way into the crowded block and found places for themselves on the floor.

The new 'digs' was Block 58, 30 metres long, eight metres wide and windowless. In the absence of bunks were four tiers of wooden shelves divided into compartments which were more like wide bookcases than beds. In space that was barely adequate for one person to sleep, three men had to cram themselves. With no room other than on the floor, the newcomers wrapped themselves in their damp blankets and finally dropped off to sleep. But after three weeks of outdoor living they at least had a roof over their heads and time to adjust to the new surroundings. Persistent rain over several days confined the airmen to the barracks, except for compulsory Appells. The other prisoners continued their work as usual.

Among the occupants of Block 58 were French, Jews, 500 German gypsy boys aged from 6 to16 years, and an accompanying horde of lice and fleas. These swarmed all over the increasingly debilitated airmen and nearly drove them mad. Also by this time 30 of the airmen were considered ill enough to be detained in the camp hospital.

This was no panacea as the five tents that made up the so-called hospital were a hot bed of infection. No anaesthetic was used, decaying matter was cut from open sores by unsterilized pocket knives and gaping, putrid wounds were covered by many-times-used paper bandages. Other than the occasional aspirin no medicines were available. Never was a place of healing filthier and corpses were removed daily by the stretcher bearers. Every morning a handcart pulled by prisoners from Little Camp did the rounds, with the bodies of those who had died during the night piled on the top.

During the final months of Buchenwald a critical shortage of coal saw bodies waiting for cremation dumped onto piles which were dotted all around the camp. Rats swarming through the piles exacerbated the threat of a looming typhus epidemic. Eventually Himmler gave permission to conduct mass burials.

"It was like hell to us and we saw many atrocities," wrote an American airman. "People were dying all the time through the lack of nourishment and typhus. The cremations of the dead took place every Wednesday and Friday. We always knew the day because that day we had half-rations of soup as they took out fuel for the crematorium."

For Phil, one memory left an indelible impression and has also been referred to later in the this book. Ordered to visit the crematorium with a message for the Kapo in charge, he descended some stairs below the main building and found himself in a small room with meat hooks around the walls. "What were they for?" he asked the guard.

"The solution to the problem, it takes only a few minutes to die. They are the lucky ones."

Visualise piano wires looped around a hook and shimmering with the blood of the last victim. Then visualise two men looped together, hanging from a hook until they stop kicking and screaming. The wall is scraped with the feet of desperate captives who have kicked out to ease the suffering of the garrotting wire which cuts through their windpipe in a slow death struggle.

Merciless guards take bets on which person will stop kicking last, and morbidly laugh as they take the bodies down in a macabre game of hangman. A small lift nearby raises the bodies to the top floor where they join the endless procession to the furnaces. All accompanied by the unmistakeable stench of human flesh that hangs over the camp.

A few days after the men moved into Block 58, bed space became available with the evacuation of a group of gypsies to another camp, although it was likely that 'camp' was a euphemism for the gas chambers. The departure freed up room in the block and the airmen were at last able to find place on the shelf-like beds around the walls. There were no pillows or mattresses, only about 45 centimetres of sleeping space and a thin blanket between three or four. But despite the fury of lice and fleas life did become a little more tolerable.

With Phil's determination that his men would not work, the days took on a monotony in which the only constantly changing factor was their continued weight loss. Along with days spent sitting on the ground outside, dozing or talking, there were nightly roll calls, insubstantial food, and the constant irritation of fleas and bedbugs. Although itching incessantly, the men willed themselves not to scratch even the smallest sore as this invited infection. Compounded by the lack of nutritious food these wounds would not heal and became open, weeping sores. To mitigate the infection the men learned to stuff the holes in their flesh with small wedges of paper. This soaked up the matter.

Every Thursday, under the supervision of the block Altester, they washed out their barracks, including the bunks, and covered the floor with quicklime, which gave off a pungent odour but maintained some semblance of hygiene. A cleaning day without sun however was a more debilitating experience. The newly cleaned bunks did not dry out and the damp would strike at shoulders and hips as it seeped through thin blankets.

Obviously with a disposition still to look on the bright side, Art Kinnis writes of this time: "Our spirits rose considerably once we were permanently installed in Hut 58, for the thought of having to spend the coming cold weather outside had been a very depressing topic. The gypsy youngsters and only a few Poles were left in the hut, so that we had bunks for our own use. Many slept on the floor, tables and benches for we found it impossible to fit the men required into the five foot space. Three in this small space could move, four barely, if on their sides, and five was absolutely impossible. A little later we were given more room and in such a position that we were able to segregate ourselves from the others.

"Conditions started to improve with this for we had our Appells just outside and sometimes inside the hut. The hut was a blessing for with our diet we could not afford to be over energetic in walking outside all day. We could now cook our toast etc on the stove, and were also allowed to make fires outside. It was possible for us all to keep our food clean and safe from prowling fingers and the gamels we had our soup in were reasonably clean. It was a pleasure to eat near a table even if we couldn't sit on the benches. The most important point however, was that the Altesters were all friendly towards us, and this proved a terrific advantage to us. The men were also each given a topcoat."

Of the bed bugs, "for such were our new friends," he says: "…we would amuse ourselves by seeing how many we could catch in our blankets and clothes. After turning our clothes inside out and running down the creases we would create a new fashion by wearing pockets facing out. In spite of this, those crawling, fast moving blood suckers were soon back again. Our arms, legs and bodies became covered with small red marks which in some cases merged to cover the whole area.

There was no relief for they made their presence felt the whole 24 hours and scratching would result in open wounds. It goes without saying that any in this condition retained those wounds for the duration of our visit."

"We soon settled into a regular routine, for we found that the time passed a little quicker. Several of us spent time planning our future homes; others who had a smattering of languages talked to other nationalities; some pit bashed. Some talked FOOD. Everyone thrived on rumours and our spirits soared according to the contents." Working parties were marched out of the camp every day after the 7.00am Appell regardless of the weather. The majority of these prisoners would either hew stones in the quarry, drag logs, or work on other utilities. But thanks to Phil's resistance they did not include the airmen.

Before moving on with the story, the following three accounts – one concerning some treatment of Jews, another of gypsy children, and the third a series of randomly inflicted punishments – illustrate the extremes in cruelty suffered by prisoners deemed to be 'enemies of the state.'

One day a party of Jews who had been brought into Buchenwald were massed for despatch to Auschwitz. These men had been forced to work in a synthetic petrol factory near Leipzig, and some had been burned terribly when the factory was bombed by the Americans. These terrified individuals were marched to the railway station and crushed into four cattle trucks. Those close to death and unable to walk to the siding were piled onto carts drawn by other prisoners, who were forced to push them along Caracho Road at double time. The strongest in the carts struggled feebly to raise their heads from beneath the pile of the dying and the dead, but many died on the trip to the station. Their bodies were simply flung through the open doors of the cattle trucks. One Pole who attempted to escape was easily captured and hung in front of the others, as an example. The hanging was a clumsy affair, and the Pole took a full five minutes to die.

The second example occurred after the airmen's move to Block 58 and the subsequent departure of some of the gypsy children already in residence.

The SS, without prior warning, hauled the remaining 250 gypsy children from Block 58, herded them into a group and surrounded them with carbine-bearing guards. These poor innocent children, many of whom had suffered castration at the hands of unfeeling butchers in the medical block, cried and called out for their frantic fathers or relatives, who were held at bay by blows from carbines or machine pistols. The

140

heart-rending sobbing and screaming still haunts many an inmate who was witness to the events of that dark day. Those children without family cried out for friends who had protected them and tended them in camp, either for reasons of compassion or even sexual gratification, while the adults moaned and wept for the children they knew they would never see again.

The crying and screaming children were hustled into a long pantechnicon vehicle and the back of the van was then closed. For the rest of that day an ominous silence hung over the camp, save for the distraught weeping of loved ones. It was a day of barbarism and tragedy that no one who was there wishes to remember or can ever forget. It was later rumoured, but never confirmed, that the pantechnicon was in fact an elaborate gas chamber similar to others in use in Germany at that time, and that the gypsy children were dead before the vehicle even left Buchenwald. While acts of the grossest perversion were committed daily throughout the camp and shock soon gave way to numbing inurement, this was an extremely soul-destroying experience for the airmen to witness.

"We had been looking, observing and talking to the many thousands that surrounded us and were convinced that the disastrous results caused by Nazi culture must run into thousands. From many of our talks with various prisoners, we learned a minute number of the countless forms of torture. Medieval methods must have been found lacking in cunning and cruelty. Men who had their finger nails bitten to the raw stage, to try to avoid having twigs set in and set alight. Salt bath was particularly trying for a chap tied such that his feet were near a roof which could be made to lower at will. The candidate was completely stripped and lowered into a tank of salt water. While suspended he was whipped with thongs until open sores appeared. Many of the victims died through drowning, due to swallowing water when their mouths opened in pain as the salt water touched their open wounds. Men were tied naked, in such a manner as to have a piece of wood between their arms and knees. In this helpless position they were whipped and kicked into insensibility. Women had string tightened around their breasts until blood appeared."

In September the numbers were boosted by a contingent of 1700 Danes. Mostly police officials, they had refused to cooperate with the German occupation forces in their homeland, instead they actively supported acts of sabotage by the Resistance. As such they had become

141

somewhat of an embarrassment whilst imprisoned at home and so were transported to Buchenwald.

Like the airmen, the Danes' own journey to Buchenwald had been an intensely challenging, and for some, a fatal, experience. From Denmark they had first been shipped to Hamburg. During their voyage in the hold of the ship the lack of ventilation, food and water was so dire that three died en route and a fourth a little later on reaching Buchenwald. Nevertheless on arrival they were described as a 'fine looking body of men,' although the rigours of camp life took their inevitable toll.

"Too fine to bear hatred to anyone, and they felt genuinely sorry that the German civilisation had sunk so low," wrote E. Jackson 78392. "They were all educated, intelligent and a fine example of the high standard of Danish culture."

They too stood up to the Germans. "When completely unarmed, they forced the goons to retract orders which, if carried out, would have been detrimental to the Danish people," Jackson continues. "It was a pleasure to know such brave chaps and the personal contact we made with them are one of the few good points about our stay in Buchenwald. They were left behind when we moved to Sagan, but the memory of their brave spirit went with us."

Their arrival must have boosted the spirits of the airmen, not the least being the willingness to share the Red Cross parcels they were permitted to receive. Anyone who has experienced the generosity of Danish hospitality will understand the gastronomic delights that may have awaited them. Along with cheese and butter and biscuits, would they have included herring (sild) and even schnapps?

Of the Danes' arrival Art Kinnis recalls: "We were on the rock pile when 1700 Danish police were brought in to be our new neighbours. We became very attached to this fine body of men and over the many years that have passed we did not forget their many acts of kindness. We remembered the food they obtained for us, their ability to help us in spite of their own problems and how their entire group joined our party when we had a memorial service for P.D. Hemmens 78286." Despite his broken arm on the cattle car, Philip Hemmens had been in reasonable physical fitness when he had entered Buchenwald only a month before his death. He had finally succumbed to septicaemia, rheumatic fever and ultimately pneumonia. The memorial service was a moving occasion, considerably enhanced by the presence of the Danes. The solemn group of prisoners, cropped heads bared and standing respectfully to attention,

142

gathered outside Hut 58 whilst a Danish 'father' conducted the ceremony. A minute's silence following a memorial address by Flying Officer Tommy Blackham and then two hymns concluded Hemmens' send-off.

The KLB Club

On October 12, 1944, the Konzentrationlager Buchenwald Club was formed. Born out of the sense of uncertainty each of the airmen was experiencing as to their fate, the KLB Club provided a formal structure to express their fears. Because none of the men had been captured by the Luftwaffe and there had been no contact with the International Red Cross at Paris, nobody knew where they were.

"We all knew the war was going well, but we could not contemplate that anyone could possibly know where we were, and that we might simply disappear without trace," writes Stanley Booker. Thus the decision was made that elected representatives of each nationality would hold formal meetings and bring a sense of purpose and order into their lives. This would help to address the constant stress, apprehension and feelings of insecurity expressed by the KLB airmen.

Randomly held discussions for post-war meetings where address lists and future activities had been proposed were formalised, and the meetings were well attended. Strict protocol was observed at all times. More than anything else, they provided a forum for the airmen's 'raison d'être' in the camp environment, their militariness and solidarity. Though few of the recommendations were adopted after the War, they formed a bond that was to last half a century after the liberation of Buchenwald. With their own Buchenwaldclubben, the Danes were fully involved in the formation of the KLB and were to play a role in future 'get togethers' including in Denmark, many years later.

The club's pin design formulated in Buchenwald is now a symbol that binds the airmen. It shows a naked, winged foot, symbolising their barefoot condition while in the concentration camp. The foot is chained to a ball bearing the letters KLB, with the whole mounted on a white star, which was the crest of the Allied invasion forces.

Throughout the challenges and traumas that beset them, Phil was going about his business within the camp. Epitomising the leadership qualities for which he had been chosen, he made contacts among certain inmates and even some Kapos, forging strategic alliances that would benefit his men.

The KLB Badge designed by the Allied Airmen while incarcerated in Buchenwald, 1944. (Photograph courtesy of the Lamason Family Collection)

One example was an association with the scientist and political prisoner, Professor Alfred Balachowsky of the Pasteur Institute in Paris, whose work at the camp included an attempt to produce an anti-typhus vaccine. Balachowsky supplied typhus-infected rabbit to the airmen, who were able to cook them and at least introduce more meat, albeit of questionable quality, into their diet. Phil's role in this is referred to later in the book during an interview with Dr Charles Roland M.D.

Along with the friendship of Professor Balachowsky, Phil's friendly overtures to the Russians had met with a kind-hearted response. The men were supplied with some bread and also clogs, enabling shod feet for the first time, although elsewhere mention is also made of the return of their own footwear.

The White Rabbit

During this time Phil had met fellow inmate and legendary British agent, the 'White Rabbit.' 'Tommy'Yeo-Thomas and 37 other agents had arrived at Buchenwald from Fresnes Prison just three days ahead of the airmen. As his extraordinary exploits are well documented elsewhere including by Bruce Marshall in 'The White Rabbit,' it is not the intention to cover them here. Sufficient to say Yeo-Thomas had lost no time in establishing networks in high places within the camp. Through his contacts Wing Commander Forest Frederick Edward Yeo-Thomas, RAFVR, GC, MC and Bar, Legion d'Honeur and Croix de Guerre, is credited by Burgess for "the prominent part he played in the lives and ultimate salvation of the airmen at Buchenwald."

But at the beginning Phil, with his customary reserve, did not warm easily to Yeo-Thomas. When the pair first met Yeo-Thomas had assumed the identity of Squadron Leader Ken Dodkin. Phil was

144

Wing Commander F.F.E. Yeo Thomas who, in Buchenwald, used the assumed identity of Ken Dodkin.

unimpressed. As he happened to know the real Ken Dodkin, he immediately distrusted the man.

Bruce Marshall's version (published in 1952) refers to "...the arrival of the more than 170 British and American airmen who arrived in Buchenwald and were herded together in the small camp without food, blankets or shelter. Their senior officer, Squadron Leader Lamason, a New Zealander with the battered-looking nose of a boxer, protested angrily to the Camp Commandant Pister and his assistant Schobert that such treatment was contrary to the rules of war as they had all been taken in a fair fight.

"These airmen were squatting miserably on the only cobbled space in the small camp when Yeo-Thomas, in search of more allies, called to see them. In spite of having passed a bitterly cold night the newcomers were cheerful. Lamason and Yeo-Thomas hit it off immediately and together they visited the two Russian colonels, who organised among their prisoners-of-war a collection of blankets, clothes and clogs for the airmen."

Writes Burgess: "When Yeo-Thomas eventually met with Phil Lamason, he introduced himself by his assumed identity. From then on, to his complete bewilderment, things did not seem to go at all well; the New Zealander instantly became suspicious and non-committal. As it

145

turned out, Lamason knew the real Dodkin quite well, having carried him on two missions before the fellow became non-operational, but Lamason was not about to let on."

Lamason also met Christopher Burney, in whom he felt he could confide, telling the SOE agent that the fellow was an imposter. Burney, surprised that Lamason knew the real Dodkin, quickly assured him that things were in order, saying there was a very valid reason for the alias. Thereafter Lamason always used the alias but was one of very few men who knew the brash Englishman's true identity.

As Phil's second-in-command, Tom Blackham has his own observations on the relationship between the two men. Mentioning their initial contact and Lamason's knowledge of the White Rabbit's true identity, Blackham's belief is that this common factor helped them at the outset to extend the rapport and degree of trust that stood them and all of the airmen in good stead. Their joint efforts would safeguard and ensure, if possible, the group's welfare and their safe transfer to normal POW camps. Blackham "knew this because Phil made me privy to much of their activities and plans and took me along on several clandestine meetings with faction leaders etc within the camp."

Yeo-Thomas being the dynamic person he was, recognised in Phil a kindred soul in leadership qualities, spirit and cold courage, and very quickly ensured that the latter got to know the most influential prisoners in the camp, his objective being to ensure the full use of the group as military men.

In his debrief interview in July, 1945, Phil stated how "I organised the British, Danish, Dutch and nationals imprisoned in Buchenwald Concentration Camp into a force under discipline for their own defence in the event of an attempt by the Germans to carry out a massacre. A comprehensive plan was made, which included the taking over of a nearby aerodrome. About 200 men in this force were armed with rifles, sub-machine guns, pistols etc, which had been assembled from parts smuggled into the camp from the armaments factory in which a large number of inmates of the camp were working. Supplies of ammunition were also being obtained."

Thus, if an emergency arose there was a possibility of the prisoners putting up some sort of resistance should the SS be given orders to raze the camp and its occupants, including themselves. The combined forces of themselves and the Russians would be divided up into units of ten regardless of nationality and each with a pilot, navigator, air-gunner, engineer and radio-operator.

Clearly, Phil was as keen as Yeo-Thomas to take part in such a 'stoush,' if one occurred. Phil concluded his debrief interview: "I was ably assisted in this organisation by a British agent who used the alias Dodkin. When I left the camp, Dodkin was placed in charge of this operation."

Arms were available should there be a need, but due to camp politics much had to be done to ensure that the powerful, warring 'mini' faction overcame their suspicions and jealousies to work under a combined defence plan for the benefit of all prisoners. There were two issues. One was a lack of arms, although it was later discovered there were arms in the camp but only the Communists knew where they were concealed. The other, Burgess states, "was the presence in Lamason's group of a so-called American flyer suspected to have been planted as a stool pigeon, and who would require to be kept in ignorance of their plans and watched." These matters were mentioned in Marshall's book.

Phil later stated that the 'unsubstantiated reference' to the American flyer should have been deleted to forestall any undeserved suspicion falling on the American contingent in the KLB. The flyer in question was their Dutch translator who had been observed talking privately with one of the German guards. This man proved to be completely trustworthy and beyond suspicion.

Then on September 9, Yeo-Thomas suffered a terrible setback. Sixteen of his 37 agents were summoned to the Tower. Two days later they were executed, dying a violent and agonising death, strangulated by piano wire and thrashing on the ends of meat hooks. This tragedy rocked the camp. Yeo-Thomas, recognising a similar fate awaited him, then removed himself and went underground to plan his escape. He and Lamason became incommunicado and two months later on November 9, the White Rabbit successfully made his escape, ultimately returning to England.

Lamason meanwhile had continued alone, single-mindedly applying himself to ensure that, in the event of a showdown with the SS and Gestapo, the group was respected for its fighting potential. "This was a major contributing factor in getting us recognised as Prisoners of War under the provisions of the Geneva Convention and being transferred to a proper POW camp in October 1944," Blackham believes. "This event

147

took place despite the SS hierarchy in Buchenwald being under orders that we were not to be released to another camp – ever!"

Firing Squad

Somewhere during this period another graphic example of Phil's outstanding bravery occurred in the most deadly of circumstances.

Interrupting a 'normal' afternoon sitting with his men outside the hut, a group of armed Nazis led by an SS officer approach them, boots crunching on the gravel and snarling Alasatian dogs straining at the leash. They ask for Lamason. Rising to his feet, Phil warily approaches the officer and quickly salutes, surprising and momentarily confusing him. "Yes, Sir?"

The officer wastes no time in delivering his message. "Intelligence says you have been inciting trouble in the camp with your men. I am here to inform you that tomorrow morning you will be shot. Is that clear?" Phil immediately protests and demands to see the Camp Commandant. He is refused and sent back to his barracks. He tells no one.

How can one imagine the agony of such a night? How can he change the certainty of the fate that awaits him? In later years, Glenys Scott dug deeper into this incident with Phil and he explained to her how he lay awake thinking as to what he could do to circumvent this fateful encounter. Maybe flattery, charm and respect would work. Phil had noticed that the Germans seemed to be receptive to such measures, he had noticed that whenever he had given the Germans his word that his men would not escape, they took him at his word. This had really impressed him. He remained the consummate leader, keeping a clear head and focussed on a strategy which might get him safely through this foreboding appointment!

Morning dawned. Appell was over, and Phil was accosted by two guards. Quickly hustled away from his friends, he was led away down a back road and into a grassy clearing. This execution was not intended for public display. The guards seemed trigger happy and the dogs were keen. He was stopped by a young officer. On being questioned, Phil confirmed that the Allied airmen are following his orders by refusing to work for the Germans. Once again he reiterated their POW status and demanded their rights.

To Mike Dorsey, Phil vividly recalled this incident: "They marched me in and I think they were going to shoot me… they called me up and stood me there with an amazing number of soldiers and I said with a bit of irony, 'I didn't realise it took about 20 guys to shoot me.' And there was this dog jumping up and snapping at my throat. But I would not step back!" Phil recalled to Glenys how "I could smell the dog's breath in my face… and I just knew that any movement backwards at all and all hell would break loose! I could not step back… and it saved my life and the life of my men.

"In those moments I stressed to the officer that my mother was a widow, my mother-in-law was a widow, and how if I was shot my wife too would be a widow. I stressed to him that the Germans were losing the war and that I would vouch for him as being an honourable officer in any war court hearings if he released me."

With 20 guns trained on Phil, the young officer considered the matter one final time. To Mike Dorsey, Phil continued, "I was looking straight at him and he looked at me and I thought he looked quite a decent guy. He looked for another minute and then he gave the order to 'ground arms' and marched them out again." Phil thanked the officer and returned to his men. That cliff-hanger encounter between these two young men, thrown together in the most extreme of circumstances, must stand as Phil's most defining moment.

Extermination Order

And then came the shocking news that all of the men were to be exterminated within the week. Not even the bed-ridden and desperately ill would be spared. The decision was made on specific orders from Berlin to Commandant Pister and was conveyed to Phil by a German Communist who had been given the information by a friend in the administration area. Pister, it seems, was reluctant to set the wheels in motion but had no option. Phil kept the news from his men who, unaware of their impending extermination, went about their daily business.

Burgess: "There is little reason to doubt that the orders were issued. The airmen were certainly an embarrassment to the Germans but their deaths would have enormous ramifications if the British found out. The killings would have to be concealed by the issue of false certificates stating that each death was the result of natural causes. But this would be a lengthy process."

149

Phil immediately sought out Yeo-Thomas and Christopher Burney, among others, but after lengthy discussions they concluded "there was precious little that could be done to avert a mass execution."

"So how did the miracle that saved them occur? How did the airmen secure a transfer from Buchenwald when the records clearly stated transference was never an option?" Burgess asks. He attributes this to Christopher Burney, the SOE agent and camp interpreter. Like Yeo-Thomas, Burney, an interpreter and former commando subaltern, was a tough nut to crack. He too had undergone extreme torture and solitary confinement at Fresnes prison before being thrown into Buchenwald.

As an interpreter with free access to Little Camp, Burney was well known to the Allied airmen, who regarded him as a solace and an inspiration. He was also in frequent contact with Yeo-Thomas. In turn, Phil's senior officer status gave him access to the Main Camp where he would meet and liaise discreetly with Burney and members of the powerful International Camp Committee.

Thus a decision was made to smuggle out a note which would be delivered to the Luftwaffe hierarchy. It would advise that a group of aircrew personnel were being illegally detained in a concentration camp. With the threat of death imminent, time was of the essence. A trusted prisoner on an outside working party at the nearby Luftwaffe airfield succeeded in getting the message out of the camp. It requested that an officer pass the information to Berlin and/or the Luftwaffe to intercede on behalf of the men.

Apparently the message got through, for shortly afterwards an outraged Hermann Goering made stern approaches at the highest level, and obtained the immediate transfer of the airmen to Luftwaffe control. Miraculously the gamble had paid off. As Burgess describes, Phil would recall the moment when Yeo-Thomas informed him that the information had not only reached the Luftwaffe, but had also reached London.

With some disbelief he enquired of Yeo-Thomas, "How on earth did you know it has reached England?" Yeo-Thomas smiled. "We heard it on the BBC news last night, courtesy of our secret radio." And then in a reference to the somewhat 'patchy' relationship between them, he said, "You must learn to trust me, Phil. We'll soon have you and the chaps out of here. Must go… talk with you later." Lamason, for once in his life, was gobsmacked.

150

Luftwaffe Intervention

Another player in this saga of life and death must be mentioned. A German officer named Hannes Trautloft. A fighter pilot whose successful missions had included the Battles of France and Britain Trautloft, on Goering's orders, was later given responsibility for the inspection of all of Germany's daytime fighter planes. In late 1944 a rumour reached him that a large group of Allied airmen were incarcerated in Buchenwald Camp. Under the pretext of making a first-hand inspection of the aerial bombing damage near the camp, Trautloft decided to investigate. On leaving, the Luftwaffe officer was hailed from behind a fence by a captured US airman, Bernard Scharf, and informed in fluent German of the men's whereabouts and predicament. Scharf begged for rescue. Intervention by the outranked SS guards proved fruitless. Trautloft's adjutant duly confirmed the story from Phil and transfer proceedings were implemented.

On the morning of October 14, 1944, a tall, sharp-looking civilian arrived from Dulag Luft in Oberursel on the outskirts of Wiesbaden. This was the interrogation centre and transit camp for captured Allied aircrew. Once considered a place of dread, this venue now had a welcome significance.

Puzzled, when ordered to assemble in the Main Camp, the group were understandably nervous about the change in routines. With the exception of those in hospital, they were marched behind Phil down through the camp and herded into a large canteen building. Here, the civilian stood facing them, accompanied by two Luftwaffe officers. For most it was their first sight of a Luftwaffe uniform. The man held up his hands and called for silence.

"Gentlemen, I would ask that you listen very carefully to what I have to say," he began. "I am here from Dulag Luft. Do you know where that is and what it means?" A few of the men nodded. This was the centre where captured men were sent for interrogation before transfer to more permanent POW camps.

"Recently it came to the attention of the Luftwaffe that you were being held in this place and were brought here, so the SS tells me, by mistake." The howls of derision from the airmen echoed round the room. Once more the civilian raised his hand in a gesture for silence.

"I have brought you here for two reasons. You will all be released from this place and transferred to a prisoner of war camp, this time under Luftwaffe control." As an instant hubbub greeted this news, it was Phil

151

who held up his hand for silence. "Thank you Squadron Leader," said the civilian. The men were then informed the transfer was conditional only on completing the required information on some Red Cross forms. "This is necessary to prove your identity and status, and must be fully completed. I am instructed to inform you that should any of you choose not to complete this formality you will remain at Buchenwald as a political prisoner." Chillingly he added, "And I hardly need tell you what that means." The speaker could barely contain his disgust with the camp and its administrators.

The small stack of forms embossed with the familiar Red Cross symbol was passed around amid groans of exasperation from the men as they read the questionnaires. Here again was the all too familiar dilemma on what information to provide. Back in England, Intelligence staff had already briefed them about the contents of these spurious forms. Not only did they require personal information, but also details on their squadrons, aircraft and operational movements.

Phil was consulted. "Sir, we've already been told not to fill out these bloody forms. What should we do?" The small crowd pressed around him. Phil's mind was already made up. "We all know the origin of these forms and it is not my intention to instruct any of you to go against orders. I will just say this. It is up to each man as to how much information he provides and how much of it is correct. I must, however, remind you that we are in an extremely dicey situation. There is nothing you can say now that will change the result of the war."

Phil was well aware that the contents of earlier forms already filled out on arrival were not only known to the Germans, but were out of date. "For my own part I will provide nothing other than my name, rank and number." Crucially, Phil already knew of the extermination orders and typically was keeping it to himself.

Amidst a mood of anger and confusion one of the men confronted the German telling him it was against orders for them to sign. With blazing eyes the German shot back, "You are NOT, I repeat NOT, in a position to argue young man. Either you fill in the form or you stay here. I am trying to help, but that help depends entirely upon you!"

With no uniforms, no tags and nothing to prove who they were, this was a sticky situation. Was the German bluffing? The men were caught in the life-challenging predicament of remaining at the camp or defying their King's regulations. For the majority the thought of undergoing another winter in their life-testing conditions proved too much.

152

Following Lamason's advice which had been passed around, they complied with the German's request. Correctly filling in their names and numbers, and supplying bogus information for addresses, squadrons and types of aircraft flown, they handed in their forms.

Not everyone agreed with Phil's stance and Texan-born Stratton Appelman, determined to provide only his name, rank and number, issued a direct challenge. Appelman had arrived in the camp from different circumstances, which at one point saw him officially recognised as a prisoner of war by the Germans. He had later lost his status when he joined the group bound for Buchenwald. Nevertheless he was adamant that the men should follow his example and give only the required information.

Appelman announced that he would do everything possible to report anyone who co-operated with the Germans in what he considered to be a violation of standing military orders. Several of the men sided with him in refusing to complete the forms. The German officer then explained that those who co-operated would leave Buchenwald the very next day. He could not be responsible for those who didn't.

Overcome with repugnance at the thought of aiding the Germans and filling out the forms, 30 of the men stood firm, giving only bare information or refusing altogether. Enraged, the German then separated the dissenters from the rest of the men. One of them was Phil's fellow-New Zealander, Malcolm Cullen.

Years later Stratton Appelman was more conciliatory. "If Lamason remembers the incident I describe, I hope he will remember my youth," he wrote when recalling his experiences. Having extensively studied prisoner behaviour by then, he recognised his own behaviour as trying to restore self-esteem lost as a result of being a prisoner…"With all that experience behind me, I know now that the KLB Club was fortunate to have Lamason as its leader."

Readers can only guess at the impact of the airmen's circumstances and the pressure they were under in this fraught situation. Caught in the cross-fire of conflicting behaviour, they should not be judged for their reactions.

Cullen writes of tossing and turning in his unaccustomed bed after he and his colleagues were isolated from the main group. They wondered if their defiant actions would be their undoing but were more cheerful the following morning, having decided to stick to their guns. That day each was harangued by the German individually, but all he received was "a polite negative from each of us." Hoping they would have more sense, the German departed.

"I must say that as we marched away this time to our old barrack, my spirits had reached such a low ebb, and the thought of staying behind while most of the others were sent to a proper camp made me shudder."

For the next few days the airmen were on tenterhooks as they awaited their fate. Those who had partially or totally refused to fill out the bogus forms were filled with agonies of uncertainty. Then on the afternoon of October 18 came the breakthrough. A list of names was sent to the block of those required to report to the main gate the following morning. The only ones to remain behind were the 14 in hospital. To the profound relief of Cullen and his fellow dissenters, their names too were read out with the others.

Few slept that night. Up early the next morning, many attempted to shave themselves with several well used razors that had been retained. The blunt blades and driving rain outside did nothing to dampen their excitement. Then came the return of their old civilian clothing and most of their effects, the clothes hanging like sacks from their emaciated frames. Outside in the rain the SS guards stood them in files of five for a final headcount.

Even then reality must have been hard to comprehend. But no! To the men's intense relief the gates beneath the dreaded tower were swung open to reveal a Luftwaffe Hautpmann in full uniform. Their joy on seeing that uniform was almost tangible. The Hauptmann stood in front of the men, looked at the leaden sky and grunted.

"Gentlemen," he said, "please break your ranks and go back inside out of the rain." To have such civility from a German was unbelievable to the men. Quickly they scattered inside where the Hauptmann addressed them in soft, precise terms. In an almost dream-like state the men listened. Unbelievably there was mention of Red Cross parcels, the Geneva Convention, prisoner of war status, even beds with sheets. Things they had hardly dared to contemplate whilst in Little Camp.

Reaching the transport train to see the familiar '40 hommes/8 chevaux' painted on the sides of cattle trucks temporarily unnerved the men, as memories of their previous transportation were reawakened. But no. Instead of overcrowding in stinking, fetid conditions there was fresh straw on the floor, a stove, two guards, and an open door. First class travel? Almost.

154

Their ultimate destination was not immediately disclosed. But as the distance from Buchenwald increased and the train built up speed, the men's concerns dissipated. Comforted by the warmth of the stove, the rocking movement and the hypnotic click-clacking of wheels on rails, the exhausted group fell into a deep, undisturbed sleep.

All that remained on their minds were concerns for their 14 sick comrades in hospital and the sad memory of the death of Philip Hemmens. Later, they were to lose Flight Lieutenant Levitt Clinton Beck.

Meanwhile, on their three day journey to Sagan the men began to actually enjoy the ride. Chunks of bread and sausage meat and ersatz coffee were handed out, and there were 'relief' stops. As earlier suspicions were erased with the miles, singing began. The guards, one with a mouth organ, joined in and the singing of 'Lili Marlene' by one of the airmen helped to cement the relationship. In an unprecedented gesture of goodwill, prisoners were given cigarettes and they all enjoyed a smoke together.

Stalag Luft III, Sagan

An armed guard company dressed in Luftwaffe field blue, greeted the airmen as the doors of the cattle trucks were rolled open at Sagan. Stretching cramped limbs, the prisoners disembarked onto the platform into misty, sweet-smelling, morning air. Here, they looked onto pine forests bordering the massive air force camp, Stalag Luft III, which sprawled over several hectares in a clearing hewn from the pines. Sincerely, their former guards wished the men 'Guten abend,' before they were marched uphill by the Luftwaffe to their new surroundings.

The men's condition apparently shocked the Luftwaffe authorities whose attitude to the Gestapo and the SS was already one of contempt. Once photographed and registered, the men were given an overwhelming reception. Unbelievably, there were hot showers, a set of underclothes and a complete airman's uniform. Finally, on reaching East compound, awaiting them were a bunk, clean sheets and two blankets. Topping off their arrival, each was handed a Red Cross parcel. Quickly they found a quiet, secluded corner in which to examine the contents.

This unforgettable experience was recalled later by Stanley Booker. "Needless to say, the parcels were quickly devoured and shortly afterwards many of us were violently sick. At last we felt secure, into a

Some of the Allied Airmen of Buchenwald pictured on their arrival at Stalag Luft III in October, 1944, after their release from Buchenwald. (Photograph courtesy of the Lamason Family Collection)

proper, organised routine. However, the greatest thrill was not the food, as relatively little as it was, but the sheer joy was being able to write that first Red Cross letter home, to hopefully let our loved ones know we were alive and well."

Despite the feelings of security noted by Booker, it was obvious to the authorities that the cruelty of the Buchenwald experience was not to be shaken off easily. Certain reactions were noticed: on their first parade, as each prisoner passed the German NCO for a headcount they instinctively stiffened as if expecting a blow; resident prisoners were asked by the newcomers how many went 'for the chop' each week and were horrified to learn that 'chop' meant execution; nor were the resident POWs able to believe the 'normal' conditions of a prisoner lying in their own excreta, the lampshades made of human skin and a hospital where 'patients' were treated as guinea pigs. Such stories were beyond their comprehension.

On November 29, 1944, news reached Phil that Levitt Beck, a fighter pilot with the USAAF, had succumbed to purulent pleurisy at Buchenwald. He broke the news of the 'vibrant' young fellow's death to the men. Beck was a fine saxophone player who had also cheered his comrades with his jazz. The following day they sadly gathered to attend his memorial service.

Whilst at Sagan Phil, in one of his oft-quoted escapades, noticed 'a fine milk cow' in the vicinity and quickly took advantage of the situation. Obviously the camp was lax on security, as Phil not only managed to break out, find, and then bring the cow back to camp and milk it and feed his comrades, which put goodness into them immediately. Here the frothy nectar was quickly downed by the men. The men revived markedly in the next few days but sadly this routine faltered when, as Phil recounted to Glenys, "the Kapos with their hunger for meat, slaughtered and cooked every part of the beast!"

The following comments on life at Sagan are recorded by Ken Chapman. Arriving at his new, 12-man billet just in time for supper he sat down to a bowl of soup, followed by a 'good bowl' of hot potatoes, meat, vegetables and a dessert. "What a relief. I was very tired. The boys had fixed up my bed. Jerry, a room-mate, gave me a pair of pyjamas and with three blankets and white clean sheets it was paradise. Overall, the standard German food issue was limited to small quantities. However, thank God, we were able to make up the deficiency on Red Cross food. What a joy to us to be able to share in the Red Cross parcels we had for so long been denied. The good variety of food included powdered milk, spam, salmon, some cheese, two chocolate bars, soap and cigarettes.

"There were sporting activities which included golf and well attended soccer and basketball matches. However the men were definitely not in any physical condition for strenuous sport. A 'very fine theatre' with an orchestra and lighting was in constant use with numerous performances of a high standard. Education was a 'big thing' in the camp and any subject imaginable could be studied. Three well stocked libraries and regular church, catered for all literary tastes and denominations. 'Quiet rooms' catered for lectures and private study. Sexual 'shadow' libraries were also in existence and were fully used. Letters, few as they seemed, came in daily. I eagerly awaited a letter from home, but my luck was never in.

"Each of the eight barrack blocks had a kitchen, and vegetable gardening was encouraged, the seeds supplied by the Red Cross. In the 'Camp Kitchen' NCOs cooked the daily soup and issued rations. Hot showers were weekly and cold showers daily."

Barbed wire surrounded the camp and to retrieve golf or foot balls from the outside a special Red Cross cloak had to be worn. Chapman felt the menacing presence of the barbed wire keenly. "No one can realise the effect this detestable piece of equipment has on one, separated from the outside world for weeks on end." Continuously armed 'Goon' boxes, 20 feet off the ground and overlooking the compound, were spaced at intervals around the wire. At night searchlights in the guards' boxes scanned the whole vicinity.

Inside the compound the prisoners were 'pretty free' and were not pestered. "But Germans were strolling around all the time keeping an eye open for anything untoward. They were dressed in blue overalls, with an inevitable screwdriver in the belt and a torch after dark. These types were known as 'ferrets.' They often made themselves a nuisance and were always crawling under huts and creeping stealthily around at night."

Weeks move by. "November 16, my darling wife's birthday. I write her a letter. Not much is happening." Cold and snow set in and ice skating is a popular sport. Christmas approaches. "Well it's Christmas again, shall we get Christmas parcels?" Chappy wonders. Luckily 7500 American Christmas parcels arrive and everyone is hopeful of a share. On Christmas Day an 11.00am Appell gives the prisoners the chance of a lie-in. At New Year 3500 parcels arrive from Britain.

More significantly, January heralds the Russian Offensive. Morale soars. As the Russians approach, "great was the spirit of the camp and everyone was speculating as to our possible liberation." On Wednesday January 27, Russian guns could be heard in the distance and amidst the chilling cold, expectant men were preparing for a move out.

The Long March

"There was always the possibility of being moved so we set to work to convert our kitbags into haversacks to carry our belongings. We were told 20 pounds was the maximum a man could carry so we arranged our packs to hold that amount. Food and cigarettes were of major importance, and for these we made due allowance. No one thought we'd be moved, but on the evening of Saturday 27 January, 1945, at about 2100 hours, we had the order to prepare to move out immediately."

Flight Sergeant Ray Perry from Western Australia shares his recollection with Colin Burgess: January 25: "Rumours were rife around the camp that we were going to be moved towards the west. For those of us who had been in Fresnes Prison, we wondered if we would be moved away from liberation again.

"Although it was illegal to do so, many of us converted our kitbags to rucksacks by sewing on a pair of braces for straps. Being mid-winter and very cold, we knew we would want to carry as much clothing and food with us as possible – the Germans were by now so disorganised that we knew it would not be easy to survive any march in this weather. We were getting frequent falls of snow. Some of us thought that if the snow continued and froze we would be able to carry our gear easier if we made a sledge from a wooden box, with wooden runners fastened underneath."

The camp prisoners were moved out, at intervals, by compounds. First the South, followed later by the West and Centre compounds, and then the North and Belaria. Finally, at 8.45pm on January 27, came the order for the East compound to prepare for immediate evacuation. Phil was not entirely happy with the move out into the snow and unable to understand why the Russians wanted to move west. But as time dragged on into the night the fully-clothed men dozed off in their barracks. Finally at 6.00am the following morning they began moving out of the camp. Those at the end became the last Allied servicemen to evacuate Stalag Luft III.

Although the cold, lightly snowing conditions were not conducive to escape attempts, Phil's order to his men was clear. "No escaping, no heroics. Forward, stay together and help each other." He was remembering the murder of 50 officers from the camp following the ill-fated Great Escape only ten months previously.

Ray Perry described how "it was snowing lightly over the camp. We moved towards the Red Cross store to get a parcel each, which I stacked on my sledge and, as we were the last, we starting throwing some parcels over the fence to some Russian prisoners in a nearby compound. There was still quite a bit left in the store when we moved out."

Moving in a 12 kilometre single file towards a weak dawn streaking the eastern horizon, the men passed guards with machine guns, dotted at 100 metre intervals along the muddy quagmire of a road. High snow drifts piled up along the roadside, fenced them in. At its conclusion, this horrendous, mid-winter ordeal would cost lives, as already weakened men died from exposure and exhaustion. Loads were discarded and precious diaries and souvenirs left to be trodden underfoot by those that followed. Following Phil's instructions, the airmen maintained their encouragement and support for the weaker members of their desolate group. At night they slept in barns, churches and halls, bartering for bread and using cigarettes as currency.

Chapman's account captures the 'human element' of their departure and the first day and night of the march. "Food was divided, clothes were packed, and all was ready although not as ready as we should have been for we were, I admit, unprepared. We never thought it would happen. Delays began, an hour at first, then two more hours. We tried to sleep, some lads cooked potatoes while others made two cakes. We had plenty of flour and barley to leave behind. These when cooked were delicious, potatoes with margarine and salt. Thick honey on the cake.

"Some lads made sledges to carry their kit, and huts were torn up for wood etc to do so. Food we could not pack strewn about. Cigarettes by the thousand left behind. At last, about 0500 hours we went out for a final check and then we left. Oh how sorry we were to leave good food, cigarettes and clothes because we could not carry them. My pack must have weighed 40 pounds, for at the gate we were issued with a Red Cross parcel each and some 20,000 of them were left behind.

"I was in a room with Phil (Max) Bear and we were sharing all food. We had a suit case and this we slung on a pole carried over our shoulders. It was daybreak by the time we left the camp, an endless line of prisoners with the Luftwaffe guards alongside, some with dogs to prevent any lines of escape. We had 10 minutes rest about every 90 minutes. Snow was thick on the ground. We passed the occasional convoy going to the front and the civilians eyed us with curiosity. They appeared very docile.

"At 12.30pm we halted for lunch and at such an inconvenient spot, on a hill with a blizzard blowing. We ate bully beef, a couple of biscuits and had a smoke. Oh we were a miserable crowd. Even the guards seemed fed up and they soon sought protection in our ranks.

"About 3.30pm we entered a village called Flalbain and a few citizens handed us hot coffee for which we were very grateful. In the centre of the place we halted. We were pretty well exhausted and longed for a good rest. I met several French POWs and managed to buy a sledge for several packets of cigs (cigarettes). This easily took our two bags and the case. After about two hours wait we slowly moved forward, learning that some lads were being put into the local church for the night. In about another three hours during which we bartered with the civilians for bread etc (I managed to get a swig of Schnapps) we moved into the school.

"It was a large place, four storeys and well lighted. We were terribly crowded, 20 of us in a small box room, 12 ft by 8ft. I was lucky and slept on top of a cupboard. It was soon very dirty due to the snow thawing on boots. After a hasty meal of bully beef we got to sleep, learning we were staying at the school all the next day also.

"This was Monday, January 29. We managed to get some hot water and made some coffee. It was difficult to get a wash, water was scarce. It was cold outside, so most of our day was spent indoors. At evening we were very short of bread, the Germans had not issued us with any and there seemed little hope from this source. I got outside, many lads cooking on improvised stoves. A considerable amount of bartering with German civilians was going on over the wire – coffee, chocolate, and cigarettes being in big demand for bread, the chief necessity. My luck was in and I obtained a full loaf and a bit for two knobs of chocolate and some cigs. We were pleased, and after a meal we went to bed again, having to get up at 5.30am to resume the trek."

The ordeal continued for a further four days, with daily distances varying between 20 and 30 kilometres. The prisoners were forced in a meandering westerly direction, as the Russian and Allied forces on two fronts continued to exert their squeeze on the Germans. They sought sleep in schools, barns, churches, a glass factory, even open fields, and dropped their weary bodies into whatever accommodation was available. They endured freezing winds and blizzards, many dying from a combination of exposure and exhaustion. Kit items and even food littered the roadsides as loads became too heavy for the weary marchers to bear. Precious diaries and treasured souvenirs were discarded, trodden into the icy slush by the feet of desperate men whose sole thought was of survival. To witness German guards pausing for their ten minute halts to eat bully beef and chocolate from (presumably discarded) American Red Cross parcels, only exacerbated their distress.

The following story is provided by Graeme Simmonds. It was told to him by Phil during one of their many conversations.

"Phil was no longer officer in command of the 166 airmen. With mixed codes of service, Army, Navy and Airforce, it was most likely that an Army officer outranking Phil had been given command over the hundreds of prisoners about to march deep in towards Germany. Despite this change in command, Squadron Leader Phil Lamason kept his mind sharp for the good of all the men on this long march. It was a trek to take them to their unknown destination, trudging through knee deep snow in blizzard conditions without any respite made for distressing and challenging conditions. Once again as he had done so many times, Phil found an answer.

"Moving to the front rank of about eight men wide, Phil issued instructions to tramp down the deep snow for five minutes only. Then they should peel off and return to the rear of this long column. The next eight men would do the same. This way the snow would pack down to create an easier walkable surface for everyone. This solution worked for everyone except the German guards who, armed with rifles, were posted to walk outside the column and keep order. These 50 year old soldiers were unable to keep up with the younger men in the knee deep, icy conditions. The prisoners took their rifles and told them to fall in at the rear of the column. This trek was pure survival for all. But more was to come.

"One late afternoon after a long day's march the weary column trudged into a small town. Here they were met by the mayor, the Burgermeister, who proceeded to address the prison officer in command and issue his orders for the night. The men were to stay in a fenced off area capable of containing large numbers. The temperature was minus ten degrees, night was coming on and there was no head cover. The prison officer in command accepted that this was their lot for the night and indicated he understood.

"Out stepped Phil. Standing immediately in front of the officer and confronting the Burgermeister, he delivered an uncompromising message. Rather than perish outside in freezing conditions they would burn down the town to stay alive if they had to. It must be remembered that the prisoners were now in possession of the rifles and they outnumbered the elderly, worn-out guards, by a ratio of 50:1. With the German's full attention by now, Phil continued. 'You have schools, churches, public meeting halls. Get them open and get them heated and you will save your town tonight.' Recognising that Phil meant business, the Burgermeister immediately complied and the men gratefully enjoyed a night's warmth." There is a sequel to this story.

"Phil said when he finally entered one of the buildings and stood in the doorway the warmth hit him. Exhausted, he slid straight down onto the floor and was instantly asleep. No one was prepared to wake him as he lay across the doorway. They all stepped carefully over him 'til morning.'" Later Phil told Graeme if he hadn't acted instantly he believed half or more would have died as they lay out in the freezing conditions. The quick thinking and decisive action had saved many, maybe hundreds, of lives that night and Phil had once again demonstrated outstanding leadership skills in the face of adversity.

Stalag IIIA, Luckenwalde

At Spremburg the column was split into two. While many were eventually diverted eastward to avoid the oncoming British forces, others, including Phil and his men, were entrained for a one day, 100 kilometre journey to camp Stalag IIIA at Luckenwalde, in Poland. Enduring a sleepless night on another long train of over-crowded cattle trucks, they arrived to find a rundown camp with little food and substandard shelter. Left to forage for themselves, the men set about finding food and firewood. There were few guards.

Luckenwalde was about 35 miles from the centre of Berlin and due south. A POW transit camp, it was already housing British, American, French, Poles, Russian, Norwegian, Serbs and Italians. A group of 1500 RAF NCO's (Non Commissioned Officers) also arrived with the allied airmen. Having trekked for three weeks from near Breslan, east of the Oder River, they were in an exhausted state. The men spent eight weeks at Luckenwalde, from February 5 to April 1, 1945.

A de-lousing process greeted the tired and dispirited men on their evening arrival. As this coincided with an air raid warning, an accompanying loss of lighting and a long, two hour wait, Ken Chapman was not a happy 'chappy.' "In much discomfort, with no seats and grossly over crowded, we waited from about 2000 hours – 0430 hours for this shower. Oh! How depressed and miserable we felt." Later however, "our shower was very good, but we were too tired to appreciate it." Then the men were searched before being ushered to their barracks. Here there was more bad news. "A climax was yet to come for our living quarters proved to be the worst hovels imaginable. When I stood before my future bed at 0530 hours on Monday February 5, I could have wept like a child. There was just bare nothing, only boards to sleep on and facing this sorry state of affairs we finally went to bed."

Conditions were indeed trying. Three barrack blocks accommodated the 1300 men, mainly RAF officers, in the camp. Each block, divided in half and separated by a washroom, housed 180 men. Three tier bunks combined to hold 12 men. Worse still, only two German blankets were supplied, presumably to each tier. Coal supplies were inadequate for the two stoves per block, lighting and food were poor, and no eating or cooking utensils were supplied. A very unhygienic lavatory was

163

available outside. Due to the goon inability to count properly, Appells were unduly lengthy, for the tired and weakened men. Lacking the energy for exercise, most spent the day on their beds. Eventually, when the coal issue ceased, bed boards were torn up and burnt and sacks of straw were substituted for sleeping on.

But as time went on, and with Red Cross parcels arriving at the rate of one per week, morale was gradually improving, although the food was still not plentiful. Nevertheless cooking activities were also providing tasty additions to meals. Sports events were organised, and with a sunny late March, 'the lads even took to sunbathing.' Optimism was in the air. "Well, that just about brings me up to date," Chapman writes on April 1. "We begin April in good spirits and hope 'ere long the war will be over and we'll be coming home for a really good feast."

During the next three weeks, April 1-22, change was in the air and speculation was rife that the war was ending. Courtesy of the Germans, the men were supplied daily with the War Communique and, with map in hand, could follow the advances on all fronts. On one day the men were given hot showers, waiting in their birthday suits for their steam-cleaned clothing to arrive. On another, they were given X-rays. The guards too, were more affable. On Wednesday, April 11, came news of a move to Mooseburg, but not before the inevitable search and head count. Here they were serenaded by a solo Norwegian flautist who played first the British, and then the Norwegian national anthem.

The move was short lived… On the journey back to Luckenwalde, after much dialogue and bartering for food with nicotine-starved guards and two nights in a cattle truck punctuated by the sound of American bombers en route to Berlin, the men were returned to Stalag IIIA. The Russian offensive on the Oder began the following week and as Burgess writes, "suddenly it was all over as the victorious Russian, British, and American forces finally overwhelmed the remaining pockets of German resistance and liberated the many thousands of exhausted but exultant POWs."

Liberation

Cullen: "The big worry was who would get there first, the Russians or the Yanks. One night at about 11.00pm we heard something. It wasn't quite a sound but could be felt, like an approaching thunderstorm. The air seemed oppressive and menacing. Then it was more distinct this time, a low rumble in the distance. The barrack was deathly still as every inmate listened. They must be coming, that was the thought that throbbed in every brain…"

The following detailed eye witness account is narrated by RAF Bomb Aimer Bill Taylor who had baled out over Italy on July 13, 1944, and ended up at Luckenwalde. "On April 19, 1945, the German guards were seen to be leaving the watchtowers and withdrawing from inside the camp. At 6.00pm on April 21 someone shouted 'The Russians are here!' We rushed outside to the wire fence and there was a Russian Scout Car with a Russian officer waving a tommy gun to our cheers. Behind him were three T34 tanks. We were liberated, or so we believed.

"For three days we were free to go outside the camp, mostly foraging for food. An American war correspondent returning from Berlin found us and informed the SBO (Senior British Officer) that he was surprised to find British and American POWs here." Knowing that Allied Headquarters were unaware they were at Luckenwalde he promised to inform them. On April 24 the Russians closed the gate and put armed patrols around the perimeter fence. No one was allowed out of the camp and this caused great tension. The next day the Americans from the River Elbe area sent six Army lorries to evacuate British and American personnel. The Russians allowed them to take some of the sick and wounded and sent some of the lorries back empty. The next day the Americans returned, but this time the Russians turned them all back and fired shots over their heads. We were now prisoners of the Russians and the word 'hostage' began to be heard."

During this time prisoners began to take their chance and make a dash for freedom but some were rounded up by the Russians and brought back to the camp. This state of affairs continued through until VE Day on May 8, 1945, with inmates experiencing further water and food shortages.

Taylor and some others decided to 'borrow' some bicycles from some Italian inmates and make a dash for it. They managed to get through the fence and began pedalling, even waving to a guard. Later they were stopped by an American officer with a lorry who, having ensured they were American or British, offered them a ride to freedom. Or so they hoped.

"At the very moment we were ready to move off on the American truck, a Russian scout car arrived with two very angry Russian officers and ordered us back to Stalag IIIA camp. As the American truck made its way very slowly towards the camp, prisoners were climbing out of

165

ditches, from behind trees and hedges, and we pulled them onto the truck. We were almost within sight of the camp when the American officer got out, had a look round and told the driver to 'turn around, my orders were to get a load and get them out.'" Taylor was on his way. Eventually arriving at the American base they were just in time to hear Churchill's unforgettable broadcast saying the war in Europe was over, "tomorrow will be VE Day."

At the time of liberation the subject of whether the prisoners had actually become hostages of the Russians had a sequel, as Bill Taylor recalls: "Although we suspected at the time there was an element of truth in the rumour we were about to be held as hostages by the Russians, many years later I discovered some documentary evidence. An extract from 'The Victims of Yalta' by Nikolai Tolstoy (1977) reads: 'A Russian broadcast stated that British and American prisoners in Luckenwalde Stalag IIIA were being held as hostages because the Allies were unjustly attempting to retain Russian soldiers captured in Normandy fighting for the Germans. A month was to pass before the Russians allowed the prisoners who remained in Luckenwalde to be repatriated.'"

Phil took matters into his own hands and made a break for freedom during the protracted Russian versus American negotiation process. He is officially recorded as having arrived 'safely back' in England on May 14, 1945, to start Repatriation as No 12PDRC. In the account to Mike Dorsey he tells that a jeep came along. Phil was in civilian clothes. He stepped out and put his hand up but the 'very nervous' driver who happened to be a war correspondent, wouldn't let anyone on board. "I did contemplate taking it over," Phil recalled, "but he said he'd go back a few miles and then three or four tanks arrived and drove us back home."

During his repatriation back in England, an NZPA (New Zealand Press Association) correspondent quoted the following during an interview with him. "To say the Russians 'captured' the camp is more or less accurate for, although they allowed the prisoners to forage for themselves, they would not allow the American trucks to enter and take them to the airfield. Squadron Leader Lamason and his navigator decided that they had quite enough of life behind barbed wire, so they escaped and made their way to the trucks.

"The Americans could not do enough for them. They fed them lavishly and plied them with cigarettes and deposited them at

166

Hildersheim airfield. Today Squadron Leader Lamason is looking little the worse for his experiences and is in good health."

The reference to Lamason and his navigator may not be correct as there is no mention by either that they departed together. Chapman earlier refers to Max Bear who he had teamed up with at Luckenwalde but states at the end: "I'm off on my own to join up with the Americans 30 miles away. We hear there are 100 American lorries two miles off but the Russians won't let them in – off I go... the Yanks take us back to Seheuebeck over the Elbe. It's VE Day. Then it's on to Hildesheim, by air to Brussels, by air to England and home May 15-19 to my darling mother, wife and my bonny son."

Neither does Cullen refer to Phil in his final words: "May 20 the Russian convoy pulled out and headed west with all the British and American personnel and after a hazardous trip along the Berlin-Leipzig Autobahn during which we had to negotiate about six demolished bridges and road blocks, we arrived at the Elbe. We packed our small kit on our backs and walked over the pontoon bridge to where the American trucks were waiting for us. Within another two hours we were driving into a big ex-Luftwaffe camp and were counted in and billeted by midnight. Then today is May 24, 1945. All I await is an aircraft to fly me back to England."

While there is no written account of Phil's immediate post-war activities in Britain, he did later speak of them to Glenys Scott. There are references to meetings with Churchill and the King, another flyover of Windsor Castle for old time's sake and of a friendship with Princess Elizabeth. Phil is quoted as saying he was asked to take part in the Okinawa bombing of Japan but the RNZAF declined the invitation believing he should return to New Zealand. Job offers in Britain will be covered in his post-war narrative. All of these references are tantalizing threads in the tapestry of his life.

The question of the extermination order papers has since raised questions. Did they exist? Glenys Scott confirms that Phil told her he saw them, signed by Hitler himself, from Berlin. Mike Dorsey has two comments to make. He writes that all he has heard is the story of Phil's verbal revelation of his long-held secret to KLB members in 1985. Secondly he has also heard that one of the authors of '168 Jump Into Hell' "eventually found the actual paperwork for it in Germany." Dorsey surmised that the 'finder' may have been the book's co-author Art Kinnis. He has since had contact with Kinnis' son and grandson but

167

the conversation petered out without any result. Current efforts by the writer to contact them have met with a similar result. Dorsey also mentions another theory:

"Another argument that one of the airmen gave is that their/his Buchenwald file was stamped with the German translation for something equivalent to 'not to be transferred to any other camp.'" Here Dorsey is referring to the DIKAL papers which were known to exist and were sighted by a member of the group. These are referred to earlier in this story. Meanwhile back in 2012 a series of online commentators challenged the authenticity of the extermination order but to no conclusion. Does this matter then still remain a subject for debate? All that is known is that Phil Lamason was advised in person of the extermination order. It is pertinent also to remember what Phil himself said about this incident in a television interview at the time of the publication of Max Lambert's book in 2005: "I knew what the Gestapo interrogations were like and I figured that the fewer people who knew about this order the better."

Looking back now at the immediate post-war era, it is clear that the world was on the threshold of a new order. The demise of Hitler and the Nazi regime was already occurring. The Russians as former allies of Britain were now flexing their muscles in the post-liberation negotiations. European power was disintegrating and Communism was about to become the philosophic adversary of the United States of America. In this new order, a monumental shift in the global balance of power was underway.

Phil meanwhile was heading for home. It would be another 40 years before his shocking story would be broken to an unknowing world.

A Family, the Farm and a Life Long Lived

"Phil's family were the salve to his soul" - John Lamason 2016

The Homecoming

It was September 4, 1945, when Squadron Leader Phillip Lamason DFC and Bar arrived back in Wellington, New Zealand, on board the 'Orion.' The troopship had departed Liverpool on August 7, for a 27 day voyage via Panama and Balbao. The 'troops' were service personnel comprising 1337 New Zealand former Prisoners of War, along with an Australian contingent and Royal Navy officers and men – about 5000 altogether.

It had been a tough voyage marked by controversy and discontent. Allegations of overcrowding, poor food and sleeping conditions surfaced as soon as the ship arrived, and many of those on board were quick to air their grievances to the press.

For a start, it was reported that some 150 New Zealanders had refused to embark at Liverpool once they had seen the accommodation. However a 'number of airmen and several soldiers decided to continue with the voyage because their anxiety to get home outweighed their dislike of the conditions.' This is at odds with another account, in which the officer tasked with inspecting the conditions before the ship sailed, had reported to the officer in charge of prisoner repatriation that the accommodation was adequate. The officer in charge was Major-General H. K. Kippenberger.

Complaints ranged from overcrowded sleeping quarters and bed bugs 'as big as kangaroos,' to inadequate toilets for the number of men, two changes of diet only – 'fish to bully beef and bully beef to fish' – re-stewed tea, and the price of commodities such as chocolate and cigarettes that men had to buy at the canteen with their own money. All of these allegations were refuted by the master of the 'Orion,' Captain A.G.C. Hawker, who vigorously defended the 'scurrilous and incorrect attacks' in a September 5 interview about the conditions on board his vessel.

Phil's role on board the 'Orion' is not specifically documented and there are no records that suggest that he was one of the officers in charge

The RMS Orion

of the subordinates on board. However the New Zealand official returning dates do at least confirm that Phil was amongst the servicemen travelling on the 'Orion.' In one interview many years later he is quoted as saying that his arrival back in New Zealand occurred the day after the bomb was dropped on Hiroshima on August 6, 1945. That particular day was in fact misreported. That day was in fact the day before Phil's departure from Liverpool in the UK aboard the 'Orion' for his return voyage to New Zealand.

Phil is also known to have been placed in charge of an extremely recalcitrant group of men who were ex-Prisoners of War. Trish Simmonds recalls being told by her father that the behaviour of these men on the Liverpool wharf was so extreme that he had considered banning them from coming on board.

"They were actually fighting on the wharf and out of control, breaking things up and to get them focused and on board was difficult. The authorities thought Dad would have strategies to control them. He had announcements made over the wharf with loud speakers saying that the ship would leave at a certain time and that anyone not on board would be left behind." Yet again, Phil's well-known leadership qualities were being called upon.

The 'Orion' is the only ship with the press coverage to support these events. Research indicates that an Australian and another New

170

Zealander had overall responsibility for those servicemen on board. It seems likely that Phil was in charge of the RNZAF component.

The 'Orion' was met in on arrival in Wellington Harbour by a 'welcome home' entourage headed by the Prime Minister Peter Fraser. The men disembarked at the wharf sheds where a rapturous welcome awaited them. The September 5 edition of the Evening Post records their arrival: 'Each was announced over a public address system as he passed into the section of the shed where next-of-kin were waiting, and there were several 'bottle-necks' in the traffic as kitbag-laden soldiers were almost knocked off their feet by the welcoming rush of wives, parents, children and friends. Several of those waiting to welcome their men had large banners of greeting and formed a triumphant procession out of the shed with them.' Welcoming music was provided by the Trentham Military Band. 'Elaborate arrangements' were also made for the Australian and Royal Navy personnel in clubs, theatres and private homes.'

There is no evidence that Phil's return was marked by a welcome party so it may be assumed that he was among the 88 Hawke's Bay and Gisborne men who proceeded north via the 9.40am Gisborne Express. Envisage the scene when the train chugged into Napier in the early afternoon of September 5, 1945, Joan would have been waiting on the platform.

Off jumps a uniformed, blue-eyed young man. Phil is home. What, in these brief moments, is he anticipating? Is this the newly-married sweetheart he left behind or has the smooth, unworried countenance he remembers been altered now by lines of worry?

While Joan sees the still-handsome, strapping, broad-shouldered man she had bid farewell to four and a half long years ago, the deprivations of Buchenwald would have taken their toll. He would have been thinner. But more importantly, what of the hidden toll that none can see and only the victim can know? Time would tell. For couples who have been parted in times of uncertainty and with death always on the shoulder, post-war reunions must rank amongst the most precious but also the most challenging of experiences. So it's not hard to picture them, arms outstretched in their first embrace after so long apart.

Joan's separation had been fully occupied. With her job, sporting activities including 'rep' basketball and the welfare of her own and Phil's mother, being busy helped the time pass. Daughter Trish

Phil and Joan Lamason pictured soon after Phil's return to Napier, New Zealand, in September, 1945. (Photograph courtesy of Lamason Family Collection)

describes her mother as being "capable and social, with a strong personality."

So how would Phil have regarded the home country he had returned to, New Zealand barely post-war?

In similar scenes replicated nationwide, society was adjusting to the influx of young men coming home, whilst coming to terms with the loss of those whose graves lay elsewhere. A bitter-sweet moment in social history.

After six years of war New Zealand was tired. Taking up the mantra of his late predecessor Michael Joseph Savage that 'where she stands we stand,' Prime Minister Peter Fraser had abandoned his former position as a conscientious objector to wholeheartedly support England and the War effort. Troop numbers were built up to form the Second New Zealand Expeditionary Force under Major General Bernard Freyberg, with 76,000 men overseas at the end of 1943. The government also passed the Emergency Regulations Amendment Bill which placed all the resources, the knowledge and the power of the community 'at the disposal of the state.' At home patriotic New Zealanders intent on 'doing their bit' adapted to a 'rationed reality' as farm products became the national version of 'the sinews of war' and were shipped off to 'Mother England' in ever increasing quantities. As the War continued, British demands on New Zealand commodities increased, leading ultimately to a reduction of domestic rations and eventually living standards.

In 'New Zealand In The Twentieth Century,' historian Paul Moon records that between 1939 and 1945 the War had sucked out a third of the national income, within that period the New Zealand contribution had risen to an astounding half of its national income. So for homecoming soldiers their land, still in the grip of shortages, was flowing with less milk and honey than when they had departed. Nevertheless the vivid green countryside, mountain ranges, uncluttered beaches, all devoid of bombsites and the outward ravages of war, must have been a welcome contrast.

Meanwhile, on arrival there was a discussion to be had. Phil's English 'connections' had made him a proposition. A farmlet in Berkshire awaited him if he would be a Lead Pilot for the development of the new Heathrow Airport in London. Phil's role was to plan the flight paths in and out of the airport and train the pilots into service. This was to commence the following year in 1946 and he and Joan would make their home in post-war Britain. It would be a life in an environment in which he obviously felt at home. He had also been offered a Captain's job with British Overseas Airways Corporation (BOAC), and also a test pilot's job with Shorts, the planemaker for whom he'd flown during the War.

Whilst still in Britain it seems that Phil was very keen to embrace these exciting offers. But first he must return home to his patiently waiting wife and ask her opinion. Maybe he underestimated the challenges the women in his life had faced during his absence. If so, it was soon pointed out. Phil's mother was a widow, his mother-in-law was a widow and his wife had been much closer to widowhood than she realised. The message was clear. It was prudent that Phil should decline the influential offers and return home to take care of them.

It seemed that the New Zealand Government sided with the family. Having been advised that he had 'seen enough of war,' Phil was debriefed by Government officials and commended by Prime Minister Fraser for his exploits and survival in the War effort. However, the offer of a position with the Ministry of Agriculture in Wellington was declined .On December 13, 1945, Phil was formally discharged from the RNZAF.

With 2743 fully trained pilots sent to serve with the RAF in Europe, Middle East and the Far East, the RNZAF's contribution to the War was definitely a statistic for the nation to be proud of. As well, another 1521 airmen were retained in New Zealand as instructors and staff pilots.

In the context of post-war adjustment, the combined family decision that Phil should not return to Britain was one he had to come to terms with. In hindsight, even though he would never have swapped his family life on the land and knew it was the right thing to do, there is a family recollection that this was a decision "he felt to the end of his days."

Phil's enthusiasm for the Heathrow offer suggests that in the intervening five years his world view had broadened. This was inevitable. Given the breadth of personal experiences – from Buchenwald to Buckingham Palace – this gritty, strong-minded Kiwi had demonstrated his ability to deal equally with adversity and diversity and with the associated individuals. Yet, by turning his back on Britain and the wide world, he was committing to familiarity and re-establishing the priorities which were to bring him lifelong satisfaction.

The return to normal life by War veterans deeply scarred by trauma has the common theme that the subject was never – or seldom – discussed. Anecdotal evidence backs this up with Phil Lamason and is confirmed by his son John, who says "Dad never talked about the War to the family." Certainly, in his compelling documentary 'The Lost Airmen of Buchenwald' aired in 2011, journalist Mike Dorsey comments that "Lamason remained scarred by his experiences."

Flying anecdotes were another forum altogether. A willing recipient was Phil's son-in-law and fellow airman Graeme Simmonds. A former farming neighbour recalls that the subject would come up amongst the men of the district at community gatherings when "Phil would

174

occasionally volunteer tantalising little snippets of information." It was the same with his club or business associates where "a yarn over a whisky" – or three – always commanded an appreciative audience. But the War stopped there.

In the nineties, Phil's role in the story of 'The Lost Airmen of Buchenwald' began to emerge. But it was not until towards the end of his long life that, in a series of gripping conversations, Phil would finally reveal his story. Until then only the occasional reference to a deeper and more sinister layer of experience would offer a glimpse of what lurked beneath the surface. The favoured recipient was his family friend Glenys Scott. But more than 60 years were to elapse before he disclosed that information.

Family, Farm and Community

With the decision made to remain in New Zealand, Phil, in his characteristic way "just wanted to get on with it," to tackle life and charge ahead. This meant getting back to normality, accepting his new circumstances and most importantly resuming married life. The Lamasons settled in with Joan's mother at 61 McDonald Street, Napier, where their life together was soon presented with another very welcome adjustment. Patricia Jean Lamason was born on July 2, 1946, cementing the family togetherness. She was the first of five, to be followed by John, Robert, Cheryl and Billy.

The new family's time in Napier was just the first step. Phil's thirst for his own land had remained undiminished and government assistance was at hand. In preparation for mass demobilisation and to assist returning servicemen in their adjustment to civilian life, the Fraser government had established the Rehabilitation Board. Among the initiatives a land resettlement ballot scheme met with 'overwhelming enthusiasm.' New Zealand servicemen had 'lived by the sword and thousands of returning soldiers were now prepared to live by ploughshares.'

After Phil declined the offer of a career in Wellington, the Ministry of Agriculture was still keen to acknowledge his War effort. His entry into the farm ballot scheme was paradoxically unsuccessful, so he reconciled for his next request, to live in a "warm place" and work as a livestock inspector with the New Zealand Ministry of Agriculture. He was posted to Dannevirke. Although there were changes of abode during their lifetime, the move to Dannevirke and surrounds in 1948 would be Phil and Joan's last. Here in this rural farming district they would put down roots.

Dannevirke is a country town about two hours south of Napier. It is the hub of an extensive farming district with the eastern hill country bounded by the Pacific Ocean featuring a proud history of long-established, multi-generation large sheep station farms. The inland, higher rainfall area flanked by the Ruahine mountain range to the west, is the dairy farming belt. These Ruahine Ranges, so familiar to Phil in his Smedley cadet years, would have been a sense of homecoming.

Dannevirke's name refers to its early settlement by Danish immigrants, many of whom forsook their land after a mid-nineteenth century skirmish on the German border and the subsequent encroachment of the victorious foe. Their sturdy, hard-working presence combined with predominantly, but not exclusively, English pioneer stock laid the foundation of the 'no frills,' kind-hearted and down to earth community-minded town that it is today. It was a locality where the Lamasons could settle and feel at home.

The first move for Phil and Joan was to a house in the town with their two children, John having been born in 1947. As a small child he was stricken with the polio in the epidemic which was sweeping the country. This left him with a permanent disability which was never an impediment. John engaged fully with life, becoming a champion swimmer, a Queen's Scout and a top-class badminton player. The Lamason grit was again overcoming the odds.

During this time Phil's a lot of work was checking dairy cow herds for tuberculosis. This condition must have been quite prevalent as John recalls "Dad having to shoot a lot of 'TB' cows." Post-war rationing of commodities including building materials, was still the norm, as Phil discovered when he decided to build a garage for his car. Unable to buy corrugated iron for the roof, he had no option but to resort to malthoid, a heavy duty building paper.

During this time two memorandums from the Department of Internal Affairs written on September 23, and October 1, 1948, indicate there was a small matter of identity to sort out. When Phil had been posted by the RAF as 'missing' he was deemed to have been a casualty of the Army, due to a soldier having been allocated the same number. Further investigation however revealed that NZ.403460, 23.9.48 was indeed Squadron Leader Phillip John Lamason of the RNZAF.

176

View westwards across the Lamason Rua Roa Farm towards the Ruahine Ranges, with the Tamaki River in the foreground. (Photograph courtesy of Mike Harold)

In 1950 a 30 hectare farm purchase marked the fulfilment of Phil's boyhood dream of achieving farm ownership. In rural New Zealand the post-war fifties was a time of transition when 'old' was overlapping with, and gradually giving way to 'new.' The kerosene lamps and candles of the pioneer era were ushered out as power poles marched up gravel roads to transform households. For the housewife new 'mod cons' brought another dimension to the daily routine. The coal range gave way to an electric stove, the washing machine replaced the copper, and the nightly home-killed mutton roast was more easily removed from the 'fridge' than from the outside meat safe. Communication was streamlined with the arrival of the local telephone exchange and 'party line' linking groups of neighbours.

It was also the era of the 'baby boom.' The time when the country's returned servicemen 'got down to business,' – as it were – increasing the fifties population by 400,000. Helped by the many soldiers working to develop their balloted farms, the sheep numbers in New Zealand rose by 40%. Mother England's appetite for wool, meat and dairy from the pasture of 'Britain's backyard' became a driving market force, accounting for 90% of New Zealand's export earnings.

In New Zealand, Maori refer to Turangawaewae, 'the land on which we stand.' For Maoridom land is the essence of one's identity, and Phil's newly acquired land in the Rua Roa district near Dannevirke, was to become his Turangawaewae. His 'place to stand.' In time, with the purchase of two more adjacent farms, which he joined together, Phil would own 165 hectares. In a poignant gesture and tribute to his War

177

time farming friend from Scotland, "old Mr Cadzow," Phil named his property "Glen Devon."

In this Rua Roa district, Phil Lamason was destined to live out the rest of his 93 years in a post-war life that would deliver what he held most dear; the family and the farm. In Rua Roa he would know joy, tragedy, the achievement of farming success and the bittersweet warmth of reconnection with Buchenwald mates. Slowly, as the years unfolded, the Phil Lamason story would emerge to a largely unknowing New Zealand public.

With its dairy factory, school and community hall, Rua Roa was one of many small dairy farming districts typical of the times. Here the five children attended school. The two eldest, Trish and John, started at the original one roomed school where, John remembered, "the desks were arranged to keep out the rain." In such communities the fabric of social life revolved around school, the hall and district activities.

In the community Phil is remembered as being "a sociable person when he had the time, but was not involved in activities." He was also a "generous donor."

A bastion of life for rural New Zealand 'homemakers,' was the Country Women's Institute (CWI). Like the iconic individualism of 'Aunt Daisy,' the tenets of CWI fostered pride in housewifely skills from local to national level. Every small district had their branch of CWI and at Rua Roa Joan Lamason played an active role. She was secretary for over 40 years and reflected her love of flowers and gardening with an involvement in floral art and the garden circle.

On a domestic note the children recall their mother as being "quite tough." Phil preferred not to be overly strict with his kids so when some order was required the discipline fell to Joan. A leather strap was an effective measure, although the children would occasionally circumvent the punishment by throwing it down the well. In fairness to their mother, Trish admits that "John and I were pretty naughty kids."

Stories flow when the children remember their father. One response from them regarding Joan's 'toughness' is that "Dad was really soft on us so maybe Mum felt she had to make up." "Dad used to cuddle us kids on the sofa," remembers Cherry. He was a great story teller. One favourite went: "Once upon a time, when the birds ate lime, and monkeys chewed tobacco, and pigs ate stuff, to make their tails tough, there lived an anaconda..." This nightly ritual was accompanied by "lots of play-fighting." He would also sing to them. Another favourite Trish

178

remembers was a game they used to play when Phil was out fencing. They would tease him. In a scenario reminiscent of an old favourite of the era, "What's the time Mister Wolf?" the kids would "go up to Dad getting closer and closer and keep saying Hullo Father Grunt." Phil would grab them, take them to the 'dump hole' and hold them by the ankles whereupon they would be lowered into the hole, "further and further down while we all screamed." Their reaction was scarcely surprising, given that the 'dump hole' was the former offal pit and known to have rotting carcases, flies and rats. These were the days of Toby the draught horse and the dray. Trish would sit on the dray and get a wet bottom when they crossed a creek. "I loved going out with Dad."

She also recalls Phil's "delight" in silly names and "winding up the girls." This caused all sorts of high jinks with "Dad chasing the screaming girls around while he roared like a bull." Another favourite character was 'Jack the Hunter.' 'Jack' was a reference to the central character in 'King Solomon's Mines,' a well-loved story.

At one point Phil drove an orange Leyland – the 'Pumpkin Car.' Later, his grandchildren called him 'Skinny' because he was fat. Phil revelled in the "stupidity of it." When they went on holidays he loved to sing in the car which at the time was a bone-coloured Vauxhall Velox. The Kingston Trio's 'Hang Down Your Head Tom Dooley,' was a favourite. Years later Phil described these times as "the happiest of his life." The early innocence of uncomplicated relationships with his children and then grandchildren was a healing power to be cherished

Politically, this was the era of the 'Holyoake Years' in New Zealand, when the farming industry was a potent force in the economy and politics. Prime Minister Keith, later Sir Keith, Holyoake's time in office came to represent the might of the farming industry which went hand in hand with the National Party.

Keith Holyoake, a sheep farmer from nearby Pahiatua, became a 'local' with the additional purchase of a hill country property near Dannevirke. In an illustrious political career starting from the late fifties as a Member of Parliament Keith was Prime Minister of New Zealand from 1960-1972 and later New Zealand's 13th Governor General, 1977-1980. 'Kiwi Keith' or 'KJ' as he was often referred to by his supporters was a genial man who made it his business to know his constituents. However while both Phil and Kiwi Keith knew each other well, politics was never a feature of life in the Lamason household.

Above: Phil Lamason (seated 2nd from left) as a member of the AWE Board of Directors in the late 1970's. Below: Phil (seated right) pictured as a member of the Howard Estate Trust Board on which he served for 20 years, including a time as Chairman. The Board is charged with administering Smedley Training Farm. (Photograpsh courtesy Lamason Family Collection)

180

Above Left to Right: Don McDonald, Phil Lamason and Prime Minister Keith Holyoake pictured at the Dannevirke A&P Show, circa 1967. (Photograph courtesy of Dannevirke Gallery of History) Below: Joan and Phil Lamason (seated) with their family circa 1964. Pictured (left to right): Robbie, Cheryl (Cherry), Patricia (Trish), Billy and John. (Photograph courtesy Lamason Family Collection)

181

More significantly this was the era of the wool barons and the power of the producer boards. New Zealand was becoming a country of some 80 million sheep alongside a population of under two million people. Burgeoning fat lamb numbers fed the freezing industry and contributed to a buoyant farming economy in which the east coast province of Hawke's Bay was a major player.

Combining farming with fulltime employment as a livestock picker ensured a life in which Phil had few spare moments. Phil's daily work schedule required early departures to visit clients and evening telephone calls to tomorrow's clients to end it. Much of this work was in the hill country east of Dannevirke in the area of long established farmers where client relationships were valued and they returned the respect.

On his own farm Phil specialised in fat lamb breeding using a combination of Romney and Southdown genes to produce long, big-bodied sheep. Spending was prioritised in favour of quality stock and well-fertilised pasture. To a man who was highly regarded for his financial acumen, a smart new shed was considered unproductive, a 'frippery.' Phil's emphasis on the quality of his stock was consistent with the early thirst for a life on the land and his ability as a stockman.

Involvement in the wider community was underpinned by farming interests, including the Dannevirke A & P (Agricultural & Pastoral) Association, a wool company and Smedley Station. Phil served as a long-time committee member and then President of the Dannevirke A & P Show. He was also a formidable sheep and cattle competitor in the show with a reputation for his lamb weights and the quality of his 18-month steers in the 'hoof and hook' classes. Here Phil was a three times winner of the coveted Weddell Cup for a beast judged the best 'on the hoof' and then the heaviest 'on the hook' carcase.

In 1974 a group of wool growers from Central and Southern Hawke's Bay established the East Coast Wool Co-operative from the purchase of Associated Wool Exporters (AWE). The co-operative traded overseas as AWE whilst setting up New Zealand Wool Spinners, a farm to yarn farmer's pool, in the seventies. Later a wool scour was added. Phil was a director for nearly 20 years and deputy chairman. A former AWE chairman and Hawke's Bay farming identity, Bay de Lautaur had a high regard for Phil's financial astuteness, describing him as "one of the best" when it came to the minute examination of balance sheets and investment companies. Phil was also a 'moderating influence' at the board table. And then there was the lighter side. The post board meeting sessions involving a gradually diminishing bottle of whisky and Phil's flying anecdotes were highlights not to be missed. This was a routine that carried on well into the nineties. A recreational pilot himself, Bay de Lautaur would sometimes take Phil flying and occasionally hand over the controls. This is the only recorded anecdote of Phil Lamason having ever taken the controls of an aircraft after leaving Britain at the end of WWII.

Hand in hand with Phil's farming skills was a 'canny' attitude to money. "Being good at handling the money is virtually as important as the farming skills," he once mentioned in a newspaper article many years later. He also believed that while teaching young men to work the land was one thing, business acumen was another – especially in the modern era. He became a mentor to many in the District and was regarded as an advisor on agricultural matters.

Smedley Station, that significant place of his boyhood, continued to be prominent in his life. Phil was a member of the Howard Estate Advisory Board, which governed the station, for 20 years and then served as its chairman. He is also credited with changing the stocking policy on the station and "turning it around." In recognition of Phil's contribution to Smedley the Lamason family and East Coast Wool Co-operative have combined to offer the Phil Lamason Scholarship for academic study at Massey University.

Graeme Ramsden, a Dannevirke farmer, former cadet and Smedley board member, speaks of Phil with affection and great admiration. "He was tremendous fun, easy to talk to, but also a very private person." The pair would sometimes meet at the Dannevirke Club "for the odd whisky." After Phil's death Graeme made approaches at local political and RSA level to gain posthumous recognition for his bravery but, much to his disappointment, was unsuccessful.

While 'down time' was not a Lamason characteristic, rugby was the exception. A player from his Massey University days and a passionate fan of the game, Phil avidly followed local club and school rugby. He also went to great lengths to attend All Black test matches including once having entry to a corporate box in Sydney for a Bledisloe Cup match. So great was his love of the game, he was prepared to overlook the fact that the corporate owner was a German organisation. Trips to

Athletic Park in Wellington were numerous as were provincial games, attended where possible in the company of his brother Bill.

In the early Rua Roa days home for the Lamason family was an old wooden villa-styled farmhouse on their Laws Road property.

One cold April night in 1960 catastrophe evolved into yet another remarkable story of Lamason survival. Joan and Phil were out on a social occasion. Four of the Lamason children along with two friends staying over for the night, were home alone under the watchful eye of the eldest, Trish, aged just 13 years. The kids, sleeping soundly in the small hours of the morning, were oblivious of the drama that was unfolding around them.

A smouldering fire which had ignited from a malfunctioning electric blanket was taking hold in the master bedroom. Choking, acrid smoke wafted slowly and menacingly through the house. Robbie, aged ten awoke and raised the alarm. In pitch darkness and with amazing composure Trish gathered together the children as the elderly wooden house erupted in a raging inferno behind them. She then led the children along the road to the neighbour's house.

It was a major event for the district. In the pale grey light of dawn the Lamason family home lay as a pile of blackened ash and twisted corrugated iron debris in the surrounding paddock. Everything was destroyed but more importantly no lives were lost. The fire received wide publicity and the children were greatly praised. Included amongst the praise was a telegram to Trish from the then Leader of the Opposition and local Member of Parliament Keith Holyoake. "Please accept my sincere congratulations on your exemplary conduct during the disastrous fire at your home on Saturday..." he wrote.

Soon after the fire Phil and Joan built their own new home on the Rua Roa farm. Based on his brother Bill's residence in Napier city, this modern, block-built house, beautifully wood-panelled in Rimu, became the Lamason family 'homestead.' With its commanding north-east vista across the rural landscape Phil, with justifiable pride, could gaze upon the fruits of his labours.

The new, pale stoned, two storey house was set to the side of a circular drive and overlooked the farm. Over time, Joan's deft fingers established a beautiful garden with shrubs and rhododendrons fringing the driveway. With her CWI activities and love of flowers Joan derived

Above: Trish and Phil Lamason in 1967. Below: Holidays to the beach were always a highlight. Phil with his children pictured on one such occasion in the early 1960's (Left to Right): Phil, Billy, Cherry, John, Trish and Robbie. (Photographs courtesy Lamason Family Collection)

Above: The farm name with the wartime connection ...."Glen Devon" at the entrance to the Lamason Farm, Rua Roa, Dannevirke, New Zealand. (Photograph courtesy of Mike Harold) Below: Phil beside the entrance to the family's newly built home in Rua Roa circa late 1960's. (Photoraph courtesy Lamason Family Collection)

Billy Lamason, 1976. Phil described the tragedy of losing Billy, his youngest son, as being an experience that was "worse than Buchenwald." (Photograph courtesy Lamason Family Collection)

great pleasure from her efforts. Phil on the other hand is remembered as "a hopeless gardener who couldn't grow a vegetable." A manicured grass tennis court was built for the kids.

But while Phil had tremendous pride in his home and property this paled in comparison to his pride in the children. John and Billy embraced the farming life, Trish and Cherry trained as teachers and Robbie built up a successful fishing business off the Australian coast.

During these years the Lamasons upheld a cherished Kiwi tradition, the acquisition of a family summer holiday 'bach', or cottage. Their bach at Three Mile Bay in Taupo, a world-renowned trout fishing resort, became their get-away retreat. Phil loved trout fishing. For him the joy of his get-away retreat were the long summer days enjoyed by extended family and friends beside the iconic Lake Taupo. This was always a time for catching-up and retelling stories of days gone by.

Then in 1976, tragedy struck. In his prime, aged just 20 years, Phil's youngest son Billy died in a car accident when the vehicle he was travelling in collided with a bridge just below the Lamason house. Phil had already experienced his father's death by a car accident. This time his cherished son was the victim. Billy and his father were great mates. They had shared the 'larrikin' element of Phil's personality. Like his brother John, Billy had been a committed scout. He had enjoyed tennis, rugby, canoeing and his motor bike. But more importantly Billy and Phil had worked together on the farm. Phil's devastation was indescribable and an event from which he would never recover. It was a loss that he once described as being "worse than Buchenwald." John recalled in recent years how the tragic death of Billy "almost broke my father."

Rua Roa was a close-knit community and showed great support for the family. Cloaked in his loss and sharing the grief with Joan, Phil just 'got on with it' as was his custom with whatever life threw at him. Then, to compound the loss, his brother Bill, the stalwart in his life, died in the same year. Eleven years later tragedy struck again, this time with the death of his grand-daughter Sharny, daughter of Trish and her husband Graeme Simmonds. These were huge loads for Phil and Joan to bear.

Phil's grandchildren were a great pride and a solace to him. They became the next generation to enjoy the stories and the humour and to share special moments around the farm with their grandfather. There would be visits to the river for example, to "stop, and listen to the birds."

Phil and Joan Lamason with their extended family in 1991. Standing (Left to Right): Mark Taylor, Cherry Taylor, Trish Simmonds, Graeme Simmonds, John Lamason, Debbie Lamason, Joan Lamason, Phil Lamason, Robbie Lamason (holding) Sarah Lamason. Sitting (Left to Right): Matthew Lamason, Joel Lamason, Christie Lamason, Karen Taylor, Kyle Lamason, Ben Lamason, Anita Simmonds, Rowan Lamason, David Lamason, Annie Lamason, Vicky Taylor and Drew Lamason. (Photograph courtesy Lamason Family Collection)

Phil and Joan Lamason again visited Canada in August 1985 and here Phil is seen with Ed Carter Edwards and Art Kinnis in Victoria B.C.

(Photograph courtesy of Art Kinnis and Stanley Brooker from '168 Jump into Hell')

189

The Spectre of War Revisited

Hand in hand with pride in the farm and the personal tragedy of family life, the past was intervening. One hundred and sixty-six men who had given and their 'all' in the name of their countries, had suffered post-war disbelief and denials of their Buchenwald story due to a 'lack of evidence' to back up their truth. Some were still seeking recognition and redress for their war time prison experience. Somewhat to his discomfort, Phil's long-buried war experiences were beginning to emerge into the public arena.

The following is an account of the years spanning three decades and the ongoing quest for justice for 'The Lost Airmen of Buchenwald.' It was a slow process. Then, as the personal stories and documentaries became known, their story was finally broken to a disbelieving public. A painful past that was being revisited in the pursuit of justice was eventually laid bare.

In May 1987, Phil received a cheque of $13,000 from the New Zealand Government. The Cabinet in Wellington had approved a $250,000 fund to compensate servicemen held in German concentration camps in the belief this gesture would "recognise the wrong suffered by imprisonment in concentration camps in breach of the Geneva Convention," as New Zealand journalist Max Lambert later wrote in his book 'Night After Night.' Twenty-six claimants were found eligible including Phil and Malcolm Cullen, who was awarded $12,000.

This acknowledgement had been a very long time coming. In 1965 Britain had claimed reparation from West Germany and paid out its servicemen who had been held illegally in concentration camps. But when the Australian servicemen made their claim they met rebuttal, due to the lack of a peace treaty between East and West Germany. New Zealand and Canadian airmen met with the same resistance and were told their story could not be proven. It took the efforts of dedicated individuals and varying lengths of time for compensation to eventually be made. For the Commonwealth airmen this refusal to accept the legitimacy of their claim cut deep. In 'Destination Buchenwald,' published in 1995, Australian author Colin Burgess graphically summed it up: "While the passing of the years have not diluted the memories of what these men witnessed and experienced, their protracted pleas for some form of recognition and just compensation were totally rejected or ignored by a succession of chronically slow or indifferent governments. In the more extreme cases, this failure to act caused a tragic alienation

190

of these former servicemen who felt betrayed by their own political leaders. They had donned their country's uniform and left their homes to fight in a world war, and yet they were being told there was no evidence of their being held in Buchenwald and other death camps. The author would like to suggest this evidence has always been easily obtainable and in most instances is a matter of public record. No one it seems gave a damn about the men's claims."

But by then, at least, Australia and New Zealand had paid. The Canadian government meanwhile was still holding back, despite the dogged efforts of Art Kinnis, the president of the KLB Club, and others, to secure justice. Kinnis, described as a "formidable fighter for post-war justice," led a campaign to ensure the airmen's experiences were eventually recognised. Where Phil had consistently defied the Gestapo in his efforts to gain recognition of their POW status from the Germans, these post-war efforts were the next step in the quest for recognition. Formal recognition from the Canadian Government finally came in 2001 with each of the airmen receiving $10,000 compensation.

Phil had maintained contact with members of the KLB Club and in particular with Art Kinnis. In 1983, Phil and Joan travelled to Hamilton, Canada for a reunion at which he was guest speaker. Phil is pictured there with his old friends and then again two years later, when he was guest speaker at a Vancouver convention. Here, after 40 years of silence, Phil finally released the information about their impending deaths that he had carried for so long. This was a significant moment. Had he gone to Vancouver with that purpose or was it a spontaneous decision based on 'the moment?'

In the following passage in '168 Jump Into Hell,' co-author Stan Booker 78370 had this to say : "What to us was another startling jolt, that he had seen their extermination orders three days before they were to be executed and not told the men because they would have bolted. Watching Phil as his story of our past unfolded and then to see him suddenly relax and we saw the beginning of a smile. He had finally been able to get rid of the millstone he had kept to himself all those years and was now able to talk freely with some of the chaps that he had kept these terminal facts from." At this time in 1985, the fight for government recognition of their story was still ongoing.

In a series of letters to KLB members in the early nineties Art illustrates his determination to achieve recognition for his fellow airmen. "Still hunting for members," he wrote in a Christmas letter in

191

1990. Eluding him were 28 RAF, 15 USA, two RCAF, and one Jamaican. As well as trying to track them down and to ensure no one was overlooked, he was also starting to plan the book that he and Stanley Booker would later write.

During a trip to England earlier in that year Art, together with fellow KLB member Jim Hastin and their wives, had attended a club gathering in England. Barbara Yeo-Thomas, wife of the late Tommy Yeo-Thomas, the 'White Rabbit' was present. Kinnis wrote: "Barbara was a very gracious lady and we were all impressed." She was also invited to become the club's patron.

Art also met his engineer after 45 years and then went on to France to pay a visit to the "well-kept graves" of three of his crew. He also met members of the French Resistance, returned to the woods where he crashed and then to the house where he was hidden. "It was a trip that was very emotional for us and one that was very much enjoyed." Although he does not use the word, this trip could be termed a 'pilgrimage.'

His response to this experience is interesting in that Phil too could have done likewise. He had the wherewithal but clearly did not choose to do so. In fact nearly 25 years were to elapse before a Lamason 'pilgrimage' finally took place – without Phil. His reluctance to visit the past, despite the revelation at the 1985 convention, is also hinted at in a personal note from Art in reference to gathering material for his book: "It is really our hope that you two can once again drop over to meet with us again. Joan, I know you're taking good care of our 'Boss' but in all these years you have failed to get him to put pen to paper." Then in a direct appeal, "Phil, you must have a wealth of information that would be of great help to our endeavour. I have your visit to the museum." He also asks for name suggestions adding "one idea is '168 Jump Into Hell.'"

In 1991 Art put out a general request for material to write his book. "We know our story is unique and that it must be told." He urges the men to "think back to Fresnes, the boxcar and days in Buchenwald." The story would be written in two parts: Part One 'From Capture to Buchenwald.' Part Two "what Phil Lamason told us in 1983 and 1985." Among the questions to be addressed: Were those death threats real? Could we get the proof required? Who betrayed us? And most importantly, WHY THE EMBARGO ON POW FACTS? To Phil he

Above: Phil together in Sydney, 1996, with three of the nine Australian KLB members. (Left to Right) Eric Johnson, Jim Gwilliam, Phil Lamason and Keith Mills. (Photograph courtesy Lamason Family Collection). Below: Malcolm and Ailsa Cullen circa 1960's. Malcolm Cullen was the only other New Zealander among the 168 Allied Airmen in Buchenwald with Phil Lamason in 1944. (Photograph courtesy of Ailsa Cullen)

says, "Stan Booker sent outstanding material and proves what you told us in Hamilton and Vancouver."

At this time Art gave the New Zealand and Australian governments a pat on the back for the compensation recognition. "There are many still working with the Canadian, US and the British Governments... We would have thought the example of the New Zealand and Australian Governments would have paved the way."

In May 1992, he wrote to the Lamasons that the book was progressing and there had been "a fair amount of support from the gang," although not apparently from Phil. "Your story must have got lost in the mail." Then he delivers 'the surprise.' "We have had a commitment from the Canadian National Film Board and they have already started to make a 60-90 minute documentary of our KLB Club." He also makes it clear that the researcher, Roma Andrusiak, "does want to talk to you." A letter of intent is enclosed and "we will be looking forward to whatever help you can give us."

Another subtle reminder follows in the Kriegies Christmas letter of that year. Many excellent articles had been received but "there are still some marvellous incidents that remain hidden in some minds and if you can disturb and bring them into existence you'll give us all a chance to enjoy them after you have sent them."

In 1984 and then 1994 Kriegies travelled to Copenhagen to attend 40 and then 50 year commemoration gatherings organised by their fellow 'Buchenwaldklubben' inmates. The latter trip included visits to Buchenwald and France but unsurprisingly the Lamasons were not among the party. In the same year the National Film Board of Canada released the documentary movie 'The Lucky Ones: Allied Airmen and Buchenwald,' to an unsuspecting world. In it the former Allied airmen recounted their personal and collective stories before and after Buchenwald. Phil was interviewed and mentioned throughout the documentary.

Arthur J Kinnis and Stanley Booker's '168 Jump Into Hell' was published in 1999. The front cover of this compelling first-hand account lays it on the line as 'A True Story of Betrayed Allied Airmen of the KLB Club.' Described as 'a poignant, tragic compilation of personal memories and stories of the 168 Allied Airmen interred at Buchenwald,' Art Kinnis achieved what he had intended. But while there is considerable mention of Phil Lamason's extraordinary role in their story, little was contributed by the hero himself.

In a meaningful tribute to Phil, Art wrote: "In early 1994 we (KLB Club) were only too pleased to join with (fellow New Zealander) Malcolm Cullen 78388 in his effort to get some long neglected recognition for the outstanding work that Phil Lamason did for our party of 168. What Phil accomplished makes us all very grateful that he was at our helm. It was very unfortunate that the New Zealand Government found that it was too late for any action on their part. What he did for us may have gone unrecognised by the authorities but not by us. Our efforts to speak out in 1945 about our experiences went unnoticed by the Government and the military of that day, so we found our statements, which were difficult for others to believe, went into hibernation for 35 years. The fact that the latter action was not taken is difficult to comprehend, and, I think, can only have been because all of us deposed to our respective countries when the war was finished and got on with our careers as best we could."

Also in the Kinnis and Booker book, Tom Blackham, Phil's second-in-command at Buchenwald, said of their leader: "Squadron Leader Lamason epitomised all that was good in a leader and there is no doubt in my mind that his commendable, sustained effort as a front man of our group during the trials and tribulations at the hands of the SS and Gestapo was a major contributing factor in us getting recognised as prisoners of war under the provisions of the Geneva Convention and transferred in October 1944 to a recognised POW Camp... Squadron Leader Lamason, by his very strong traits of single-minded determination, selflessness, cold courage and forcefulness in the face of the very real threat to him of execution by the camp authorities because he was our leader, had quickly established himself as a legendary figure in our eyes and those of other Resistance leaders within the camp, and our standing overall was enhanced considerably as a result. His actions were completely selfless and always positive, no matter what the danger, and by direct interaction beyond the call of duty and most worthy of official recognition by the allied authorities at the end of the Second World War."

Earlier, in April 1986, Phil had received a letter from Barbara Yeo-Thomas, widow of 'Tommy' Yeo-Thomas, the 'White Rabbit.' Here Barbara expressed her gratitude that she had finally "tracked Phil down," and how "after 43 years I am at last able to write and thank you – as I have always wanted to do – for carrying back from Buchenwald

Phil with Colin Burgess in Sydney, 1996, on the the only occasion that they met together in person. (Left to Right); Phil Lamason, Ian Innes (evader), Gwen Innes, Val Burgess, Joan Lamason and Colin Burgess. (Photograph courtesy Lamason Family Collection)

the news of my husband Yeo-Thomas in that camp. Although it was not exactly 'good' news, at least I knew that he was still alive...''

'Destination Buchenwald' graphically written by Australian author Colin Burgess was also published in the late nineties but was not widely available in New Zealand. In 2004 a documentary 'Shot From The Sky' was screened on the History Channel. This covered the experience of a fellow inmate, B-17 pilot Roy Allen and also featured Phil.

'Buchenwald Flyboy' American Joe Moser then wrote 'A Fighter Pilot In Buchenwald.' Moser's account of Phil's role in the camp was significant and has already been recounted. Later, in 2011, this narrative became the basis of the Mike Dorsey documentary 'The Lost Airmen of Buchenwald.' Dorsey had his own reasons to honour Phil. He was the grandson of 'Easy' Freeman, one of the airmen saved from death at Buchenwald. Featuring Phil in person, this 'doco' confronted the truth and cemented the story. Phil was aged 91 years at the time of the interview for the documentary and, on later watching it on TV, apparently found it "a bit long."

At this time other claims were being sought.

On August 12, 2000, a German Law came into force designating seven organisations, including the International Organisation for Migration (IOM) to make payments to former slave and forced labourers but even more significantly to "certain other victims of National Social (Nazi) injustice." The funds were to be provided in equal parts by the German Government and German companies. Those eligible were "persons who were held inside or outside their own country in a concentration camp, ghetto or another place of confinement and were subject to slave labour, persons who were subjected to medical experiments, or other comparable conditions including inhumane prison conditions, insufficient nutrition and lack of medical care." Applicants "may receive up to DEM15,000."

Phil lodged his application, IOM Claim Number 1072466, with the German Embassy on April 27, 2001, stating his internment from August 20 – October 19, 1944, and his position. "I was the senior allied officer of 168 men incarcerated. I understand that the American officers held with me received $47,000 American approximately 18-months ago." On August 26, 2002, he was awarded DEM 150,000 - NZD 8036.74 to be paid in two instalments.

An interesting post-war snippet involving France and Germany was revealed in a 2001 KLB letter by Art Kinnis. A friend had sent him an article published in the New York Times of June 13, "telling of a class action suit of $75 million against the French Government for allowing their railways to be used to haul civilians into Germany to work in Concentration Camps." The French Government was getting paid "re individuals" and mileage from the German Government. The matter was put into the hands of the Canadian Government "for some sort of action." Whether it was successful is not recorded.

On December 1, 1985, the following headline appeared in the Toronto Star: 'Buchenwald PoWs seek pensions.' During the eighties the Canadian government was seeking compensation from the German government. Then, in 1985 it chose also to present a symbol of remembrance to Denmark's Museum of Resistance at Copenhagen. The chosen symbol, a parchment lampshade, was presented to the Danish Ambassador by three members of the KLB Club. On it were listed the names of the 27 airmen along with the words 'Royal Canadian Air Force

197

(RCAF),' and paintings of a Lancaster bomber and two fighter aircraft. The Canadian gesture was one of many such lampshades presented by victims of Buchenwald that were already on display at the museum.

It had been 38 years since the 168 Allied airmen and 1700 Danish policemen arrested for their loyalty to the Resistance movement in German-occupied Denmark, were herded into Buchenwald. The bonds of mutual goodwill that formed immediately had lapsed over time. Then, in 1984 at an international fishing conference, there was a chance encounter between a Dane who knew one of the policemen and a member of the KLB Club. With the Danish police connection rekindled, the presentation of the lampshade in Canada and the 1985 and 1995 visits to Denmark and the 'Buchenwaldklubben' members had followed.

One question remains. How was it that in 1985 the Canadian government presented a symbol of remembrance featuring the names of the 27 airmen, three of whom had made the presentation, but then waited another 16 years to award them compensation?

It was in 2005 with the publication of New Zealand journalist Max Lambert's 'Night After Night – New Zealanders In Bomber Command,' that shocked countrymen were finally exposed to the Phil Lamason story. Readers were reminded that 55,573 airmen who served in the RAF Bomber Command had lost their lives; that a further 9838 had become Prisoners of War and that 8403 were wounded in action.

"These guys gave their all in their efforts as they defended Britain from invasion, blasted enemy industrial infrastructure, played their part in the prosecution of Allied grand strategy and supported Allied land campaigns and targeted U-boats. To look at photos of these young, idealistic and committed young men, many of whom were out to have a lark, strikes a blow to the heart."

Readers are left in no doubt as to the conditions or Phil's heroism: "Into this hellhole on August 20, 1944, the Germans marched the shocked Allied flyers – two New Zealanders, nine Australians, 26 Canadians, 48 Britons, 82 Americans and one Jamaican…" The second New Zealand airman was Malcolm Cullen, who came from Maungaturoto, north of Auckland.

"The airmen prisoners' hair was shorn when they arrived at the camp, and the group slept in the open on cobblestones to begin with and existed on a starvation diet. Most suffered from sores and dysentery. Lamason battled these problems plus a bout of diphtheria but he was young and fit and withstood the appalling conditions well, although his weight quickly dwindled.

"A Squadron Leader and the senior officer, Lamason emerged from Buchenwald with a giant reputation. Despite the obvious dangers he stood up to the Germans, and his work as spokesman for the group, his personality, spirit and leadership skills are acknowledged in several books." Lambert also goes on to quote Tom Blackham's statement as to how Lamason "epitomised all that was good in a leader..."

Phil himself told Lambert: "It amazed me that people could be so inhuman, people from a nation that was supposed to be civilised. They hung prisoners and bet on how long the victims would continue to kick. I saw their museum while I was there – skins and heads and other bits of bodies on the walls with descriptions of what had happened to them. The inhumanity of it all amazed me."

One can only imagine the impact of these descriptions on the reader. Tellingly Lambert also comments: "Lamason however has never been honoured by his homeland for his leading role in saving the lives of the airmen in Buchenwald and didn't even rate a mention in Wynn Mason's official history of New Zealand POWs." An anecdote exists in which Phil was asked by an interviewer whether he had been in the war. The response is typical. "Yeah I got there."

That year the then 86 year old Phil Lamason was interviewed by TV New Zealand. The ensuing publicity that had catapulted Phil into the limelight was not greeted with enthusiasm. Requests for interviews were granted grudgingly, if at all.

Former Dannevirke journalist Warren Barton had in 1999 interviewed an albeit unwilling Phil Lamason – as the headline 'The Reluctant Hero' conveys. There is mention of "emaciated men, harnessed like animals pulling a wagon," and the well documented hair shaving incident. Reference too, to "men with piano wire around their necks hanging from hooks till they kicked themselves to death."

Phil's unwillingness to publicly acknowledge a past that he had carried for so many years was demonstrated by his stance on not attending ANZAC Day services. A clearer insight into his thoughts as an older man around ANZAC commemorations, was provided by farm worker Stephen Witika: "Not long after I started working with the Lamasons we were busy in the sheep-yards on the Rua Roa farm one day. Phil, although quite elderly, was still active and helping as much as he was able. It was approaching ANZAC Day and as part of the casual conversation as we worked, I enquired of him as to whether he had been at the War and whether he was planning to attend the annual parade. At the time I had no knowledge of Phil's war time experience or of his disposition towards war commemorations. 'Yes Steve, I got there (to the War)' was the somewhat blunt response, followed by a resolute 'No. I won't be going to the parade.' We kept working without further talk... then some minutes later Phil elaborated further, 'Stephen... ANZAC Day is the one day in the year that former servicemen gather to remember their colleagues who lost their lives during the War... for me there are very few days that go by when I don't think about them.'

Clearly for Phil these past experiences needed no reminders they were always there and not to be pulled out on a special day. It should also be acknowledged that this attitude was not always easily understood among his local contemporaries. It is echoed too in his refusal to address students at his old alma mater Napier Boys' High School in later years.

But amongst this long catalogue of disclosure and discovery lies an anomaly. The world had in fact been made aware of the Phil Lamason story as early as May 25, 1945. When the Auckland Star ran the "New Zealander in Buchenwald Camp" story, the information was laid out then. The story was gathered via 'NZPA (New Zealand Press Association) Special Correspondent Rec.10.30am. It was dated LONDON May 24. The assumption must surely be made that the story 'broke' in the UK and was picked up the following day in New Zealand.

As the following account demonstrates, no punches were pulled: "Every time he had kicked him or cuffed him with his fist the German warrant-officer clapped his hand to his revolver and shouted at the New Zealander: 'English officer hey?' One threatening move and the German would have shot him dead. Only the day before he had shot a young 17 year old French boy in an overcrowded truck through the hand, and then invited him to get out to be treated. When the boy left the truck this same German had shot him through the heart and had his body flung into a ditch. Squadron-Leader P.J. Lamason DFC and Bar, of Napier, remembered this incident only too well, and that is why he had to take a beating without murmur from this German guard. He was on his way to Buchenwald Concentration Camp and as the senior officer in charge of his truck he had complained of overcrowding. And for his trouble the German guard kicked him and cuffed him, shouting insults.

And then in a complete about face comes one of those extraordinary accounts when for a split second brutality gives way to compassion. Later on, "when Squadron-Leader Lamason was sitting down recovering, some stray thought must have entered the German's thick skull... He enquired from other prisoners as to what was the New Zealander's rank and learning that it was the equivalent of a Major, he summoned the Red Cross. He had Lamason's cuts and bruises treated and gave him a drink of milk. He also ordered better accommodation for his men. Then he sat down and discussed the reasons why Germany would never be defeated..."

The article backgrounds the whole story, from the 'bale out' to the handover to the Gestapo and the conditions in Buchenwald, through to the move to Stalag Luft III, and later the Russians' arrival at Luckenwalde... It concludes: "Today Squadron-Leader Lamason is looking little the worse for wear for his experiences and is in good health. He has but one thought. He wants to get back as soon as possible to operational flying..." Unlike the successive and much later interviews, this Auckland Star account is literally 'hot off the press.' Here is a young New Zealand airman with his faculties intact and a compelling story to tell. So why was Phil's heroic role in the saga of 'The Lost Airmen' not acknowledged earlier?

Another interview took place in the eighties, this one with a medical focus. Titled 'Experiences as a Prisoner-of-War, World War II,' the interviewer was Charles Gordon Roland, MD. The information was destined for the Oral History Archives, Hannah Chair for the History of Medicine, McMaster University. As the Canadian university is located in Hamilton, Ontario, it is likely that the interview took place during the KLB Club convention there in 1985.

Here it should be mentioned that the following material has been chosen selectively. It does not include other parts of Phil's narrative such as the capture, transport and arrival at Buchenwald, his leadership role in the camp and association with Yeo-Thomas the 'White Rabbit,' as these have been recounted elsewhere.

In this 32-page account, there is a discussion around memory loss. Phil frequently refers to being "a bit hazy" when trying to recollect some aspects of daily life at Buchenwald. At times his discourse is disjointed and statements linger in thin air. During a discussion concerning his association with the French scientist and medical researcher Dr Alfred Balachowsky who was a director of the Pasteur Institute, he recalls:

201

"one thing Balachowsky did say was to emphasise that anyone that is in this camp for any length of time loses their memory." The scientist then demonstrated his finding by asking a long-term inmate "who was quite a good survivor," some questions concerning his wife and family. The answers were quite confused and "he couldn't get them out." This was typical of anyone who had been incarcerated for more than 12 months. Phil himself said, "I found that (in) here, talking to people, and even myself, you get into a real haze – whether just lack of memory or the stress, which didn't help the memory. I don't know but I'm a little hazy on some of these things."

Balachowsky's scientific role at the camp was to develop a vaccine for typhus. He worked in the laboratory. Phil recalled eating "typhus-stricken rabbits" as a way of getting "a bit of extra rations." He also ventured into drinking small quantities of "pure lab alcohol which wasn't too bad with a bit of water."

The vaccine it appears, was injected to people in the block (where it was made), by a "very nasty Kapo (guard) who killed everyone who survived." These people "were fed pretty well, injected, and after two or three weeks they got better or otherwise they murdered them and then burnt them up." Once these people ended up in that block there was only one way out – through the crematorium. Phil also mentions "half a dozen blokes" whose job it was to inject everyone in the camp.

The Germans were "mighty nervous" of typhus, in particular, spreading through the civilian population…and "just kept putting injections into people. They didn't care a damn whether you had one the day before." Phil thought he had about half a dozen injections. "You'd just go out yelling and screaming and that was it."

In another recollection he mentions having diphtheria. "I was walking around and I didn't even know it. I was just feeling pretty down to it, and had a bit of a sore throat – very sore throat and I was haemorrhaging from somewhere behind the nose." Phil had a "lot of catarrh and would wake up in a big haze feeling dreadful." He staggered around, and sometimes "would walk two or three yards and have to sit down for five minutes." He was offered some sulanilimide but didn't take it because he mistrusted the connections of the Frenchman who offered it. Later, on arrival at Sagan, Phil was examined, a bacteria was 'cultured' from a throat swab and then he was "flung into hospital, in isolation for about three weeks."

Questioned about other health problems, Phil talked about his sores. "I had a few sores. They said they were diphtheria sores. Came on the leg, but not too bad. You know people had a lot of sores in Buchenwald, big sore sores. Oh they'd cover half the size of a saucer." He mentioned a lump on his thigh from a muscular injection which he had had until "quite recently." The injection was to combat the diphtheria bug.

Teeth were another issue. Phil's teeth were perfect when he was shot down, but on his return he had 13 fillings. The teeth were "sort of knocked about – I guess it was the diet... I had all these holes that appeared over 12 months." Then a comment about the cost of dentistry... "they charge like crazy and I always think that's a bill I should be getting off Germany."

Phil was asked if nightmares had troubled him, but whilst acknowledging "I have had the odd nightmare" he denied this was an issue. "...Not in the way which you mean... I don't think it's affected me at all really." Phil was asked about his contacts in the camp including Balachowsky and Jan Robert, a Dutchman. "They knew about the background of concentration camps extremely well... They had good contacts themselves through the camp and gave me an idea on who to contact to try and organise the camp." This was helpful as Phil "didn't really want it to be known that I was walking around trying to organise things." Phil did actually contact the Russians and spent a month with them. "I used to go to sleep with four Russian colonels." He also contacted the Danes, attempting to "organise the place a bit, to offer some resistance at the appropriate time." Thirty odd "genuine" British saboteurs and spies were also contacted. "Ultimately, except about three, all got hung."

The interview ends on a grisly note with a conversation about the camp's "so-called museum." It was a "formidable place." He recalls the walls lined with human skins and the preserved tattooed heads right around the building. There were "...negroes, all sorts of things... a chap had tattooed on his neck "for the hangman.'" He "remembered the skins probably more than the heads. A sort of horror fascination," but says he "would hate to go there now." At the time, "you sort of just go. There it was."

Indeed, yes, there it was. The experiences and the memories that would never leave him. This was the underbelly, the inescapable demons that lurked within, but were kept at bay. Buried, never talked about, but never far from the surface. They lay ready – like the German

SS guards – to shoot at a moment's notice. A deadly hand poised on the trigger of the subconscious. Phil was a light sleeper for the rest of his life. These flashbacks would have manifested in "the odd nightmare," but on a daily basis there were other moments too.

Rabbit stew that was never on the Lamason family menu because Phil was unable to erase the memory of the cooked, typhus-stricken rabbits. Like the extra weight that he carried, the consequence of months of starvation and his vow that he would "never go hungry again." Smaller, random incidents would also have occurred in daily life to trigger what lay beneath the surface.

Picture the following. Phil walks down Dannevirke High Street, the tall, familiar, brown-hatted figure stooped in friendly conversation with a passer-by. Approaching him, a man is walking his dog. The dog is an Alsatian. Through the town chugs the goods train, its familiar clattering presence reminiscent of a cattle truck, 90 men, two buckets and a young boy whose quest for air finds death at the hands of a crazed German Feldwebel. Think of the smoke rising from the hospital chimneys, a display of boys' striped pyjamas in a clothing store, bunks in a bedroom, a council road gang standing round a pile of rocks.

In a daily existence amongst the 'commonplace of life,' a common theme emerges. With each passing encounter a moment of innocence is confronted by 'innocence lost.' A gut-wrenching moment of a past experience is laid bare – again. Innocence lost can never be regained.

"I have always tried to put it all behind me and just get on with my life," Phil once remarked during an interview. His surroundings and his family would have helped. Nurtured by the land and its beauty, the daily splendour of farm, sky and ranges bathed in all its differing lights; the deep pride in his grandchildren, the trips around the farm when the vehicle would be stopped in a moment of solitude to listen to bird-song and a flowing river. What deeper therapy was there for a man whose family was 'the salve to his soul?'

And as always, throughout Phil's life there were lighter moments, the inevitable 'humour stories.' The 'larrikin' again. Like an incident which occurred at the Dannevirke Embassy Cabaret which was upstairs above the Dannevirke Regent Theatre in High Street. This was generally regarded in the small town as the venue where the local 'movers and shakers' held their 'black tie' functions. On one such occasion when the function was 'well and truly pumping,' Phil is recalled as holding a local identity over the balcony by the ankles and "laughing fiendishly, much to the alarm of the onlookers on the street below."

In more recent years a wartime friendship emerged in a remarkable coincidence involving Trish and Graeme Simmonds. They had attended Sunday church in their Auckland east coast community and extended the hand of friendship to a young stranger whose name was Phillip. He was a visitor from England who had come to find his namesake. To their astonishment the name-sake was "a man called Phillip Lamason and I am named after him." The young Phillip's father was Wally Runciman, Phil's Stradishall flying mate and fellow perpetrator of many pranks, including the low-flying attacks on the Bedford Canal. Needless to say his son was directed post haste to Dannevirke. Wally had named his son after Phil at the time he was still missing. In a tragic post-war incident, Wally Runciman met his death in Ireland during a flying display. His family were watching. Phil Runciman and his family now live in New Zealand.

Moving through the decades there was one 'constant' in Phil's daily life. The lifelong love that he and Joan shared for each other remained as undiminished as on their wedding day. That happy occasion on March 29, 1941 at the Gospel Hall, Napier was replicated 50 years later in 1991 with the celebration of their Golden Wedding at the batch in Taupo. And this time there was the added bonus of their grandchildren. Here were a couple who had endured much but still found much to be thankful for.

In December 2007, Phil's faith would have helped him through his last, and one of his hardest, partings. At 88 years of age, his beloved Joan passed away after suffering heart complications. They were close and loving to the end. Dannevirke resident Becky Witika, who had been Joan's personal care provider for 12 months and then continued the role with Phil, pays her own tribute. "Joan was very warm and very gentle, a wonderful woman." And in an example of Joan and Phil's enduring relationship she recalls Phil sitting his wife on his knee with his arms around her. Many years ago Joan had been tested to the limit after receiving the 'official letter' that Phil was 'missing.' and later the final message of 'presumed dead,' – she never wavered. "Phil is okay, I know he will return." Secure in the oasis of her own faith, she was steadfast.

After Joan's death, Becky's association with the family continued. She helped Phil with his cooking and shopping and later with his nursing care. Her husband Stephen was also working on Lamason farm. The

Above: There were always the 'larrikin' moments ...Phil and Joan enjoying a social occasion in Dannevirke in the early 1960's. Below: Phil and Joan on their Golden Wedding Anniversary, Taupo, 1991. (Photographs courtesy Lamason Family Collection)

birth of their son Caleb was a great pleasure for Phil who never lost his enjoyment of children.

Becky mentions Phil's "articulate and witty conversation," his blue eyes and his kindness. With her, Phil shared some of his experiences although he never mentioned Buchenwald. She was with the family when the 2011 Mike Dorsey documentary was first publically screened in Wellington. A bus from Dannevirke was laid on for the occasion and Phil was given a standing ovation.

"With Phil you felt you were in the presence of greatness." Phil would take his coffee in the lounge where he looked across the farm to the belt of trees planted as a reserve. The penetrating blue eyes could still spot a cast sheep or worse, an unwelcome visit from a recalcitrant goat. Becky recollected that after Joan's death, Phil, who had always "believed in looking forward," now found that he was looking back, often asking himself, "what could I have done better?"

Phil Tells His Story

Meanwhile another committed family friend and admirer of Phil had been busy weaving her own vibrant thread into the tapestry of Phil's life. It is time to meet Glenys Scott.

Switch back now to New Year's Eve 1999. The venue was the Lamason's bach in Taupo. On the wall of the lounge hung a picture of a Lancaster. Beneath it two people were seated on two green vinyl chairs. Deep in conversation they are oblivious to the excited group around them.

Glenys Scott writes: "It was the momentous year of 1999, when the world held its breath and wondered what the striking of 12.00 midnight would bring as the new millennium dawned in the 'Land of the Long White Cloud.' I found myself sitting in Phil Lamason's bach at Taupo, New Zealand, waiting up with family and friends for the magic midnight hour, champagne and fireworks at the ready.

"Phil and I were seated upstairs in the busy lounge, set apart on our green vinyl chairs sipping our drinks when I mentioned the picture of the Lancaster on the wall above my head. Phil began chatting about its credentials and how it was the downfall of the German Luftwaffe in World War II and won the war for us. Phil lit up as he was talking and was 'in the moment,' as he described the characteristics, challenges and advantages of the Lancaster. I listened intently and began to ask questions. Phil explained tactics and strategies of 'sorties' long ago and

Phil on his 80th Birthday September, 1998. (Photograph Lamason Family Collection)

of his dangerous encounters with a formidable enemy. I realised very quickly that this man had lived these experiences. He had seen terrible things and as he shared them, it was obvious that these episodes were still very clear in his memory. He proudly revealed that he was a World War II Squadron Leader who had flown in Bomber Command and had had first-hand experience with the Gestapo and SS."

Glenys was captivated. She was moved into another time zone. The location was just outside Paris at Massy-Palaiseau above the railway yards, where Phil was flying an Avro Lancaster early on June 8, 1944. She listened to the story of a sortie that would change his life forever and sat transfixed as Phil described the events that occurred in the air that night some 56 years previously. Feeling honoured to have the story unfold Glenys realised that this narrative had been shared with very few people.

"The series of miraculous events unfolded like a movie before my eyes. I could picture the peril, the danger, but most of all the incredible courage and strength of the man beside me." From that time on the story 'percolated.' Glenys would often be at family occasions where the pair talked and Phil would add to his stories. And then came the break-through.

"It was not until ANZAC Day, 2005, that I felt the courage to phone Phil and ask if I could sit with him and Joan to record his story." She had felt some urgency to capture the information and emphasised the need to write it down. She knew Phil did not attend ANZAC Day ceremonies as he regarded them as something he did not see to 'celebrate' or would ever forget. This was her chance.

"The whisper around town was of a 'great war pilot, war hero, very brave, a flying ace,' but not many knew the real story. Phil was a quiet hero." Phil agreed to have a cup of tea and a chat. Glenys dared not use a video or tape recorder fearing he 'might balk.' She proceeded to write frantically as he talked. "Once Phil began telling a story he was immediately back in the moment, remembering with clarity the details of what had taken place and his part in the events." Three hours passed swiftly. Joan then revealed that in their 65 years of marriage this was the first time she had heard of these stories.

"At this point Phil paused to look away, out of the window and across his beloved farm. He knew that in exposing the experiences that had deliberately been kept secret, those disturbing memories were coming far too close." Too close "to his beloved family and to the home he loved where he was now free and far from 1944."

How significant the moment. Glenys Scott's "frantic writing" had finally captured the story first hand. The groundwork for a future book had been laid at last.

In 2011, beginning to show signs of aging, and feeling the loneliness of life without Joan, Phil was diagnosed with bowel cancer. This upstanding man who, throughout his life had looked the world unflinchingly in the eye, was now confronting his own mortality. Over the ensuing 12 months he gradually weakened and was 'becoming a shadow of his former self,' as Glenys Scott writes in a continuing narrative of events.

"For as long as he was able Phil continued to farm his acres and had much pleasure in watching the improvements on the farm. His rides around the farm in the truck with his son John were important to him and he stayed in touch with stock movements."

An accomplished pianist, high school music department head and teacher, Glenys was thrilled when Phil asked if she would play for him. She would arrive after school and revisit "all the old favourites which Phil greatly enjoyed hearing and singing along to." He never tired of a song and showed real enjoyment as she played.

Always close to the surface of their friendship was the War, and time was slipping away. "Once I had delivered my repertoire for the afternoon I would sit with Phil over a cup of tea and ask him questions to explain in more detail the events he had revealed over the years. I told him I was continuing to write down his story in the hope of putting it together somehow in the future. We had many discussions about his experiences and with each visit I would learn something new."

But whilst maintaining contact and encouraging Phil with his memories, Glenys, with characteristic vigour, was pursuing another course of action. It was time that Phil received some 'formal recognition.' She wrote two letters, one to the New Zealand Governor-General and the other to Her Majesty The Queen.

As the following responses indicate, her efforts were unsuccessful. Government House dated April 12, 2012:

"Dear Ms Scott, I refer to your letter of 31 March to His Excellency the Governor-General, in which you outlined the situation regarding retired Squadron-Leader Phillip Lamason and asked whether consideration could be given in recognition of his World War II exploits. This matter falls under the purview of the Honours Unit within the Department of the Prime Minister and Cabinet, to whom I have referred your letter. They will respond shortly. Yours sincerely, Niels Holm, Official Secretary."

On April 26, 2012, came the official reply from the Executive Council Chambers – the Cabinet Office.

"Dear Ms Scott, Your letter to the Governor-General of 31 March, regarding Squadron-Leader PJ Lamason has been forwarded to this office for response. Thank you for enclosing the copies of the photographs and the documentary on Sqn Ldr Lamason…There is no doubt that Sqn Ldr Lamason's actions were exceptionally brave. As you note, his service and heroism while serving with the RAF were recognised with the award of the DFC and Bar and two Mentions in Despatches.

"However, I understand that it is not possible to retrospectively consider Sqd Ldr Lamason for a New Zealand Royal honour, such as a New Zealand Bravery or Gallantry Award. King George VI directed that no recognition of service or acts of gallantry or bravery performed during World War Two were to be considered after 1949. The Queen has followed her father's wishes in this matter, and we understand that no honours have been conferred to New Zealanders for service during World War Two since that date. Yours sincerely, Michael Webster, Deputy Secretary (Constitutional and Honours)."

The reply from Buckingham Palace dated April 25, 2012, arrived just weeks before Phil's death.

"Dear Miss Scott, The Queen has asked me to thank you for your letter of 31st March, and to say that Her Majesty was very interested to know about Squadron Commander Phillip Lamason, and that he is a family friend who has finally chosen to talk about his wartime service.

"While careful note has been taken of your request for Squadron Commander Lamason to receive an honour, I should explain that this is not a matter in which The Queen would personally intervene. As a constitutional Sovereign, her Majesty acts through her personal representative, the Governor-General, on the advice of her New Zealand Ministers and it is to them that your appeal should be directed.

"I have therefore, been instructed to forward your letter to the Governor-General of New Zealand so that he may be aware of your approach to The Queen and may consider the points you raise.

"Her Majesty would be most grateful if you could kindly convey to Squadron Commander Lamason her good wishes at this time…"

Her Majesty's good wishes were 'conveyed' to Phil on a chilly April night as he was sitting in front of an open fire enjoying his dinner. His health was rapidly declining. Glenys had arrived home from her afternoon visit and was checking the mail. Spotting the Queen's seal on an envelope amongst the letters, and with 'heart thumping,' she carefully opened the official envelope to read Her Majesty's greetings from her Lady-in-Waiting. She quickly returned to Phil's house. "He was still gazing into the fire. I placed the letter on his knee and said "read that." He looked at me with the letter and said: "What have you been up to?"

"Aged 93 years by then and without glasses he lifted it to the light and began to read, commenting on the Queen's words of greeting and remembrance. After finishing he looked up and said: "I told you so, family friend. Good, very good," and smiled. So while she would have wished for a better result, Glenys knew that he was, "just pleased with the fact that the Queen had remembered him."

Phil's mind would have flashed back to an afternoon in 1945. Buchenwald behind him now, he was back in London. Word of his exploits had reached high places. Churchill had sent for him to hear his story of survival. And then, an invitation to Buckingham Palace where he was invited by His Majesty to "…do him a favour." Would Phil, "…just one more time," be prepared to take to the skies in a Stirling that the King would provide and 'buzz' Windsor Castle? Of course. Mission completed and back on terra firma.

The King was delighted, Princess Elizabeth would walk around holding Phil's arm. She would have sensed the feeling of security around him. What an outstanding memory for an RNZAF War veteran now facing death.

There was some poignancy in the timing of this episode as on April 25, the day the Queen's letter was written, an article about Phil had been published in the local newspaper. It was written by Dannevirke reporter Christine McKay, who had been a keen follower of Phil's story and had been given some further personal insights into his time at Buchenwald. By that time he had become more prepared to discuss his experiences although as always, just in snippets. "There was no way out except as smoke through the chimney," he told her. "They tried to break our spirit. We were told to move a pile of stones from one place to another. It was

Phil and Glenys Scott pictured together at the Lamason Rua Roa farm just weeks before Phil's death in 2012. (Photograph courtesy Christine McKay)

demoralising." The "starvation diet of sawdust bread with maggots," is recalled. So too is the story of having seen the Gestapo extermination order and keeping it to himself for 40 years until revealing the information at a 1985 Buchenwald reunion. Phil died only a month after this interview was published.

It is likely that the Cabinet decision declining to recommend that Phil be considered for an official honour would not have concerned a man who had never sought post-war recognition for his wartime deeds. In his last days a characteristic determination to climb the stairs to his bedroom each night was of considerably more importance.

Glenys recognised the letting-go of the long-bottled-up memories as 'a cathartic release.' Phil knew he had a captivated listener who was seriously interested in the facts. "I told him I would travel to Germany one day and see the places he described. Talking allowed him to relax and to reconcile his memories. We did not talk much about the Jews or

213

the specific horrors of their situation, but focussed instead on the strategies and tactics for survival."

True to her word, Glenys, with John and Debbie Lamason have now travelled to Germany and a significant chapter in Phil's life has been rekindled. Glenys has also worked tirelessly to bring his story to the world. These recollections are the fruits of her endeavours. Glenys too was responsible for the involvement of documentary-maker Mike Dorsey in this narrative. The extent of the Scott-Lamason relationship has been profound.

By the end of his life, the numbers of KLB members were diminishing, but not so "Easy" Freeman whose letter in shaky handwriting written on April 3, 2012, would have reached Phil in time. "Been a long time since Buchenwald," he writes. He was "glad the New Zealanders are learning what we old cell mates have known long – Phil Lamason is a tough soldier – one that 168 were proud to serve in 1944." Freeman himself, an agitator to the last, was "still around, kicking down doors and fighting to get my other grandson out of Afghanistan."

It should be mentioned here that Joe Moser, 'Buchenwald Flyboy,' died in 2015 and was given an official send off. Surely one of the last to leave the fraternity forged so many years previously.

In one of his many tributes to his father, John Lamason, the son who had farmed nearby and was with him during the dark days, says the following. "Dad continued to farm with help from myself, still striving for greater efficiencies, not spending on unnecessary things, but accruing capital to help his family and their children." Phil used to say that a man, "should farm with a shovel, hammer and a wheelbarrow. But make sure the wheelbarrow has a steel wheel."

As the final 'bale out' drew near Phil, aged 93 years, found his peace. Visits from his son Robert in Australia and distant grandchildren cheered him in his final days. Daughters Trish and Cherry gave loving 24 hour care and were present at his death.

Phillip John Lamason died peacefully at his home on May 19, 2012.

The tributes flowed. At the funeral service, family, friends, neighbours and RNZAF personnel packed the building "to farewell a man regarded by many as one of New Zealand's greatest heroes of World War II," wrote Christine McKay. While his flying exploits and achievements were honoured, so too were the 'family man,' the father and the grandfather. Phil's youngest daughter Cherry Taylor spoke of the values that had shaped her father, describing him as a "self-made

214

man" with an ethic of hard work and a spirit of independence. "But most importantly, as a father and a grandfather, he excelled," she said.

The grandchildren remembered… Matt Lamason spoke of Phil as a hero because of "the close interest he showed in me," and also of his advice – "to be determined to be someone, make a difference, succeed in your plans and especially to be ambitious in life." He shared too the humorous experiences of working as a youth alongside his grandfather on the farm, like the day Phil "backed himself to 'gun' the Terrano up a very wet hill," only to have it jack knife and slither hazardously back to the bottom of the slope, amidst the cacophony of barking dogs in the precariously lurching trailer behind. Christie David spoke of her memories of her loving and fun-filled grandfather, recalling the drama of his story-telling. She spoke of how in adulthood she came to appreciate Phil as "a living juxtaposition – humble but often arrogant; loving but often harsh; raucous yet introverted; gentle but quick to anger; a quick thinker but impractical at times; prejudiced but open-minded." Karen Aynsley remembered especially her grandfather's love of nature, animals and his farm. She recalled a moment, when, as a child walking with Phil on the farm, how he stopped so they could quietly listen and observe a nesting skylark in the trees by the river. Kyle Lamason remembered a grandfather who was "a great role model and a gentleman," and Sarah Lamason spoke of how Phil "could command a room," and how he taught her to "realise the value of life itself." Vicki Miller described "the hair-raising ute rides around the farm, which gave him (Phil) great entertainment, while scaring the wits out of me," and how her grandfather made her feel "safe and warm, and how everything would be all right." Vicki's husband Scott Miller recounted wartime flying anecdotes which Phil – a "hero in the true sense of the word" – had shared with him. He recalled how "Phil crash-landed a Stirling bomber on an emergency field after returning from a mission, and on being told there would not be another aircraft available for a few days to get them back to home base, he and his entire crew managed to get to London for some unsolicited leave." He also recalled Phil telling him how his "request to be a Spitfire pilot," on arrival at the theatre of War, "earned him a stay in the 'lock-up base' for asking this of his Commanding Officer!" Scott concluded: "I will always have the deepest respect for you and if I could be half the man you were, I would be happy. Now it's time to show those angels how to fly!"

215

Phil Lamason's War Medals. (Photograph : Lamason Family Collection)

Perhaps the most poignant memory was shared by granddaughter Anita Taylor: "I have a memory of when I was about 14 years of age, walking down the farm with Skinny (the grandchildren's affectionate nickname for Phil) and we were discussing something we had heard on the news that morning about a violent robbery. I remember he was walking in front of me and I mumbled something like 'if it happened to me, I'd give them anything they asked for and run.' My normally relaxed, fun-loving grandfather turned on me, face red and fists balled and shouted at me 'you never, ever give in to bullies and evil people – you always stand up to them Anita!' I was shocked at his reaction and the depth of his anger my words had provoked, and ashamed of myself too. I thought about that moment a lot and understood that for him, taking the easy way out was never an option, and cowardice in any form was intolerable and unacceptable. You always do what is right and stand up to tyranny, no matter the cost to yourself. I think that code of honour and heart and courage was at the essence of my grandfather."

Letters read from the families of six of the men whose lives had been saved in Buchenwald by Phil's leadership and bravery contributed to an emotionally-charged service. Members of the Dannevirke RSA formed a guard of honour around the casket during a farewell eulogy, in a 'first' for the club.

And in a farewell gesture, an RNZAF Harvard flew overhead, dipping its wings in a final salute.

Phil Lamason RIP

Pilgrimage: Europe 2014

In 2014 John and Debbie Lamason, accompanied by Glenys Scott, travelled to Europe. Their purpose was to connect with people and places associated with Phil's past after being shot down, and in particular, to visit Buchenwald.

The Lamason story has been remarkable throughout for its twists and turns of fate and the coincidences that have emerged. Small examples in themselves have blended to make the whole compelling experience.

This was the journey, the pilgrimage, which Phil Lamason seemed disinclined to ever want to make.

The following is narrated by Glenys, John and Debbie in their own words. Each one's reaction to the people and the surroundings they encounter in the world they discover is told from the heart.

Background

Glenys: Early in 2013 John, Phil's son, received a phone call from Ngaire Nystrum (nee Hansen), residing in Denmark, who wanted to talk to the family about Phil's time in the Buchenwald Concentration Camp. Ngaire was born in Dannevirke and had lived as a child in Matamau, a small rural settlement close by. Her brother Hoani had worked for Phil as a shepherd on his farm in Dannevirke in the 1960s, doing a lambing beat. She had connected with the French Resistance family of the Kalmansons through Roger Guernon, a journalist in Paris. The Kalmanson family hid Phil and Chappy in their large chateau. Ngaire had also linked up with Francois Ydier, a French pilot who was writing a book about the history of the Plaisir bombing raid in which Phil was shot down on June 8, 1944. Ngaire persistently rang three times before the family realised the significance of the connection with their family story. So plans were made to travel to Europe in September 2014, to meet Ngaire and visit the Buchenwald Concentration Camp. They also organised to meet Francois Ydier and Denise Kalmanson in Paris. Denise is elderly now but she has heard of John and would really like to meet him.

Ngaire's insistence encouraged John to make the journey to meet Denise and François in Paris. She would drive down from Denmark to meet them in Germany at Buchenwald which she was very familiar with, having visited the Camp previously, seeking out the Lamason story.

Meeting Denise, Jean Nicolas and Antoine in Paris, September 2014

Glenys: Seventy years after the dark days of WWII, the 'Three Musketeers' (Phil's son John, his wife Debbie and Glenys), embark on the long distance, 28 hour journey from New Zealand to Paris, France.

There were two special meetings set up in Paris. The first being with Denise Kalmanson, the lady who with her family, helped Chappy and Phil shelter from the Nazis in their home near Plaisir, in occupied France, July, 1944. The second, to meet a man who lived in the town near to where Phil's plane was shot down, and who has a very special interest in this event.

Paris, September 15, 2014

Glenys: After a day of sightseeing and orientation we travelled to Rue de Bievre, near the famous Notre Dame Cathedral. The French street is in the older part of Paris and is full of character buildings and w ell-worn paths. Right beside the River Seine the taxi turns into a narrow, cobbled street. With cameras ready and high anticipation the apartment door buzzer is rung, to hear a beautiful French accent greet the small group huddled in the doorway and give instructions of how to enter the building. A door automatically opens and entrance is through a small recessed area where another door opens to let the group through into a dark lobby, locking behind them. This intricate system allows high security for the apartments all connected to one entranceway.

Called up the dark wooden staircase which consists of aged twists and turns finally rising two storeys to Denise's door, John, Debbie and Glenys gingerly make their way up the creaky stairs. There she is! Denise Diatkine (nee Kalmanson). Barely five foot in height, sprightly at 91 years of age, a lovely smile and eagerly looking at John as he approaches her. She offers her hand and John leans forward and kisses it and then warmly embraces Denise as the 70-year circle is complete. Hugs and 'bonjours' are exchanged with Denise and nephew Antoine, her sister Colette's son, as the welcoming party.

John: I felt like a child holding a wrapped present not knowing what was inside but excited all the same. Inside a dimly lit large circular staircase wound up two floors. The treads were wooden and worn unevenly, worn with age. The wall was stone and undecorated. Any expectation of grandiose was certainly not on my mind. The hand extended to me with the same care and consideration to that extended to my father 70 years ago, was so amazing, words were meaningless. It was the warmth and welcome that spoke the loudest. As I regained my composure the War story came alive through this precious, little lady. Her Jewish family were all heroes. The tensions and risks they took have enabled me to live and give thanks to Providence. Then the door opened to a most gracious and adorned room.

Debbie: As we come to the door and with much excitement, Glenys announces that this is the place, camera in hand waiting to film the special moment. Finally, as we approach Denise's door she shyly greets us on the doorstep. When she looked at John she announces in her gentle French accent, 'You are so like Phil Lamason!' The greeting is spontaneous and we finally hug each other in a special moment.

We walk into a lovely warm coloured room filled with an extensive bookcase and a beautiful rich coloured old tapestry that fills an entire wall. You can feel the love, intelligence and integrity of the people before us. It felt an unreal space. We were in history. Soon we are joined by Denise's son, Jean-Nicolas, a concert pianist who resides with his wife Artemis in Paris nearby. We did not know he existed, and he was quite overwhelmed by what he was experiencing and learning of his mother's early life as a Resistance participant.

Glenys: Ushered into a small hallway which leads into a 300-year old room laden with books roof to floor, we get a sense of timelessness and history. This room is rich with culture, music and art and becomes the setting for long overdue conversations. A huge tapestry hovers above the large cream sofa where John, Denise and Antoine share photographs of their lives past and present, putting a face to Phil in the 1940s. The beamed ceiling and library wall sets a classic scene as champagne is poured and we salute Phil on what would have been his 96th birthday. The afternoon is timeless with much chatter, recollecting and storytelling of lives well lived.

A small framed photograph of Jean-Nicolas as a boy sits prominently on the large bookcase, looking out at the gathering scene. Writings of Denise's husband, Renee Diatkine, (1918-1997) a famed French psychiatrist and psychoanalyst, grace the shelves and she speaks dearly

219

The 70 year circle is complete. Denise Diatkine, 91 years of age, meets with John, son of Phil Lamason, at her home in Paris in 2014. Denise and her sister Colette helped Phil and his navigator Ken Chapman evade capture into the hands of the Nazis by harbouring them at their Kalmanson family chateau, Chevreuse, in June/July,1944. (Photograph courtesy of Glenys Scott)

of his work and writings on childhood emotional development, still recognised to this day.

John: With Antoine interpreting for his Aunt, Denise and I shared photographs of Phil's farm and the Dannevirke District. We talked of the days in her house and she found it difficult to remember exactly what happened but said it was very exciting. There were other airmen passing through the home so the many faces were confusing but she does remember Phil and Chappy's faces with fondness. It was difficult to converse but the fellowship was warm and genuine.

Debbie: I was amazed by Jean-Nicolas because he was very touched by all that he was witnessing and could not believe we would travel so far to visit and reconnect with their family. He knew very little about the story and was overwhelmed at what had gone on in the family history of the War. Jean-Nicolas is a concert pianist who specialises in Beethoven and Chopin. He offers to give us a private recital in his home in a few days' time. Glenys was continually filming and taking pictures of the episode, recording the interactions as we were deep in conversation.

Glenys: Time goes by quickly as questions fly from one to the other, Jean-Nicolas and Antoine interpreting for all, piecing together the last 70 years since the days of hiding. A special atmosphere is in the room and the sense of time and place is impressed on all as they recount the days.

Denise is unsure of what this visit will evoke from those long ago days but is soon comfortably conversing and relating events as she can remember them, the sense of being a part of history is evident on the faces. Denise finds it hard to recall the days but clearly remembers it was a very exciting time for her and her sister Colette and brother Daniel, who delighted in the company of the Allies and being part of the intrigue of helping with the Resistance. She says she had better English in those days as her sister and herself had gone to an English boarding school and were much more able to converse with the secret visitors to their house. Denise expresses sadness at not having met up with Phil since the War and meeting his beloved Joan. She is very excited to make the connection with Phil's family, mentioning the likeness of John to his Father.

Jean-Nicolas is quite overwhelmed as he has not really heard his mother's story before. Antoine is quietly delighted about the link with his mother, who died years ago, and that she was part of the subversion by the brave Resistance fighters. He was proud for his mother and her role in history.

Finally the spell is broken and enough is said. After grateful farewells the group disperses. The meeting has had an emotional impact on us all and we leave as Denise goes off to the gym!

She had to keep her routine workout and with her daily stairs has kept herself very fit. A lunch date before our departure in two weeks is booked in. Denise waves to us cheekily out of her kitchen window high above the street and with a fine 'adieu' she is gone. We go off to dinner savouring the amazing time we have had, satisfied the connection has been made and a new friendship begun.

Francois Ydier pictured as a small child beside the wrecked tail section of Lancaster DS822 from No 514 Squadron, RAF Waterbeach. This aircraft, in a forest near Plaisir, was one of the 19 bombers shot down by enemy fire during the fateful raid on the railway-yard at Massy-Palaiseau on June 8, 1944. F/S John Clarke from this Lancaster crew ended up in Buchenwald Camp under the command of Phil Lamason. (Photograph courtesy of Francois Ydier)

Meeting Francois Ydier in Plaisir, September 16, 2014

Glenys: The next morning we meet Francois Ydier, the French former test pilot from Plaisir who, as a small child with his father, visited the site of a crashed Lancaster bomber in a forest near his town.

This wartime moment had left an impression on Francois and later, as a youth, motivated him to train for a career in flying. He worked for many years in the French aerospace industry including the Concorde, and then worked in the marine and oil industries. In retirement he embarked on a mission to find out about the men who crashed in their planes on the night of June 8, 1944, near Plaisir town, when the nearby railway yards were attacked by the Allied bombers.

He has since compiled an account of the crash sites and published a book, 'The Boy and The Bomber,[1]' detailing the profound effects the event had on his community.

Francois has painstakingly put together the individual stories of the many airmen and those on the ground who watched the fiery ordeal in the sky that night. This included local members of the famous Comet

---

[1] *The Boy and the Bomber, Francois Ydier, Mention the War Ltd., 2016.*

Line, who tried to help the survivors evade the clutches of the Nazi regime. All too often those same French citizens paid for their bravery with their lives.

A black Jaguar car rolls up to the Fertel Etoile Hotel, near the Arc de Triumph, close to where Phil was betrayed on the Champs Ellysée. Francois Ydier jumps out with an energetic step and is very excited to meet us. He is a passionate follower of War events. He has compiled his own account of the history of his experiences of 1944 in Plaisir. He promptly dumps a large tome of papers at my feet which he declares proudly as his 'Book.' "English version is coming soon!" he declares as we zoom off into French traffic and wend our way out of Paris via wide motorways familiar to any large city. Presently we arrive at a magnificent forest beside a French country town – Plaisir. The paved roadway through the woods indicates wealth and heritage. A uniformed soldier steps out of a sentry box and after a short exchange with Francois, lifts the barrier arm for us to pass through. A short drive in well-tended woodland turns towards a huge boating lake which stretches for a kilometre to the right with small row boats tied along a colourful pier. A large grassed promenade of about 10 acres surround a large water fountain with rearing chariot horses with ancient horsemen on their back, rising up out of the tranquil waters in warrior pose. This statue was of the Greek God Apollo, heralded as God of Music, Art, Poetry, Oracles, Archery, Plague (no less!), Medicine, Sun, Light and Knowledge. He is rising from the waters on a horse at sunrise, with Tritons appearing at his side in an east-west orientation.

Looking up to the left our breaths are taken away by huge fountains, vast columns of busts and statues leading 500 metres up a sweeping hill to the majestic Versailles Palace. Classical music is piped around the gardens via Bose Stereo with the quality of a live orchestra.

People wander around the vast grounds marvelling at the grand setting they are in – enjoying the ambience of the home of the great King, Louis the XIV, Sun King of France, and his successors Louis XV and Louis XVI. This Palace, in 1682, became the royal court and seat of the French political power for over a hundred years.

John: Francois was a sprightly, enthusiastic aviator who impressed me with his passion for Dad's story and desire to honour him in his book. He talked fervently, drawing deeply on his cigarettes, reminiscing about his boyhood accounts of the crashed planes. His knowledge of the War and aviation history was extensive with many anecdotes related

223

Above: John Lamason and Francois Ydier, 2014. (Photograph courtesy of Glenys Scott). Below left: The Kalmanson family chateau in Chevreuse where Phil and Chappy were sheltered during their evasion. (Photograph courtesy Kalmanson family). Below right and bottom: The house and news agency shop of Maurice Cherbonnier at Chervreuse, with the accompanying commemorative plaque, 2014. (Photographs courtesy of Glenys Scott)

with excitement. He dubbed us the 'Three Musketeers' there and then and kept up a barrage of stories linking Phil with events.

Debbie: After many emails to Francois, it was wonderful to at last meet this passionate man who honoured those who served in the War. He saw them as saving France from becoming Germany. I was delighted when he said he would take us to Versailles which was a special request on our way to Plaisir. The gardens were beyond my expectations, full of symmetrical beauty, with the extravagance of Kings. I wanted to stay and enjoy the glory of it all. I love gardens!

Glenys: With only an hour to our next appointment, we make our way up to the Palace, delighting in the ornate 'jardins' and beauty of order before us. The grandeur was not lost on us with the whole expansive gardens and lake capturing our imaginations. Kings think big! The boating lake, in the shape of a crucifix, extends for a kilometre south and is said to be seen from outer space. It created an aquifer for the parched land of the district and fully grown trees were brought to the Palace and planted entire to make the vast wooded gardens. The movie, 'A Little Chaos' starring Kate Winslet delightfully depicts the building of the 'Water Jardin' for King Louis XIV in 1682 by Andre Le Notre.

A sumptuous lunch in the Palace garden 'La Flotilles Café' is the sustenance needed to continue our journey to Francois's nearby town of Plaisir.

Driving over bridges near the town, Francois points out the railway tracks which were the target of Phil's night mission in 1944. We drive over a bridge still intact from the War. It is precariously positioned over the railway tracks targeted by Phil for demolition to frustrate Nazi transport movements.

We enter a town called Chevreuse and visit the railway station. This was the last station that Phil left as he travelled back to Paris for his secret rendezvous with the underground to escape to Britain. Phil thought it was a simple operation to get him back across Belgium and out to England to freedom. Little did he know he was on a one way trip to hell where fate and providence were to dictate his future for the next two months!

Soon we are winding around narrow streets and through ploughed countryside, a small open piece of land is the site where the Kalmanson home used to be but has been demolished since, sadly. Close by we arrive at a three storey building where Maurice Cherbonnier had his news agency.

He and his wife hid hundreds of airmen upstairs in their small house while they transferred through to the Comet Line. They were instrumental in helping many men to safety, being duly honoured with a medal for their efforts after the War.

Apparently the men made a lot of noise and needed to be hushed often. The outside toilet also needed caution to negotiate so that they were not discovered.

Into the car again we drive our way up to an old churchyard. The Church of Jouars-Ponchartrain is classic Renaissance, formerly occupied by Monks who farmed the land around it. Waiting by a small grave in the middle of the old graveyard stands a small gathering of officials from the local Council to give tribute to a brave airman. This is where Robbie Aitken is buried, Phil's mid-upper gunner killed as he jumped too late from the burning aircraft after firing late to help his crew escape. He is buried where he was found, a Scotsman far from home yet at rest in this beautiful French countryside. Phil named his second son after his dear friend. Robbie Lamason is a deep sea fisherman currently living in Cairns, Australia. The town honoured 'Robbie' Robertson Roy Aitken, just 22 years, by naming a road after him: 'Chemin de l'Aviateur Aitken.'

John & Debbie: A real sense of privilege for being there was our main impression of this place. The care of the townspeople to tend the grave sites of the fallen was very evident in their appreciation of what the Allies secured for the French.

Glenys: After paying our respects, our entourage drive into Plaisir town and park in front of the idyllic Town Hall. With its quaint turrets, dormer windows and classic French architecture, it is an excellent example of the Baroque style of the 17th Century.

We are immediately drawn to the beauty of the building and are impressed that this is where we are being hosted by the local Mayor and dignitaries.

After gathering on the promenade, a group of 20 people walk in procession to the town cemetery nearby. A strong Frenchman leads the way carrying in his arms a large wreath of flowers in the French colours of red, white and blue.

We solemnly walk along the path to Tommy Dunk's gravesite in the hot, 34 degree, afternoon sunshine, thinking of the night of the June 8, 1944. The rear gunner was from Rhodesia and met his fate in the back

226

:Above: Francois Ydier, Debbie Lamason, John Lamason and Roger Guernon beside the grave of Phil Lamason's mid-upper gunner, Robbie Aitken, in the churchyard at Jouars-Ponchartrain, 2014. Left: The local French community acknowledged the supreme sacrifice made by Robbie Aitken by naming the road adjacent to this cemetery to "honour him and other Allied servicemen who fell on French soil." (Photographs courtesy of Glenys Scott and Francois Ydier)

We solemnly walk along the path to Tommy Dunk's gravesite in the hot, 34-degree, afternoon sunshine, thinking of the night of the June 8, 1944. The rear gunner was from Rhodesia

The commemorative medallion and book presented to John Lamason by the Mayor of Plaisir in the official civic reception at the Plaisir Town Hall, September 16, 2014. (Photograph courtesy Glenys Scott)

of the Lancaster staring into the fire from the German Messerschmitt. A big game hunter, Tommy had flown with Phil on many missions and was a valued crew member and friend. With words of consolation and affectionate reflection the group says a prayer, lays the flowers and returns to the Town Hall for refreshments and for a formal ceremony where we presented a letter from the Mayor in Dannevirke, Mr Roly Ellis, acknowledging the link between our towns through Phil.

The afternoon was finally celebrated with 'The Kiwis' singing the New Zealand National Anthem, with the Maori verse being most popular in the rendition. The Mayor, Mrs Josephine Kollmannsberger, graciously handed John a gift which contained a book of Plaisir town history and a boxed medal honouring Phil for his bravery in the battle over their town. Many French saw the Allies as being the only help to liberate them from the Nazi regime which had divided their country into the Occupied and Vichy zones. The victory by the Allies was seen as a victory for France and for freedom.

John: I was humbled to think how the town's executive honoured us and, although the speeches were in French, one was overawed by the reception and respect they gave us in connection with Dad. Mayor Kollmannsberger was gracious in her words and said it was important that we remember what these men did for their country.

Glenys: We travel back into Paris buzzing with impressions of the wonderful day. We are hosted on our last night in Paris by Jean-Nicolas and his wife Artemis, both piano teachers and virtuosos in their own right. Their home has three grand pianos! Jean-Nicolas proceeds to play my favourite piece: Beethoven's Sonata No:13 and we toast our new friendship with more champagne and fellowship. He is giving a special concert soon featuring music by Chopin and Beethoven, so is practising hard for his big night on stage in Paris.

And so to Germany…September 19, 2014

Glenys: A swift taxi ride takes us to the Gare de l'Est, (East Gate) railway station, in the 10th Arrondissement, Paris. Phil also exited the city this way but in very different circumstances! A bullet train awaits to travel into Germany. Capable of 330km/hr our pilgrimage to Buchenwald is rapidly taking us into the heart of the country, the site of Phil's Death Camp experience 70 years previously. It must have felt a very long way from home at the time, as it does to us now.

Stuttgart:

Before we go to Weimar, we stop off at Stuttgart to stay with Glenys's exchange student from 2008, Steffi Schultz. Her father, Christian, is a fabric merchant who imports cloth from all over the world. Their clothing business has been in the family for two generations. The family treated us very warmly and provided great hospitality for our short stay.

John: Upon learning of our journey to Buchenwald, Christian commented that he was embarrassed by what took place in his country in World War II, as were most Germans concerning the Nazi regime. He said it was a dark period in their country's history which should never happen again.

Glenys: Steffi gave us a tour of her ancient city and was then off to the Oktoberfest Beer Festival in Munich. Remembering Phil and his five day journey standing in a cramped, claustrophobic cattle cart, we stand for the last two hours of our trip into Weimar city, the home of Goethe,

John and Debbie Lamason with Ngaire Nystrum in Weimar, Germany, 2014. Below: The end of the railway line at Buchenwald 2014. The 'Blood Way' is where thousands of desperate prisoners were herded during the years of WWII. (Photographs courtesy Glenys Scott)

231

Hayden and Schiller. Bach played music here and Liszt directed; Von Webber composed, adding to its rich cultural history.

Glancing out the window it was possible to see old railway tracks which may have been used in the 1940s. What took Phil five days to achieve was a five hour trip for us. Tired and appreciative of modern transport, we settled into our lush 4½ star accommodation at the Grand Hotel Russischer Hof.

We meet up with Ngaire Nystrum, the friend of the Lamason family who has linked them together with the Kalmansons and the French pilot, Francois. She has driven down from Graasten, Denmark which is close to the German border, and is taking us to Buchenwald to guide us around the site. She recalled how her brother Hoani had thoroughly enjoyed Phil's companionship when he worked on the Lamason farm.

Weimar, Germany, September 20, 2014

Glenys: Weimar township is a quaint collection of convenience stores, statues of famous sons and cafés for miles. They celebrate their history of high cultural achievement yet there is the shadow of the dark days of WWII – the lowest point being in the form of Buchenwald Concentration Camp, just eight kilometres away in the Ettersburg hills. There is a statue commemorating Goethe and Liszt, and the Elephant Hotel where Adolf Hitler would stay.

Buchenwald, Weimar, Germany, September 21, 2014

Glenys: On waking, it was but a few seconds to realise we were going to be visiting the place which was the reason we were on this side of the world. Feeling unwell, I pushed myself to get ready for the day which was to help us understand and unpack the past around Phil. Quietness prevails as we travel by car on our short trip to Buchenwald.

We travel with high expectation up the hill to the memorial site of the Buchenwald Camp. We come across the Blood Road (Caracho Way) where thousands of desperate prisoners were herded from train carriages to walk the last kilometre to their fate. Signs of rotten sleepers and old railway tracks litter the brick landing where the trains left the bewildered, dishevelled passengers at the mercy of the guards and dogs as they disembarked their cramped, stinking carriages.

232

Above: The corroding railway lines at Buchenwald Camp, 2014. Below: Buchenwald Tower and main gate, 2014. (Photographs courtesy Glenys Scott)

233

Above: Almost placid in its innocence, the freshly painted crematorium at Buchenwald, 2014. Below: A small set of wooden steps sat in the corner, the obvious last step those poor souls took on earth. Buchenwald, 2014. (Photographs courtesy Glenys Scott)

Above: The ovens in the Buchenwald crematorium, 2014. Below: Guard tower and remnants of an old electrified boundary fence, Buchenwald, 2014. (Photographs courtesy Glenys Scott)

US President Barak Obama, German Chancellor Angela Merkel and Buchenwald survivor and writer Elie Wiesel, during their visit to Buchenwald in 2009.

The Buchenwald visitors' centre is a well laid out area using the Gestapo accommodation alongside to create an impressive sweeping driveway, a stark contrast to the pitiful conditions less than 20 metres away through the barbed wire fence.

Approaching the Guard Tower on a calm autumn morning it was difficult to imagine the horror experienced once through the gates leading under the Observation Block which greeted the captives. To the left of the gates was a door with a well-worn stoop. The windows of the building had black metal boxes over them with air holes allowing no view out and little light in. This was the notorious interrogation building where many prisoners were beaten and incarcerated for months on end in a space the size of a small cell, just 2x3 metres wide, with a bed and bucket.

There were 30 of these small cells in the Block and evidence of clubs and instruments of torture present. A famous prisoner kept in the Gate House cells was Leon Blum, a prominent Jew who had been a former Prime Minister of France.

236

Paul Schneider was a Pastor of a Confessional Church. His friend Reverend Martin Niemoller, who was cofounder of his Church, sums up the plight they faced as political prisoners: "First they came for the Communists, but I was not a Communist, so I didn't speak up. Then they came for the trade unionists, but I was not a trade unionist, so I didn't speak up. Then they came for the Jews, but I was not a Jew, so I didn't speak up. Then they came for me and there was no one left to speak for me."

Walking through the gates as a free person where many others had been forced and degraded was a surreal moment. Before us was a vast, barren wasteland of approximately 20 acres. This was where the barracks were situated which housed the desperate and dying horde of over 40,000 people. Strewn with stones, debris and bits of broken brick, the ground is testament that something monstrous has occurred on this seemingly cursed land where nothing dares to grow. New life is beyond what this earth has endured and as the cool, autumn breeze blows across the expanse, a cold shiver goes right through me as I look out to the far trees on the boundary to 'Little Camp.'

To my right stands the ominous crematorium, freshly painted and almost plausible in its innocence as it stands boldly as a main structure to survive the years. The large chimney stack now clear above the skies, the last belch of smoke long since risen full of souls to the heavens. Entering this building was strange as there was no main door or obvious entry considering the numbers of people who had entered there.

A small door led us into an examination room which had grating like sheep battens on the floor of a woolshed. A scale for measuring height was up against the sky blue wall processing a line of prisoners through 'health checks.' Meanwhile a Nazi soldier would stand in a small cupboard behind the scale and shoot the unsuspecting person through the back of the head. Then I understood the need for the grating which was to catch the blood as the Kapos would load the bodies into a large metal hod, wheeling them away to be burned.

Below this sinister room was a much darker chamber. Walking down the concrete stairs one was aware of the only way out being as you came in. Phil had described this room to me in detail, noting the meat hooks gauged about half a metre apart along the white washed wall. A chill ran right through me. A small set of wooden steps sat in the corner, the obvious last step those poor souls took on earth. The black drain pipes were evil looking as they snaked across the ceiling from the mortuary above.

This is where Phil was sent to take a message to a Kapo one day, and found men hanging by piano wires, two at a time, garrotted around the neck till dead. This execution took about seven minutes to achieve unless the victim kicked hard enough to force the wire through their windpipe and shorten their struggle. Phil was furious at this method and voiced his disgust, shouting at the men involved. He said they were better to shoot the poor beggars than allow this slow suffering and called them inhumane, merciless and despicable. Many were tortured this way then placed in a lift which raised them up to the ovens above to be consumed by the fires.

These ovens were working 24 hours a day, every day, according to Phil, with pungent smoke belching humanity out over the camp with a constant sickening stench. He likened the smell to badly burnt bacon. The local town of Weimar must have smelt this in the air when the wind so directed it towards the culpable 'civilisation' nearby.

Needing air and some semblance of humanity, I made my way down the hill to the Gallery where prisoner art works were kept from the years of captivity, 1938-1945. Images of human suffering and desperation stand out from the walls of exhibits. Pencil drawings, paintings and clay sculptures depict daily scenes from the camp of emaciated skeletons and gaunt faces. Next door is the museum full of photos, machinery, papers… (The Germans were fastidious with lists and numbers, many of these very records incriminating them later with war crimes).

Spoons, sketches, handmade chess sets, musical instruments, buttons, metal plates, cups, clothing and hauntingly, the shoes of little children, litter the displays of a past generation gathered here as an eclectic humanity of nations.

Air – I needed air after looking into so many doomed faces gazing out at me. A time when the world went mad.

I found a roadway near the electric fence on the boundary and followed it down beside thick bush. A guard tower loomed every 50 metres – security was tight in 1944 so there was no way out through these high powerful electric fences!

Good humouredly, Phil had taunted the Russians to have a go at breaking through the fence in large numbers stating that he would be right behind them!

238

Beside these towers were dug out bomb shelters. In case of attack the guards could scurry into these for protection. Still functional, they were well made and had stood the test of time. This was one very secure perimeter and with guards and loaded weapons at the ready, the prisoners would have had no show at penetrating it.

Little Camp:

Glenys: Time for Phil's 'Little Camp,' where his group spent their first weeks, mostly out of doors. This Camp was down the bottom of the large field, directly opposite the Gate Tower but far enough away with the barracks in between to keep them out of sight. John is standing there waiting in deep thought as I approach.

Some 5000 prisoners were kept in this area of cramped conditions with a horde of gypsy children (Roma) who ran stealing and pilfering all they could. The first thing I noticed were the large latrine trenches and drains still visible near the entrance to the precinct. It was unbelievable that these few ditches were enough to toilet 5000 people! Phil said the smell was putrid and always pervading the air. Having no shoes, the men walked constantly through mud and on stony ground, grids of small ridges of rocks protruding and hurting their feet, making movement slow and painful. The ground was striated with rocks. I lay down on this ground from a promise I had made to Phil and felt how the stones dug into your thigh and hip making sleep difficult. Knowing he had slept like this for three weeks out in the open I appreciated the discomfort he and his men had faced. A skinny body would make it even more unpleasant and the chance shelter in a barracks with wooden boards would have been a welcome reprieve.

Baled up in wire crates at the bush edge were remnants of human existence. Pieces of leather, broken crockery, bricks, buttons, metal and stones were relics from this hard Camp where utensils were difficult to come by and treasured if owned to feed one self. A spoon was a luxury.

The Little Camp Memorial

Glenys: The Little Camp Memorial is testament to the special role this small area played in isolating and breaking prisoners' spirits with its Spartan environment.

U.S. President, Barak Obama visited this site in 2009 with the Chancellor of Germany, Angela Merkel and Eli Wiesel, a former prisoner who remarkably survived numerous near death moments in the

In memory of the Allied Airmen of American, British,
Canadian, Australian, New Zealand,
and Jamaican nationalities, incarcerated here
from August 20 to November 28, 1944.

78286 Lt. Levitt C. Beck, Jr. USAAF
and 78383 F/O Philip Hemmens RAF
did not survive the horrors of Buchenwald.

Lest We Forget

k·l·B cluB

Above: The Little Camp memorial plaque to the 168 Allied Airmen of Buchenwald. Below: The Goethe Oak stump with stones of remembrance, Buchenwald, 2014. (Photographs courtesy Glenys Scott)

240

Camp. Tributes are written on marble slabs, a tree grows out of a cage representing the captive's ability to break free of the oppressive enemy. Looking back at the foreboding Gate House, the desolate landscape feels as if a large monster has devoured human beings in a monstrous rampage leaving a barren wasteland of rubble.

Solemnly we pay our respects to the plaque honouring the 168 Allied airmen and remember Phil and his loyal mates who were kept captive here some 70 years ago. We gather back at the main gate and a cold wind reminds us of the same season Phil was in Buchenwald; we pull our coats closer around us, shivering more from the bleak atmosphere on the Ettersburg than from the actual cold. This infamous place has revealed enough to us of the conditions Phil was subjected to in 1944, against his will... and forced to survive to ensure his life continued, and made it back to his beloved family far away. The odds of this happening must have been doubtful for most of the time; an indomitable determination to stay alive was essential.

John: The mixture of disbelief and amazement that human beings would construct such a place and that one could survive such atrocious conditions. This was a feat of mental and physical endurance which was nothing short of a miracle. The bleak, inhumane atmosphere still prevailed on the landscape some 70 years later. With no topsoil on the land it was very like the surface of the moon. For young Prisoners of War what would it have been like to wake in the morning and pinch oneself and ask, 'Is this real?' And 'yes,' this is real because of the hunger pangs and cold. Only the young could really survive and only then with great determination to do so. The discipline to keep your mind positive and perform routine habits as in even marching to the latrines, were ways of keeping sane. To sing songs and make merriment amidst this dire situation was testament to the spirit of the men. The handcart was a vivid symbol of the tortuous debilitating futility that pervades the place.

Debbie: I was particularly moved to tears at the Prison Gallery where I found the replicas in pottery of the real shoes of the prisoners. I cried thinking at the sheer loss of humanity that had occurred in the camp. It shocked me and left a long and lasting impression on me.

The pictures of the roll calls or Appells showed people perished at most of these daily gatherings. Death and brutality were obviously an everyday occurrence.

241

Walking past the derelict dog kennels it is still evident that the threat of savage attack was ever present. Alsatian dogs were allowed to rip people apart on order and posed a constant terror.

The Goethe Oak stump is still seen, laden with stones of remembrance and signalling the fall of the Third Reich. Bombed in the attack on the Gustloff Armament Works, the oak tree is a gnarled relic, used to celebrate the downfall of the Nazi regime in totality.

Glenys: As we drive away from the camp I feel privileged to be a free person and live in a democratic country. The mist is coming in for the evening, enveloping the slopes of the mountain, clouding out the memories of our witness. The two Allied airmen who did not leave the camp are in our thoughts. Hemmens and Beck both perished from the poor camp conditions they were exposed to. Hemmens had struggled from the time he arrived, with a badly broken arm which weakened his chances to withstand the harsh conditions. Beck died of dysentery before he could be transferred out of the camp.

We visit the huge Buchenwald Bell Tower memorial as we leave town and are dwarfed by the liberation statue celebrating the freeing of the camp at 3:15pm, on April 11, 1945, by U.S. General George Paton.

We are glad to leave this grim, grief filled place to the birds, realising how blessed we are to live in a free land, still disbelieving this could happen in a civilised country.

After a whirlwind trip of music and culture through Czechoslovakia, Austria, and Italy, we arrive back in Southern France and make our way back to Paris for a final week of farewells.

Farewells

Glenys: Finally on October 7, we travel to Denise's home in Notre Dame, excited to meet our special friends again and share our findings at Buchenwald. Just down the Rue, 50 metres, is the former handsome home of President Pompidou. I wonder if he realised that he had lived so near a Resistance fighter!

Joining our group is Cousin Lawrence, who is Daniel's daughter, Denise's niece. She is a mother and author in her own right, who would like to write her family's story one day. A sumptuous luncheon is shared with crisp napkins and best silver. Beef heart tomatoes drizzled in olive oil followed by scallops in parsley sauce with jasmine rice.

Above: Pictured together in Paris, Jean Nicolas (son of Colette Kalmanson), Debbie Lamason, Denise Diatkine, John Lamason and Antione Poliet. (Photograph courtesy Glenys Scott). Below: Colette and Denise Kalmanson with Ken Chapman (centre) and Phil Lamason (right) pictured while these two young Allied Airmen were supported by this family during their evasion in 1944. (Photograph courtesy of the Kalmanson family)

243

John savoured the special cheese and of course the compulsory champagne to wash it down. It is a timeless afternoon of further piecing the story together, creating a special bond between us all and building a solid friendship for the future. All too soon the magic spell is broken and we bid farewell with promises of future visits and continued contact. The group disperses with 'adieus' aplenty after photos have recorded the memorable meeting.

John: In a far more relaxed atmosphere, we treasure the time relating Dad's escapades after the War and what he achieved in his life. Connecting with the wider part of the family was an added bonus.

The fact they embraced us has created a firm friendship and we can leave knowing we have finally connected the story full circle.

Glenys: Satisfied, we leave reluctantly, with Jean-Nicolas escorting us through the streets to a waiting taxi. Our journey to the opposite end of Paris to our Hotel awaits as we prepare for our final farewells.

Across town another home is opened to us as we join in a final meal with Francois and friends Geraldine Cerf, whose mother was Ann Marie de Dudzeele, who organised transfers for the Resistance. Her grandmother was the Countess of Montenegro, the quality of her character shining through. Geraldine had just lost her beloved husband only two months previously.

Also present is Francis Cuillerier, a man who was a child when Phil stayed hidden at his house. As a boy he played soccer and chess with Phil. Francis fondly remembered his time with Phil who clearly impressed him as a young man.

Josselyn Lejeune Pichon, whose father went into Buchenwald and never came out, is there too. She especially wanted to join our group for closure and the comfort of being with people related to her father's fateful destination. She was engrossed in the conversations of the night, taking in every word, gleaning insight and savouring the fellowship.

We luxuriated in the beautiful décor and ambience of the host, where history is recounted and we dine together in the vibrant yellow and white kitchen. A rich boeuf bourguignon has been prepared for us to eat and we taste it with relish. Kinship comes to mind as we are united by the fateful events 70 years earlier. We are all drawn together in a story of survival and succession, in the thriving generations now living free lives across a very changed world since 1944. Again we embrace and fond

During a trip as part of the launch of his book, The Boy and the Bomber, Francois Ydier visited John and Debbie Lamason on their farm near Dannevirke, NZ. Pictured together in February 2017, as members of Francois's "New Zealand Lancaster Family," are (left to right): Francoise Ydier, Glenys Scott, Francois Ydier, Mike Harold, Debbie Lamason, Ngaire Nystrum and John Lamason. Photo courtesy of Christine MacKay.

farewells are given with warm hugs of new friendship. Promises are made of returns and contact to be kept until we meet again.

John: The wine flowed freely complimenting a wonderful meal and topping off an amazingly rich, historical adventure. We had a toast for absent friends and then to much hilarity and laughter, Glenys played the ukulele and sang a song she had written, celebrating our story.

Debbie: A great celebration of fine food and fine people made our long trip worthwhile. As we savoured our last moments of time, our statuesque host, Geraldine, graciously served us and interpreted the vibrant conversation around the table.

Above: Geraldine Cerf whose mother, Ann Marie de Dudzeele organised transfers for the Resistance including helping with the movement of Phil Lamason and Ken Chapman in 1944. Below: Josselyn Lejeune Pichon, Glenys Scott and Francis Cuillerier together in Paris 2014. (Photograph courtesy Glenys Scott)

A Final Reflection

Glenys: And so, we have completed our pilgrimage to the place which played host to one of the worst periods of human history. That Phil had 'kept his head' when in a place where the hordes of hell were pounding all over it, is astounding. At just 25 years of age he marshalled his men together to survive, by holding his nerve and establishing his presence as leader. Like a courageous rugby captain of the 1st XV, he used his influence and physical stature to lead his men to 'not step back,' and battle through the odds to return home safe and sound. He was the man for the hour, decisive in his decision making and cool under pressure.

Phil struggled with his faith throughout his long life. From contradictory hardness from his father, to the inhumanity of war, then finally to the peace of green pastures and his beloved family.

Phil considered it all. He acknowledged that he was kept safe in the War – except for one bullet that nicked him in the neck, he was physically unscathed by combat. Asked if he ever prayed while flying, he shrugged and said, "I guess so." And in his last days he would ask to sing favourite old hymns along with the piano. He had wrestled with his faith, pondering it all, coming to a peaceful reconciliation in the end.

May 19, 2012. Ironically, the day Phil passed away was the day of the Queen's Diamond Jubilee Flypast in London where she was seen acknowledging the planes through the decades in a fitting salute.

A great story, yet a great testament to the strength of the human spirit and what 'ordinary' people can do when faced with daunting odds.

This is just one of the miraculous stories to emerge from World War II.

So, if there be any redemption from this story, if there be any future from this grim episode, let it flow from the thousands of lives living today because of the survival of these brave men. Within the heart of each one of us is the wellspring to hope again, to learn from suffering, to press on in the noble journey to right injustice and be people of restoration.

In Winston Churchill's timeless words, 'Never, never, never give up!'

Phil did not see himself as a hero but whenever he talked about Buchenwald, a steely look would come into his eyes, his mouth would tighten, he would look away to the side and say, "I would not step back."

247

Writer's Acknowledgements

Writer Hilary Pedersen at book signing event in New Zealand, April 2017. Photo courtesy of Mike Harold

My thanks to the following for their input into Phil Lamason's biography:

The Phil Lamason Trust for inviting me to write Phil's story. Striving to meet expectations and present the man as he was has been a challenging and rewarding assignment.

Trust chairman, researcher and writer Mike Harold, BA (Victoria University), proof reader Sherynn Harold, BA (Massey University), writer and the 'Keeper' of the story, Glenys Scott (BEd Massey University), and especially award-winning Wellington photographer and designer Sal Criscillo. This team have held the process together. Their dedication and combination of skills has ensured that the project has remained on track and achieved the desired outcome. Thanks also to Catherine Keating for her help on the final proof read.

The Lamason family for their support: Trish and Graeme Simmonds, John and Debbie Lamason, Cherry Taylor and Robbie Lamason have provided anecdotes and insights into their father (and father-in-law) that have enhanced the family picture. Graeme and Phil's shared knowledge as aviators has contributed significantly to the fund of flying stories including at RAF Stradishall, for which Phil's wartime history was famous. I also acknowledge the wider Lamason family sources for supplying early historical background information, anecdotes, photographs, correspondence and newspaper articles about Phil as this biography project gathered momentum.

In particular my thanks go to Mike Dorsey for again honouring Phil by agreeing to write the Foreword to this book, and also for the use of information sourced from his film documentary, 'The Lost Airmen of Buchenwald.'

To the writers whose published books include references to Phil's Buchenwald experiences: Colin Burgess' gracious offer of access to 'Destination Buchenwald' with its 'straight from the horse's mouth' account of events was of immeasurable assistance. Thanks also to Max Lambert for material used from 'Night After Night,' and to our French connection, writer Francois Ydier ('The Boy and The Bomber'), and researcher Franck Signorile, who have provided detailed information around the period of the crash, evasion and capture.

I acknowledge the information collected in the work of Art Kinnis and Stanley Booker ('168 Jump into Hell'), Joe Moser ('Fighter Pilot in Buchenwald') and Ken Chapman (diary), all of whom provided excellent insights and intensely personal accounts of their shared Buchenwald experiences. I record also my appreciation for information sourced from 'The White Rabbit,' by Bruce Marshall. For valuable background material in the wider post-war context of the times, I acknowledge Paul Moon's 'New Zealand in the Twentieth Century: The Nation, The People.'

For research assistance and clarification of Phil's RNZAF and RAF records, my thanks go to John Hamilton, ONZM, MVO; Air Vice-Marshall RNZAF, Retd. Chief of Air Force for RNZAF, 2002 – 2006. For their contributions into aspects of Phil's family and community life, my thanks to Pat Magill, Bay de Lautour, Graham Ramsden and Becky Witika. To Pat Portas and the Smedley Station Trust for willingly providing access to the property, personnel and records and to archivist Phillip Rankin at Napier Boys' High School for his research.

But finally, I cannot close this narrative without expressing once more, my gratitude to Mike Harold. No words can adequately describe his gigantic role in an undertaking that has proved to be so much greater than we ever envisaged.

Hilary Pedersen
BA (Massey University).
Hawkes Bay daily newspaper journalist 1984-2002.

The Phil Lamason Heritage Centre Trust (Inc)

Phil Lamason Heritage Centre Trustees, the writer and special guests pictured together in Dannevirke, New Zealand at the launch of "I Would Not Step Back..." in February 2018. (Left to right): John Lamason, Ailsa Cullen (widow of Malcolm Cullen, the only other New Zealander among the 168 Allied Airmen of Buchenwald in 1944), Debbie Lamason, Ngaire Nystrum (key supporter of the biography project), Hilary Pedersen (writer), Glenys Scott, Mike Harold, Sandra Cordell and Nicky Roberts. (Photograph courtesy Dave Murdoch)

In 2015, as an outcome of considering how Phil Lamason's heroic and inspiring War story could be accurately preserved and presented for historical purposes, The Phil Lamason Heritage Centre Trust (Inc) was established. After discussions with the Lamason family and members of the wider local community the Trust, which has a Charitable Purpose, was formed with the following goals:

o   To accurately preserve and promote a wider understanding of the Phil Lamason War Story.

o   To work collaboratively with other local heritage groups to create a modern story telling facility, in which Phil Lamason's and other important local stories can be shared and preserved.

The Trust greatly acknowledges the support and generosity of the Lamason family for vesting this story in the Trust for the benefit of supporting preservation of heritage stories in the local district. Special thanks to the Monty Fairbrother Trust for their funding support for the writing of this biography. The Trust acknowledges the efforts and huge amounts of work done by our very dedicated writer Hilary Pedersen and photographer/layout designer Sal Criscillo. We deeply appreciate the interest and help of Mike Dorsey and his special contribution in writing the Foreword to this book. A very big thanks to all the many contributors from local through to national and international sources for your interest and help in securing resources which have made this project possible.

The biography, "I Would Not Step Back...," is the first project initiative undertaken by the Trust. We are very interested to receive feed-back and are particularly interested to make contact with individuals, groups and organisations who are interested in helping the Trust work towards our other stated goals.

Signed by the Phil Lamason Heritage Centre Trustees 2017: Mike Harold (Chairman), Glenys Scott, Nicola Roberts, Sandra Cordell, Lee Bettles and John Lamason.

Website: www.phillamason.com

Facebook: Phil Lamason Heritage Trust

Names and Nationalities of Allied Airman Detained in Buchenwald 1944

List of the Airmen and their nationalities with their Buchenwald number. Information courtesy of '168 jump into Hell' and KLB Club records.

New Zealand

78388 Cullen, M. F. (Malcolm)

78407 Lamason, P.J.(Phil)

Australia

78427 Fairclough, M.F.(Mervyn)

78423 Gwilliam, J.R.(Jim)

78421 Johnston, E. (Eric)

78381 Light, K.W. (Kevin)

78379 Malcolm, T.A. (Tom)

78405 Mills, K.B. (Keith)

78426 Mills, R.N. (Bob)

78356 Perry, R.W. (Ray)

78442 Whellum, L.K. (Les)

Jamaica

78393 Guilfoyle, M.A. (Mike)

Canada

78440 Atkins, H.(Harold)

78378 Bastable, H. (Harry)

78364 Clark, D. (Don)

78406 Crawford, J. (John)

78434 Compton, G.A.E. (Edward)

78361 Carter-Edwards, E. (Ed)

78418 Fulsher, F.W. (Frederick)

78394 Gibson, W.R. (Bill)

78438 Grenon, L.T. (Leo)

78412 Harvie, J.D. (John)

78430 Head, L. (Les)

78436 Hetherington, S. (Stan)

78422 High, D. (Dave)

78424 Hodgson, T.R. (Tommy)

78429 Hoffman, C.R. (Dick)

78391 Kinnis, A.G. (Art)

78404 Leslie, D.E. (Don)

78373 McLenaghan, J.R. (Ralph)

78374 Prudham, J.E. (Pep)

78395 Scullion, P. (Patrick)

78372 Shepherd, E.G. (Ernest)

78428 Smith, J.A. (James)

78343 Sonshine, E.R. (Joseph)

78402 Walderam, W.A. Willie)

78431 Watson, E.C. (Earl)

78342 Willis, C.E. (Calvin)

Great Britain

78390 Angus, J.W. (Jack)

78342 Barham, L.P. (Leonard)

78384 Baxter, S. (Stuart)

78344 Bennett, G. (Geoffrey)

78380 Blackham, T.H. (Tom)

78370 Booker, S.A. (Stanley

78365 Bryden, R. (Bob)

78409 Chapman, E.W. (Ken)

78433 Chinn, A.J. (Albert)

78385 Clarke, J. (John)

78346 Davis, E. (Eric)

78410 Dowdeswell, P. (Philip)

78403 Eagle, D. (Douglas)

78352 Fernandez, J.J. (John)

78386 Gould, T. (Terrance)

78414 Harper, R. (Robert)

78420 Heggarty, P.W. (Patrick)

78383 Hemmens, P.D. (Philip)

255

78347 Hughes, R.R. (Ronald)
78401 Joyce, R.W. (Reg)

78389 Lucas, I.J. (Lewis)

78413 Measures, D.K. (Dorak)
78371 Osselton, J.N. (John)

78419 Phelps, E.K. (Edward)
78408 Rowe, A. (Andrew)

78443 Spierenburg, S.A. (Dutch)
78376 Taylor, R.J. (Ralph)

78439 Watmough, G.F. (George)

USA

78357 Allen, R. (Roy)

78196 Bauder, W.F. (Warren)
78336 Bowan, C.E. (Chas)

78318 Carr, F.W. (Frederick)
78285 Chessir, D. (Douglas)
78319 Coffman, J.D.

78316 Dearey, R.W. (Ralph)
78267 Edge, W.L. (William)
78309 Friel, E.J (Edward)

78280 Hanson, J.T. (John)

78326 Hilding, R.D. (Russ)

78321 Horrigan, R.J. (Roy)

78279 King, M.A. (Myles)

78339 Ludwig, E.F. (Everett)
78290 Masters, L.O. (Lovell)
78266 Mikel, G. (George)

78392 Jackson, E. (Edgar)

78400 Kay, W. (William)

78435 MacPherson, A.J. (Alexander)
78375 Mutter, N.E.S. (Neville)
78362 Peirson, F. (Frank)

78387 Reid, J.D. (John)

78345 Salt, F. (Frank)

78416 Stewart, J.A. (Jim)

78377 Vincombe, V. (Frederick)
78399 Wesley, L. (Laurice)

78287 Alexander, W. (William)
78286 Beck, L.C. (Levitt)

78340 Bozarth, J.W. (James)
78278 Chalot, J.A. (John)

78308 Coats, B.A. (Basil)
78277 Crouch, M.E. (Marshall)
78269 Denaro, J. (Joe)

78313 Fix, E.E. (Karl)

78359 Freeman, E.C. (James)
78354 Hastin, J.D. (James)

78350 Hoffman, R.B. Robert)
78337 Hunter, H.E. (Harry)
78363 Larson, M.E. (Merle)
78348 McClanahan, J.H. (John)
78298 Mauk, W.E. (William)
78307 Mitchell, G.E. (Gerald)

78341 Jordin, D.F. (Douglas)
78382 Leverington, R.L. (Ron)
78417 Marshall, W. (Wilfred)
78366 Nuttal, C.W. (Cyril)

78411 Percy, D.C. (Douglas)
78415 Robb, I.A. (Ian)

78397 Sharrate, W.D. (William)
78425 Taylor, P.D. (Peter)

78396 Ward, J.D. (John)

78437 Williams, L. (Llewelyn)

78314 Appleman, S.M. (Stratton)
78283 Bedford, R.L. (Richard)
78295 Brown, R.W. (Robert)
78284 Chapman, P. (Park)

78271 Cowan, F.K. (Frank)
78324 Dauteul, D.F. (Donat)
78300 Duncan, J.H. (James)
78349 Fore, J.W. (James)

78312 Granberry, W.L. (William)
78334 Heimerman, L.A. (Lawrence)
78281 Horwege, G.L. (Glen)
78272 Johnson, R.T. (Robert)
78301 Little, B.S. (Bruce)

78299 Martini, F. (Frederic)
78338 McLaughlin, D.G. (Whitey)
78369 Moser, J. (Joe)

256

78288 Pasha, A.M. (Arthur)
78351 Pederson, J.W. (Charles)
78331 Phelps, B.F. (Byron)

78292 Reynolds, L.J. (Leo)

78327 Robertson, C.W. (Charles)
78323 Smith, J.W. (James)

78332 Shearer, D.R. (Donald)
78276 Sypher, L.H. (Leroy)

78293 Vallee, E. (Edward)

78333 Watson, J.P. (John)
78297 Wilson, P.J. (Paul)

78322 Zeiser, J. (James)

78320 Paxton, S.K. (Keith)
78289 Pennel, S. (Sam)

78335 Pelletier, A.J. (Arthur)
78317 Richey, G.T. (Thomas)
78358 Rynerd, W.H. William)
78353 Scharf, B.T. (Bernard)
78268 Straulka, P.A. (Paul)
78329 Thompson, W.A. (Warren)
78310 Vincent, E.H. (Edwin)
78294 Williams, W.J.
78367 Wojnick, R.J. (Ray)

78309 Friel, E.J. (Edward)

78315 Pecus, S. (Steve)
78325 Petrich, M.R. (Michael)
78296 Powell, W. (Bill)

78311 Ritter, E.W. (Edwin)

78370 Salo, L.H. (Laurie)

78330 Scott, G.W. (George)
78273 Suddock, D.E. (Dwight)
78360 Vance, I. (Ira)

78328 Vratney, F. (Frank)

78355 Ward, R. (Robert)
78368 Zander, A.E. (Arthur)

Glossary

Military and War-time Terms

ANZAC   Australia New Zealand Army Corps – the name given to the troops from these two countries involved in the Allied, Gallipoli campaign of 1915 in WWI. ANZAC Day, 25 April, is the annual commemoration day for the war dead, in both New Zealand and Australia.

Appell   German - Abbreviated from 'Appellplatz' meaning roll call.

Blitz   The Blitz, derived from the German word Blitzkrieg (lightning war), used to describe the Nazi air bombing raids over Britain between September 1940 and May 1941. .

Bomber stream   The tactic adopted by the RAF whereby large numbers of bomber aircraft flew in tight formation at the same speed, along a common route to the target. Each aircraft was prescribed a height and time to minimise the likelihood of collision. Typically, a raid involving 600-700 bomber aircraft might fly in a rectangular airspace 8-10 miles wide, 4000-6000 feet deep and take an hour and a half to pass over a target.

Bowser   English term for a petrol (gas) tanker.

Browning   Name given to a machine gun manufactured by the Browning Company.

Caught in the cone   The experience of being in an aircraft which has been caught in the crossed beams of two or more round-based enemy searchlights and rendered especially vulnerable to enemy anti-aircraft gunfire.

Circuits and bumps   Flying short, continuous practise courses or loops, which involved a touchdown and take-off as part of each completed circuit.

Cobba   Slang term for close friend or mate.

Commando   Soldier trained for special operations

CO   Commanding Officer

Cop it   To have been the subject of and damaged by an enemy attack.

CU   Conversion Units which were established for the more specialised training of aircrews.

D-Day   Code name given to the massed Allied landing on the beaches in Normandy, France, 6 June 1944

DFC   Distinguished Flying Cross. Britain's 3rd highest wartime award, presented for "an act or acts of valour, courage or devotion to duty whilst flying in active operations against the enemy."

Dogtags   The Individual identification discs worn around the neck by all military personnel.

Erks   Slang term for Air Force ground crew.

Feldwebel   Non-commissioned officer rank in the Luftwaffe.

Flak   Exploding shells fired at Allied aircraft from enemy ground based anti-aircraft guns.

Flying Fortress The Boeing B-17 four engine bomber which was the premiere aircraft for the United States Army Air Corps in WWII.

Funkspiel (German - radio play) The name given to the counterintelligence operation carried out by Nazi intelligence in WWII whereby captured radio operators in France were forced to send false messages to British intelligence. It also allowed Nazi intelligence to intercept messages and convey mis-information thereby disrupting the activities of the Resistance movements.

Gamel A bowl for soup.

Goons Allied Prisoner of War term in WWII for the guards in the Prisoner of War camps.

Incendiary shell. Ammunition used for the creation of fires.

HQ Headquarters

KLB The Konzentrationslager Buchenwald (KLB) was the group formed on 12 October 1944 by the 168 allied airmen wrongly incarcerated as Prisoners of War in Buchenwald concentration camp.

Knackerbrod A crisp German whole grain bread which was an essential part of their military ration in WWII.

Kriegies Short form of Kriegesgefangenen, the German word for prisoner of war in WWII. The term was commonly used by allied prisoners of war to describe themselves.

Legion d'Honneur Croix de Guerre The highest French award for wartime bravery.

Luftwaffe The air force component of the German Wehrmacht military forces in WWII.

Luger German hand-gun or pistol.

Mentioned in Despatches A special mention of a specific person's act of bravery in a military report destined for higher command consideration.

Merchant Navy A term bestowed by King George V on the fleet of non-military ships involved in the support of the War effort.

Morse Code An electronic method used to communicate information over a distance by using an internationally recognised alphabetical and numerical code which combines sequences of short and long signals ('dits' and 'dahs') to form messages. This was especially important as a communication tool in WWII.

NCO Non-Commissioned Officer

OTU Operational Training Unit where airmen were prepared with the details necessary for active air service.

Pathfinders Specialist airborne forces developed by the RAF in WWII whose job it was to fly ahead of bombers on operations and mark the targets with flares to guide the aircraft accurately to target.

POW Prisoner of War.

RAF Royal Air Force.

RAFVR The Royal Air Force Volunteer Reserve was the principle group through which volunteer airmen were recruited into the RAF during WWII.

RCAF Royal Canadian Air Force

RNZAF	Royal New Zealand Air Force
RSA	The Royal New Zealand Returned and Services' Association (commonly called The Returned Services' Association) is a voluntary welfare organisation established during WWI to aid the rehabilitation of servicemen returning to New Zealand.
Schmeisser	A machine gun widely used by German troops in WWII.
Second New Zealand Expeditionary Force	The title given to the military force sent from New Zealand to support the Allied efforts in WWII.
Shells	Bullets and explosives fired from larger guns.
SOE	Special Operations Executive. The British organisation developed during WWII to conduct sabotage, espionage and reconnaissance in occupied Europe and also help the Resistance movements with their operations.
SS	The Schutzstaffel was a paramilitary organisation of Nazi Germany in WWII. It consisted of several constituent groups including the Gestapo and Sicherheitsdienst (SD) whose role was to detect potential enemies of the Nazi state, neutralise any opposition to ideology, police the German people for their commitment to Nazism, and collect domestic and foreign intelligence. The SS-Totenkopfverbande (SS-TV) ran the concentration and extermination camps.
U-boat	Abbreviation of the German 'Unterseeboot' (undersea boat) meaning a submarine.
USAAF	United States Army Air Force
Very Pistol	A small pistol for firing flares as target markers or for distress signals.
WAAC's	Women's Army Auxiliary Corps
WAAF	Women's Auxiliary Air Force which was established in WWII as a means by which a large number of women could be directly involved in a wide range of roles (excluding combat flying), with helping the War effort.
Whitley	A twin-engined medium bomber aircraft similar to the Wellington bomber, which was in service for the RAF from the start of WWII. Manufactured by the Armstrong Whitworth Company, this aircraft was superseded by the heavy four-engined bombers as the War progressed.
WWI	The historical event known as The Great War or World War One.
WWII	The historical event called World War Two which spanned the years 1939-45.

RAF Aircrew Ranks WWII

The RAF aircrew rankings in WWII in ascending order of seniority were:

Non-commissioned Ranks
Sergeant (Sgt)
Flight Sergeant (FS)
Warrant Officer (WO)

Commissioned Rankings	*Equivalent Army Rank*
Pilot Officer (P/O or Plt Off)	Second Lieutenant
Flying Officer (F/O or Fg Off)	Lieutenant
Flight Lieutenant (F/L or Flt Lt)	Captain
Squadron Leader (S/L or Sqn Ldr)	Major
Wing Commander (Wg Cdr)	Lieutenant Colonel
Group Captain (Gp Capt)	Colonel
Air Commodore (Air Cdre)	Brigadier
Air Vice Marshall (AVM)	Major-General
Air Marshall (AM)	Lieutenant-General
Air Chief Marshall (ACM)	General

Non-Military Terms

A & P Show   The Agricultural and Pastoral Show of farm livestock and produce. Still a prominent annual event in many of New Zealand's rural communities.

Bledisloe Cup   The Rugby football trophy keenly contested annually between the national representative teams of New Zealand (All Blacks) and Australia (Wallabies).

Docking   The sheep farming management practice of removing lamb tails and also the process of male lamb castration.

Dog–trialing   Competitions in which interested sheep farmers and their dogs contest against other farmers and their dogs to establish the best working dog.

Hectare   A unit for measuring land area. One Hectare is 10000 sq metres.

Hoof and hook.   A competition term used in a New Zealand farming wherein the contesting farmers have their animals judged in both the live and the slaughtered context.

Lambing beat   The management practice on New Zealand sheep-farms for farmers to routinely make daily checks on their flocks of ewes (female sheep) and their progeny during the birthing season.

Livestock buyer.   A job related to farming wherein an agent purchases livestock on behalf of an interested buyer party.

Livestock inspector.   A job in which personnel with the appropriate training work to ensure compliances are being met on farms in regard to the health and well-being of the farm animals.

Lorry   British term for truck.

Paddock   Commonly used name in New Zealand farming for a farm field.

Pantechnicon vehicle   An enclosed vehicle or van designed for the transportation of furniture.

Richter Scale   The scale used for measuring the magnitude of earthquakes.

Sluicing claim   An area of ground, legally acquired by a prospector during the New Zealand gold rush era, on which the miner was able to use running water to extract the gold from alluvial soils and gravels.

Steer   A castrated male bovine animal.

Stockmanship   The application of a learned set of skills for the purposes of husbandry and management of animals in a farming context.

Ute   Abbreviation of 'utility truck," which is a commonly used term for a small, decked vehicle used on New Zealand farms

Information Sources

COVER DESIGN:
Topics Design – The Creative Partnership combining images from the book. Based on the design of the hardback edition by Geo Casper Chong and Glenys Scott.

THE MAKING OF THE MAN
Books
Lindsey, Ivan and Lorna. (2012). *In the Heavens Above – British Commonwealth Air Training Plan.* Wilsonscott Publishing, Christchurch.
The Cyclopedia of New Zealand (Nelson, Marlborough and Westland Provincial Districts). (1906). The Cyclopedia Company Ltd., Christchurch,
Ross, Squadron Leader J.M.S.. (1955). *Royal New Zealand Air Force.* Historical Publications Branch, Wellington. Chapter 4.
Jessen, Don. (2016). *Vintage and Iconic Aircraft – New Zealand Collections,* David Bateman Publishing, Auckland, NZ.
Thomsen, Kevin. *Smedley Station – 75th Jubilee 1931-2006.* (2014). Central Design Print, Waipukurau,
Simpson, Tony. (1974). *The Sugarbag Years – An Oral History of the 1930s Depression in New Zealand.* Alister Taylor Publishing
Newspapers and Periodicals
Grey River Argus, Saturday 15 August 1885.
Grey River Argus, Vol LVII, Issue 9910, 23 February 1898
West Coast Times, Issue 6342, 16 November 1886,
West Coast Times, Issue 9536, 12 April 1893.
West Coast Times, Issue 2924, 16 August 1878.
West Coast Times, Issue 10538, 7 April 1897.
Inangahua Times, 24 January 1912
Timaru Herald, Volume XXV, Issue 1552, 18 October 1876, Page 6
Hawera & Normanby Star, Volume XLII, 16 February 1922
New Zealand Herald, Volume LXXIII, Issue 22359, 4 March 1936,
The Scindian, Napier Boys' High School, 1932
The Scindian, Napier Boys' High School, 1938
Evening Post, Volume CXXIV, Issue 141, 11 December 1937
Reports and Official Records
New Zealand Defence Archives, Upper Hutt. Second World War Air Force Service Records. Records of LAMASON, Phillip John. NZ403460:
   RAF Airmans / Womans Record Sheet (Active Service) RAF Form 1560
   Record of Career, Officers and N.C.O. Aircrew (Form AF 381)
   RNZAF Report on Flying and Ground Training (Form 1587)
   RNZAF Officer's Record Card (Form 373)
   RNZAF Certificate of Service and Discharge
New Zealand Electoral Roles 1905/06, 1911 and 1914. www.ancestry.co.nz/
Arnold Haig Convoy Database, *HX Convoy Series.* www.convoyweb.org.
Siri Holm Lawson, *Convoy HX 132.* www.warsailors.com
New Zealand Army WWI Reserve Rolls 1916-1917. www.ancestry.co.nz
Websites

www.cambridgeairforce.org.nz	Wings over Cambridge, *RNZAF Stations, Airfields and Depots North Island.*
www.wikipedia.org/	Training aircraft information
www.ancestry.co.nz/	NZ Electoral and Military Rolls.
http://paperspast.natlib.govt.nz	Newspapers past; The Cyclopedia of NZ 1906.
http://nzetc.victoria.ac.nz	Newspapers past.
http://www.findmypast.com	NZ Electoral and Military Rolls.
www.warsailors.com	Convoy HX 132.
www.convoyweb.org.	HX Convoy Series.
www.geneallogy.rootsweb.ancesrty.com	Wreck of the 'General Grant.'
www.teara.govt.nz/en/biographies	Richard John Seddon.
http://www.napier.govt.nz/services	Hawke's Bay Earthquake 1931.
http://www.nzine.co.nz	Sugar Bag Years – NZ in The Depression.
http://paperspast.natlib.govt.nz	Massey College. Diplomas and Prize List.1938.

Correspondence and Letters

8 March 1936   Letter from Phil Lamason to his Mother.
November 1912   Letter from William Hopkins to Mr Junk.
Assorted letters, cards, births, deaths and marriage certificates provided by different members of the wider Lamason family.

Research, Interviews and Recounts

Glenys Scott, friend of Phil Lamason and family
Patricia and Graeme Simmonds, daughter and son-in law of Phil Lamason.
Cherry Taylor, daughter of Phil Lamason.
Pat Magill, boyhood friend of Phil Lamason.
Pat Portas, Chairman, Smedley Trust Board, 2016
John Hamilton, ONZM, MVO; Air Vice-Marshall RNZAF, Retd .Chief of Air Force for RNZAF, 2002 – 2006.
Phillip Rankin, Archivist, Napier Boys' High School, 2016

WAR AND NEW HORIZONS

Books

Thompson, Wing Commander H.L..(1956). *New Zealanders with the Royal Air Force (Vol II) – Official History of New   Zealand in the Second World War, 1939-1945.* Historical Publications Branch, Department of Internal Affairs, Wellington.

Reid, Richard (2012). *Bomber Command. Australians in World War II.* Canberra Department of Veterans' Affairs.

Adams, Spencer and Whitehouse, Jock. (1996). *Royal Air Force Stradishall 1938-1970.* The RAF Stradishall Memorial Trust. Square One Publication, England.

Hall, Archie. (1985). *We, Also, Were There.* Merlin Books Ltd, Great Britain.

Ydier, Francois. (2016). *The Boy and the Bomber.* Mention the War Ltd, Pudsey, UK.

DVD/Video

Dorsey, Mike.   (2011).   *The Lost Airmen of Buchenwald.*   Interviews and commentaries.

Television New Zealand Limited. *(2005). Forgotten Hero – Ex RAF bomber remembers WWII .*
Harvey Lilley, Colin and Ewan McGregor. BBC1 (2012). *Bomber Boys.*
Newspapers and Periodicals
The Globe and Mail, Toronto, 1 September 2007. *Gerald Musgrove Eulogy.*
The Globe and Mail, 16 February 2007. Bourdon, Buzz. *Gerry Musgrove DFC WOP/AG and Bomb Aimer RCAF, No. 15 Squadron RAF,*
The Telegraph,UK. 12 November 2000. Eden, Richard and Oaks, John. *French Never Forgot Lost Wartime Airman.*
The Dominion, 24 April 1999. Barton, Warren. *The reluctant hero.*
Reports and Official Records
The National Archives (UK) Kew, *RAF Records 1941- 1944*
    AIR27 203: Report Nos 35, 36, 37, 40, 41, 43, 44, 71, 72
    AIR27 204: Report Nos 1, 2, 3, 4, 5, 6, 7, 8, 9, 10, 11, 12
    AIR27 1349: Report Nos 16, 17, 20, 21, 23
    AIR27 1350: Report Nos 1, 2, 4, 5, 8, 10, 12, 14, 16, 26, 27, 28, 29, 30, 31
    AIR27 2141: Report Nos 4, 7, 8, 9, 10
London Gazette: 15 May 1942; 19 April 1944; 22 May 1945
Websites
https://en.wikipedia.org/wiki/World_War_II Outbreak WWII in Europe, Battle of Britain, The Blitz.
www.218squadron.wordpress.com_218 (Gold Coast) Squadron Association. *218 (Gold Coast) Squadron, 1936-1945, History.* Acknowledgement of Steve (Smudger) Smith, No.218 (Gold Coast) Squadron Association Historian, 2016, for management of this website.
http://nzetc.victoria.ac.nz/ New Zealanders with the RAF
www.514squadron.co.uk 514 Squadron. *Losses,*
www.427squadron.com 427 Squadron Association. *No 23 Operational Training Unit (O.T.U.), Pershore Worcestershire, UK.*
www.dnw.co.uk/auction-archive Dix Noonan Webb, special collections archive 27 June 2002:
www.rafcommands.com/forum RAF Commands Forum. *A Kiwi Called Lamason.*
www.evasioncomete.org/ *The Comet Network.*
www.telegraph.co.uk Eden, Richard and Oaks, John. 12 November 2000. *French Never Forgot Lost Wartime Airman,* The Telegraph, UK.
www.214squadron.org.uk Scantleton, Vern. *214 Squadron, Personnel.*
https://www.raf.mod.uk Information on RAF No 15 Squadron, Mildenhall, WWII
http://www.wartimememoriesproject.com/ww2/ Information on RAF Mildenhall, WWII
www.forces-war-records.co.uk Information on RAF Mildenhall, WWII
https://etherwave.wordpress.com Transcript of The Butt Report, 18 August 1941
https://en.wikipedia.org Butt Report summary; Information on Sir Arthur (Bomber) Harris.
http://www.bbc.co.uk/history Sir Arthur (Bomber) Harris Information.
www.raf.mod.uk Sir Arthur (Bomber) Harris Information.
https://en.wikipedia.org/ Avro Lancaster, Vickers Wellington and Short Stirling aircraft details.

http://www.militaryfactory.com   Avro Lancaster, Vickers Wellington and Short
Stirling aircraft details.
http://www.defensemedianetwork.com   Clark Gable WWII service – Robert F
Dorr, 2010.
https://en.wikipedia.org/wiki/List_of_air_operations_during_the_Battle_of_Europe
Bombing Raids
http://www.raf.mod.uk/history/famousraids.cfm   Bombing Raids
https://www.thegazette.co.uk/   Military Award citations.
http://www.cieldegloire.com/_001_borchers_w.php Information on Walter Borchers
https://en.wikipedia.org/wiki/Walter_Borchers   Information   on   Walter
Borchers
https://www.dnw.co.uk/auction-archive/special-
collections/lot.php?specialcollection_id=221&lot_id=77055 Dix Noonan
Webb Auction listing of John Marpole DFC medal, Flying log. (June 2002),
DFC Citation.

Interviews and Recounts
Glenys Scott, friend of Phil Lamason and family.
Patricia and Graeme Simmonds, daughter and son-in law of Phil Lamason.
John Lamason, son of Phil Lamason.
John Hamilton, ONZM, MVO; Former senior commander in the RNZAF, Chief of Air
Force 2002-2006.

INTO DARKNESS – BLOODY, BLOODY BUCHENWALD

Books
Burgess, Colin. (1995), *Destination Buchenwald*. Kangaroo Press, Kenthurst, NSW.
Kinnis, Arthur and Booker, Stanley. (1999) *168 Jump Into Hell*. Victoria, B.C.,
Canada.
Lambert, Max. (2005), *Night after Night: New Zealanders in Bomber Command*.
Harper Collins, Auckland.
Marshall, Bruce. (1952), *The White Rabbit - The Story Of Wing Commander F.F.E.
Yeo-Thomas*. Evans Brothers Ltd, London.
Moser, Joseph F. and Baron, Gerald R. (2009) *A Fighter Pilot in Buchenwald*. Edens
Veil Media, Bellingham, W.A.98225
Ydier, Francois. (2016), *The Boy and the Bomber*. Mention the War Ltd, Pudsey, UK.
Mason, W, Wynne. (1954) *Prisoners of War – edited by Howard Karl Kippenberger*.
Historical Publications Branch, Department of Internal Affairs, Wellington
NZ.
Tolstoy, Nikolai. (2012) *Victims of Yalta: The Secret Betrayal of the Allies, 1944–
1947*. Pegasus, New York.
DVD/Video
Dorsey, Mike. (2011) *The Lost Airmen of Buchenwald*. Interviews and commentary.
Television New Zealand Limited. *(2005) Forgotten Hero – Ex RAF bomber
remembers WWII*. Mark Crysell interview with Phil Lamason.
Diaries
Chapman, Kenneth. Unpublished personal war diary, 1944-45.
Cullen, Malcolm. (1994) *Twelve Months Story*. Unpublished personal POW diary
covering experience as an Allied Airman in Buchenwald, 1944-45.

267

Official Reports
Lamason SPG Report (3 July 1945) M.I.9/S/P./.LIB/192 – Phil Lamason's liberation
file (POW/evasion) The London Gazette, (Supplement) 27 June 1944
Newspapers and Periodicals
The Dominion, 24 April 1999. Barton, Warren: *The reluctant hero.*
Auckland Star, 25 May 1945. Volume LXXVI, Issue 122. NZPA Special
Correspondent, London. *New Zealander in Buchenwald Camp*
Auckland Star, 6 September 1945.Volume LXXVI, Issue 211. *Horror Camp. Pilot's
Experiences. Prisoner in Buchenwald.*
Websites
http://www.vintagewings.ca/VintageNews/Stories   Dave O'Malley; 'A Terrifying
Beauty – the Art of Piotr Forkasiewicz.'
http://www.evasioncomete.org/   Airmen of the Marathon Transaction (Musgrove);
Person(s) Captured during His Escape (Lamason & Chapman)
https://en.wikipedia.org/wiki/Buchenwald_concentration_camp   Buchenwald
Camp
http://www.holocaustresearchproject.org/othercamps/buchenwald.html Buchenwald
Camp
https://en.wikipedia.org/wiki/KLB_Club   KLB Club formation
https://en.wikipedia.org/wiki/Stalag_Luft_III   Stalag LuftIII
https://www.raf.mod.uk/history/TheLongMarchHistory.cfm   The Long March
https://en.wikipedia.org/wiki/The_March_(1945)   The Long March
https://stalagluft3.wordpress.com/   Stalag LuftIII
http://nzetc.victoria.ac.nz/   New Zealand Prisoners of War
https://en.wikipedia.org/wiki/Stalag_III-A   Stalag 3a Luchenwalde
http://www.aircrew-saltire.org/lib175.htm   Bill   Taylor   recount   Stalag   3a
Luchenwalde
http://www.bbc.co.uk/history/ww2peopleswar/stories/   Stalag   3a
Luchenwalde
https://heyhamilton.com/stalag-iiib-george-altmans-pow-experience/   Stalag   3a
Luchenwalde
https://paperspast.natlib.govt.nz/newspapers/auckland-star   New   Zealander   in
Buchenwald Camp; Horror Camp. Pilot's Experiences. Prisoner in
Buchenwald.
http://www.wartimememoriesproject.com/ww2/pow/powcampLog entries of F/Sgt
Donald Edward Thomsett - Stalag 3a Luchenwalde Liberation.
Letters and Correspondence
Watkins, W.D.   Letter to Joan Lamason from RAF dated 8 June, 1944, advising
Phil Lamason is missing.
Franck Signorile   French Researcher and Historian with special interest in the
personnel of the French Resistance – email 28 April 2017 new information
regarding Lamason betrayal to Gestapo in 1944.
Interviews and Recounts
Glenys Scott, friend of Phil Lamason and family.
Patricia and Graeme Simmonds, daughter and son-in law of Phil Lamason.
John Lamason, son of Phil Lamason.

268

FAMILY, FARM AND A LIFE WELL LIVED

Books

Moon, Paul. (2011). *New Zealand In The Twentieth Century – the Nation and the People.* Harper Collins, NZ.

Burgess, Colin. (1995). *Destination Buchenwald.* Kangaroo Press, Kenthurst, NSW.

Kinnis, Arthur and Booker, Stanley. (1999) *168 Jump Into Hell.* Victoria, B.C., Canada.

Lambert, Max. (2005). *Night after Night: New Zealanders in Bomber Command.* .Harper Collins, Auckland.

Marshall, Bruce. (1952). *The White Rabbit - The Story of Wing Commander F.F.E. Yeo-Thomas.* Evans Brothers Ltd, London.

Moser, Joseph F. (2009). *Buchenwald Flyboy – as told by Gerald R. Baron.* Edens Veil Media, Bellingham, W.A.98225

Mason, W, Wynne. (1954). *Prisoners of War – edited by Howard Karl Kippenberger.* Historical Publications Branch, Department of Internal Affairs, Wellington NZ.

Jackson, Sophie. (2013). *Churchill's White Rabbit – a true story of a real life James Bond.* The History Press, UK.

DVD/Video

Dorsey, Mike. (2011) *The Lost Airmen of Buchenwald.* Interviews and commentary.

Newspapers and Periodicals

Hawke's Bay Today, 26 August 2010. Doug Laing: *Duty clear for man of the land.*

The Dominion, 24 April 1999. Barton, Warren: *The reluctant hero.*

Hawke's Bay Today, 25 April, 2012. McKay, Christine. *Phil Lamason. Humble Pilot.*

Auckland Star, 5 September 1945.Volume LXXVI, Issue 210.PA. Wellington. *Crowded Ship. Bitter Complaints.*

Auckland Star, 6 September 1945.Volume LXXVI, Issue 211. *Horror Camp. Pilot's Experiences.   Prisoner in Buchenwald.*

Evening Post, 5 September 1945. Volume CXL, Issue 57. *Men's Complaint. Ship Conditions. Boat Kiwis Walked Off.1500 Home Again.*

The Dominion, 4 April 1960. *Girl 13, Saves Six from Fire.*

Dannevirke Evening News, 4 April 1960. *Averted by Polio, Victim and Sister.* Also: *'Example to all Young People.'*

Dompost, 26 May 2012. Tracey Chatterton. *War hero had core of steel (Obituary)*

Hawke's Bay Today, 22 May 2012. Christine McKay. *Hero treasured family and friends.*

Hawke's Bay Today, 26 May 2012. Christine McKay. *Final Tribute – Phillip John Lamason*

Reports and Official Records

New Zealand Defence Archives, Upper Hutt. Second World War Air Force Service Records. Records of LAMASON, Phillip John. NZ403460:

> *RAF Airmans / Womans Record Sheet (Active Service) RAF Form 1560*
> *Record of Career, Officers and N.C.O. Aircrew (Form AF 381)*
> *RNZAF Officer's Record Card (Form 373)*
> *RNZAF Certificate of Service and Discharge*

Dannevirke Fire Brigade   1960 *Log Book of call-outs.*

Hannah Chair for the History of Medicine.Oral History Archive. Mc Master University, Hamilton, Canada.

18 August 1985. *Experiences of Prisoners-of-War, World War 2.Phillip Lamason.* Interviewed by Charles Gordon Roland, MD.

Websites

https://paperspast.natlib.govt.nz/newspapers/　　Auckland Star, Evening Post (1945)

Letters and Correspondence

11 May 1986　Barbara Yeo-Thomas letter to Phil Lamason

13 November 1987 R.M. Miller, Commissioner of Concentration Camp Fund, NZ Department of Social Welfare letter to　　Phillip J. Lamason.

19 October 1991 KLB Letter Art Kinnis to Phil Lamason

May 1992　KLB Letter Art Kinnis to Phil Lamason

November 1994　Letter from Barbara Yeo-Thomas to Phil Lamason

5 May 1995,　'Buckingham Palace' her Majesty the Queen. Thanks and best wishes to servicemen attending RAF Mildenhall reunion.

26 August 2002 .International Organisation for Migration (IOM).Payment advice notice.

23 September 1948 NZ Department of Internal Affairs letter to Phil Lamason.

1 October 1948, NZ Department of Internal Affairs letter to Phil Lamason.

12 July 2006　Franz-Josef Birkel, Defence Attache, Embassey of Federal Republic of　　Germany. Letter to Mr Trevor E. Gollan.

12 April 2012　Niels Holm, Secretary to the Governor General of NZ. Letter to Glenys Scott.

25 April 2012　Miss Jennie Vine, Deputy to the Senior Correspondence Officer, Buckingham Palace. Letter to Glenys Scott conveying best wishes and thanks of Her Majesty Queen Elizabeth II.

3 April 2012　Easy Freeman. Letter to Phil Lamason.

Undated (circa 2011)　Ailsa Cullen. Letter (card) to Phil Lamason.

Interviews and Recounts

Glenys Scott, friend of Phil Lamason and family.

Patricia and Graeme Simmonds, daughter and son-in law of Phil Lamason.

John Lamason, son of Phil Lamason.

Bay de Latour, former Chairman AWE, prominent farmer and colleague of Phil Lamason.

Graeme Ramsden, a farmer and colleague of Phil Lamason.

Dick Bedford, former US Airman and Buchenwald survivor.

Becky Witika, caregiver/home helper of Phil Lamason in his later years.

Eulogies

Matt Lamason, grandson of Phil Lamason.

Christie David, granddaughter of Phil Lamason.

Anita Taylor, granddaughter of Phil Lamason.

Karen Aynsley, granddaugher of Phil Lamason.

Kyle Robert Lamason, grandson of Phil Lamason.

Sarah Lamason, granddaughter of Phil Lamason.

Viki Miller, granddaughter of Phil Lamason.

Scott Miller, grandson-in-law of Phil Lamason.

PILGRIMAGE
Interviews and Recounts
Glenys Scott, friend of Phil Lamason and family.
Patricia and Graeme Simmonds, daughter and son-in law of Phil Lamason.
John and Debbie Lamason, son and daughter-in-law of Phil Lamason.
Francois Ydier, retired French pilot, Plaisir, France.
Acknowledgements
Ngaire Nystrum (nee Hansen) from Graasten, Denmark.
Denise Diatkine (nee Kalmanson), Paris.
Antoine Poliet, Paris.
Jean-Nicolas Diatkine, Paris.
Mayor Josephine Kollmannsberger, Plaisir.
Geraldine Cerf, Paris.

Printed in Great Britain
by Amazon